Freud and the *Sexual*

Freud and the *Sexual*:
Essays 2000–2006

Jean Laplanche

Editor and Textual Reviser:
John Fletcher

Translators:
John Fletcher, Jonathan House, Nicholas Ray

Copyright © 2011 by International Psychoanalytic Books
All rights reserved.
First Edition

Cover photo by Trish Mayo

Cover image: Bacchante, 1894, sculpture.
Frederick William MacMonnies (American, 1863–1937).
Marble, 86-1/2 x 31 x 33-3/4 in. (219.7 x 78.7 x 85.7 cm.)
Collection of the Brooklyn Museum,
Ella C. Woodward Memorial Fund, 06.33.

ISBN 978-0-615-57137-9
Library of Congress Control Number: 2011944629

CONTENTS

Acknowledgements vii

Foreword 1

1. Drive and Instinct: distinctions, oppositions, supports and intertwinings 5

2. Sexuality and Attachment in Metapsychology 27

3. Dream and Communication: should chapter VII be rewritten? 53

4. Countercurrent 83

5. Starting from the Fundamental Anthropological Situation 99

6. Failures of Translation 115

7. Displacement and Condensation in Freud 133

8. Sexual Crime 139

9. Gender, Sex and the *Sexual* 159

10. Three Meanings of the Term 'Unconscious' in the Framework of the General Theory of Seduction 203

11. For Psychoanalysis at the University 223

12. Intervention in a Debate 229

13. Levels of Proof 235

14. The *Three Essays* and the Theory of Seduction 249

15. Freud and Philosophy 267

16. In Debate with Freud 275

17. Psychoanalysis and Psychotherapy 279

18. Incest and Infantile Sexuality 285

19. Castration and Oedipus as Codes and Narrative Schemas 303

Bibliography 311

ACKNOWLEDGEMENTS

To the *Fondation Jean Laplanche: Nouveaux Fondements pour la Psychanalyse*, at the Institut de France, for the support and financing of the current translation.

To Presses Universitaires de France, publishers of the French collection of Jean Laplanche's works which provided the original text for the current translation: *Sexual: La sexualité élargie au sens freudien: 2000-2006*. Where appropriate the date and venue of the first publication is given at the beginning of each essay. An early version of the translation of Essay 10 was published in *The Unconscious: Further Reflections*, ed. José Carlos Calich and Helmut Hinze (London: International Psychoanalytic Association, 2007). The translations of essays 7, 13, 15 and 16 appeared in *Sitegeist* no 5, Winter 2010.

To Professor Jean Laplanche for his generous participation in the translation process. On a number of occasions the original text was revised and the revised text forms the basis of the current translation.

Each essay was worked on by two translators with editorial oversight and revision. The lead translators for each essay were:
    John Fletcher for no. 10;
    Jonathan House for nos. 3, 4, 5, 7, 9, 9-Appendix 1, 13;
    Nicholas Ray: Foreword, 1, 2, 6, 8, 9-Appendix 2, 11, 12, 14, 15, 16, 17, 18, 19.

I would also like to thank Dr. Nicholas Ray for his extensive contributions towards the final harmonization of the translations.

John Fletcher

Jean Laplanche is Professor Emeritus of Psychoanalysis at the Sorbonne (Paris VII), Scientific Director of the *Œuvres complètes de Freud* (1988–) and author of *Hölderlin and the Question of the Father* (1961), *The Language of Psychoanalysis* (with J.-B. Pontalis) (1967), *Life and Death in Psychoanalysis* (1970), *New Foundations for Psychoanalysis* (1987), *Essays on Otherness* (1999), the seven volumes of *Problématiques* (1980-2006), *La révolution copernicienne inachevée* (1992), and *Entre seduction et inspiration: l'homme* (1999).

Translators:

John Fletcher is Associate Professor in the Department of English and Comparative Literary Studies at the University of Warwick, UK. He has edited three previous volumes on the work of Jean Laplanche: *Jean Laplanche: Seduction, Translation and the Drives* (with Martin Stanton), *Essays on Otherness*, *Jean Laplanche and the Theory of Seduction*: Special Laplanche Issue of *New Formations*, no. 48, Winter 2002–3. He is the author of a number of essays on the work of Jean Laplanche and of *Freud and the Scene of Trauma* (Fordham University Press, forthcoming).

Jonathan House, MD, is a psychoanalyst in private practice in New York, Lecturer in Psychiatry and Psychoanalysis at Columbia University, where he is also Training and Supervising Analyst at the University's Center for Psychoanalytic Training and Research.

Nicholas Ray is Lecturer in Critical and Cultural Theory in the School of English at the University of Leeds, UK. He is the author of *Tragedy and Otherness: Sophocles, Shakespeare, Psychoanalysis* (2009).

FOREWORD

The present volume comprises most of my writings from the period 2000 to 2006. As with the previous volumes, *La révolution copernicienne inachevée* and *Entre séduction et inspiration: l'homme*,[1] the articles are not classified according to theme. Some of the texts, such as "Three Meanings of the Term 'Unconscious'" and "Gender, Sex, and the *Sexual*", have an innovatory aim with respect to theoretical matters (i.e. metapsychology). The title of the latter article leads me to justify the volume's overall title: what I call the '*sexual*'[2] is everything that emerges from the Freudian theory of an enlarged sexuality, and first and foremost what is called 'polymorphous perverse' infantile sexuality. Once we have understood the way in which Freud enlarges the notion of sexuality – beyond the simple union of the two sexes (to the extent that the *sexual* may often be auto-erotic) – we can only smile at the ubiquitous claim that there exists a modern 'sexual freedom', triumphant at last, and possibly even thanks to Freud himself.

On the other hand, one is perplexed by Foucault's approach; for, having relegated Freudian sexuality to the field of heterosexual genital union, he revels in the discovery of 'non-sexual' and even anti-sexual pleasures which are already amply described by Freud in 1905

---

1 *La révolution copernicienne inachevée* (Paris: Aubier, 1992); *Entre séduction et inspiration: l'homme* (Paris: Presses Universitaires de France, 1999).
2 [*Editor*: Laplanche invents a neologism in French by transforming the German component adjective *Sexual*- into a free-standing noun, in pointed contrast with the standard French term *sexuel*. (In German *Sexual* mainly appears as a bound adjectival root in combination with a noun, e.g. *Sexualtrieb* – sexual drive, *Sexualtheorie* – sexual theory). This is an attempt to register terminologically the difference between the enlarged Freudian notion of sexuality (*le sexual*) and the common sense or traditional notion of a genital sexuality (*le sexuel*). This terminological innovation can't really be captured in English as the German term *Sexual* coincides exactly with the spelling of the standard English term 'sexual', rather than contrasting with it as in French. The translators have chosen to signal Laplanche's neologism by italicizing *sexual* – pronounced with a long 'a': *ahl*].

(read the *Three Essays*!) under the heading of infantile and/or perverse sexuality.

In short, the *sexual* is not exactly what we think. It is much more complex and much more repressed, sometimes buried within barely formulated fantasies.

Although not every text in the present volume bears upon this theme, by using this slightly strange term, which is, nevertheless, extracted from Freud, I have sought to affirm the primacy within psychoanalysis of a unique and specific 'variety' of sexuality. It is this that is at the heart of the notions of the drive, the unconscious and even the 'death drive': the sexuality that, in infancy at least, can transform any region or function of the body, and even activity in general, into an 'erotogenic zone'.

It would, however, be one-sided to reduce this enlarged sexuality to the polymorphous perverse sexuality of early childhood.

This anarchic sexuality, whose fate is sometimes close to the 'sexual death drive', has another, more stabilising fate, and one to which Freud attached the name 'renunciation of the drive'. The path of renunciation is not purely negative. It is the path of binding within the field of genitality and, more generally, the path of sublimation. This is what Freud calls 'the Eros of the divine Plato', and it is no less erotic for all that. We have touched on this theme in an earlier volume, under the title of "Sublimation and/or Inspiration".[3] It is essential that this fate, which is by no means always conformist, not be forgotten.

---

3 "Sublimation and/or Inspiration", trans. John Fletcher and Luke Thurston, in *New Formations*, no. 48, Winter 2002–3.

Essays

1

**DRIVE AND INSTINCT:
DISTINCTIONS, OPPOSITIONS, SUPPORTS
AND INTERTWININGS**[1]

Although this is a presentation for a conference on the theme of 'homosexuality and adolescence', I am by no means a specialist in adolescence. What I'm presenting here is a re-examination – which is no easy task itself – of a certain number of presuppositions. It is thus a clarification, which, within our discipline, is primarily and of necessity a catharsis – something for which psychoanalysis has a powerful and continuing need. Stoller, with his great freedom of thought and in his own occasionally very amusing manner, compares current psychoanalytic theory to the Pantheon of imperial Rome where coexisted the temples of Isis and of Jupiter, a few early Christian churches, the temples of Mithra, and so on. In psychoanalysis too we add little temples, private mansions, and supplementary shrines onto the Freudian forum, without worrying about their coherence. A pinch of the symbolic, a dash of leaning-on, a knob of the negative, a small measure of seduction, a sprig of transitivity – all without worrying ourselves about what it is we are building upon or how these cohere with it.

---

1 First published in *Adolescence*, 2000, vol. 18, no. 2, pp. 649–668.

1 — Thought cannot properly take place except on the basis of distinctions, even if it is later to establish relations between what have been distinguished from one another. Today's topic requires the clearest possible distinctions.

I should like to take up the terms of Colette Chiland's article in *Adolescence* where she enjoins us "to be clear about the terms we use" and, in harmony with the paper by Jean Bergeret that follows it, to make a distinction between homosexuality and homoeroticism.[2]

I might also have appealed to the gender/sex/sexuality triad, which also seems to me to be essential today. However, this will have to wait for another occasion when I can take account of the notion of gender; for, briefly put, in Freud's key formula concerning homosexuality – "I (a man) love him (a man)" – he varies each term except the first, which is to say the gender of 'ego': "I (a man)".[3]

I shall say a little about 'translation' and 'terminology' and a little about 'concepts', but I shall also say a great deal about reality as it is viewed by psychoanalysis. For both the conceptual problem and the problem of translation have pervaded our psychoanalytic world for almost eighty years. They have done so in a confused fashion, but this is a confusion that also exists in the real. As I like to say, with a touch of irony, 'theoretico-genesis recapitulates ontogenesis'.

Let's begin with the simplest matter: the translation of the Freudian word *Trieb* by 'instinct'. Ever since Strachey's edition, which is now very old, 'instinct' has been the principal English translation of *Trieb*. In French we have had *'instinct'*, or in a manner that really mixes apples and oranges, *'pulsion ou instinct* [drive or instinct]', as Marie Bonaparte was able to say in a single breath. The issue here is not one of purism, or of mechanical translation. For an immense number of concepts German has two words – one of Latin origin, the other of Germanic origin. Thus, for 'conception' it has both

---

2 1989, vol. 7, no. 1.
3 "Psycho-Analytic Notes on an Autobiographical Account of a Case of Paranoia (Dementia Paranoides)" (1911c), *SE* 12, p. 63.

Auffassung and *Konzeption*; for 'morality' it has both *Sittlichkeit* and *Moralität*. These words often have analogous derivations, one from Latin or the Romance languages and the other from Germanic roots. German speakers can either choose to use them as pure synonyms or to inhabit the difference and enlarge it, so as to make out of it a conceptual distinction. But, even if they do occupy or dwell on each word very differently, the risk of them collapsing back into one another is always present. This is certainly the case for *Trieb* and *Instinkt*, which I shall henceforth translate as 'drive' and 'instinct' respectively.

What is the case with Freud? Does he distinguish these two terms or concepts? He certainly never combines them, he never opposes one to the other, and he never really compares them. And we shall see that there are ambiguities in Freud apropos of *Trieb*, apropos of the drive. But things are clearer with respect to instinct, or *Instinkt*. Freud only uses this term rarely, but he does so in a consistent manner, very often to refer to instinct in animals: "If inherited mental formations exist in the human being – something analogous to instinct in animals – these [primal fantasies] constitute the nucleus of the Ucs."[4] (Clearly he could not have said, "If there exists something analogous to the drives of animals"). Or consider this: "the little human lacks most of the survival instincts found in animals".[5]

The most piquant passage for our purposes today is from "Psychogenesis of A Case of Homosexuality in a Woman". It concerns a father who, albeit with some misgiving, brings his daughter to Freud for analysis. Here is the relevant passage in Freud:

> There was something about his daughter's homosexuality that aroused the deepest bitterness in

---

[4] "The Unconscious" (1915e), *SE*. 14, p. 195.
[5] [*Editor*: This is the paraphrase of a statement made by Freud about the lack of 'realistic anxiety' in human infants: "It would have been a good thing for them if they had inherited more of those life-preserving instincts" , "Lecture 25: Anxiety", *Introductory Lectures on Psychoanalysis* (1916–17), *SE* 16, pp. 407–8].

> him, and he was determined to combat it with all the means in his power. The low estimation in which psychoanalysis is so generally held in Vienna did not prevent him from turning to it for help. If this way failed, he still had in reserve his strongest counter-measure: a speedy marriage was to awaken the natural instincts [*Instinkte*] of the girl and stifle her unnatural tendencies.⁶

You can see the opposition here. This is a young girl who is not far past puberty. A speedy marriage must, finally, awaken her natural instinct (this is clearly a matter of *Instinkt*, of 'complementarity' as Philippe Gutton would say) and choke off her 'tendencies' – that's to say, her unnatural *Triebe*.

We can see the pernicious effect of unifying the two terms under the single heading of 'instinct'. In Strachey, in Marie Bonaparte, and in a lineage that persists even in France, one finds this general confusion within both the language used and the understanding of Freud's own usage.

A unification of the two terms under the heading of 'drive' is no less dangerous, however. So it is in Lacan, according to whom Freud "never wrote the word" instinct.⁷ Ever since Lacan, drive has occupied the entire field. Furthermore, it has been interpreted loosely as 'drift' [*en dérive*] by Lacan, through a play on the English word

---

6 "The Psychogenesis of a Case of Homosexuality in a Woman" (1920a), *SE* 18, p. 149.

7 [*Editor*: "La lecture des écrits analytiques et les traductions officielles de Freud (qui n'a jamais écrit ce mot) nous mettant de l'instinct plein la bouche, peut-être y a-t-il intérêt à obvier à une rhétorique qui obture toute efficace de concept." Jacques Lacan, *Écrits* (Paris: Editions du Seuil, 1966), p. 834. It receives a face-saving English translation as: "Reading analytic writings and official translations of works by Freud (who never wrote the word 'official') that use the term 'instinct' right and left, it is perhaps worth obviating a rhetoric that obturates the concept's effectiveness", which has the effect of rewriting Lacan's assertion *(Écrits* [1966] trans. Bruce Fink (New York: WW Norton, 2005), p. 708)].

'drive', for we are henceforth 'all-adrift', in the realm of the 'pure drive'. But drifting/deriving[8] from what? For if the drive does not drift/derive from the *instinct*, how can one say that it 'derives' at all?

There is also a folding back of terms in Freud's own work. I have emphasized this point ceaselessly for thirty years. Especially in English, 'drive' is collapsed back into 'instinct' or, sometimes, the two form a sort of mixture: the 'instinctual drive'. In support of the claim that this confusion is present in Freud (side by side with the distinction) I could note the fact that he never protested against Strachey's translation and that he rarely, if ever, thematised the opposition between drive and instinct. The closest he gets to such a thematisation is the following famous passage from the opening of *Three Essays*. The word 'instinct' is not used but it is certainly present in what Freud refers to as "the popular view" of sexuality:

Here is the key passage:

> Popular opinion has quite definite ideas about the nature and characteristics of this sexual drive [*Geschlechtstriebes*]. It is generally understood to be absent in childhood, to set in at the time of puberty in connection with the process of coming to maturity [*J.L.: each of these terms is important*] and to be revealed in the manifestations of an irresistible attraction exercised by one sex upon the other; while its aim is presumed to be sexual union, or at all events actions leading in that direction. We have every reason to believe, however, that these views give a very false picture of the true situation. If we look into them more closely we shall find that they contain a number of errors, inaccuracies and hasty conclusions …

---

8 [*Trans.*: The French verb *dériver (de)* can mean either to derive from or to drift].

> The popular view of the sexual drive [*Geschlechtstriebes*] is beautifully reflected in the poetic fable [*J.L.: this is Aristophanes' well-known fable*] which tells how the original human beings were cut up into two halves – man and woman – and how these are always striving to unite again in love.[9]

This passage, which is fundamental to our concern here, only finds its true resolution in the distinction between drive and instinct. And yet, in spite of what he writes in *Three Essays*, in spite of the veritable 'drift' [*dérive*] (to take up this term) that he proposes with respect to infantile sexuality, Freud will frequently tend to collapse the drive back into an instinctual model. I shall not take up the extensive developments I have made in order to demonstrate this in *Le fourvoiement biologisant de la sexualité*.[10] We shall return to it partly later on. I shall simply allude to two points:

Firstly, the model of tension reduction and of *homeostasis* is an instinctual model. It is a consistent model in Freud from his first writings on the 'actual neuroses', where he gives a very precise mechanistic version, through to "Instincts and their Vicissitudes".[11]

Secondly, Freud will rehabilitate the *myth of Aristophanes*, the myth of *complementarity*, in his theory of the 'life drives', which can reasonably be considered, in that final version, as 'life instincts'. Here is how, fifteen years later, Freud takes up the myth of Aristophanes, not to criticise it this time but to adopt it in relation to the 'life drive'. I shall quote only the last part of the pertinent section, since the beginning is more complicated. As you know, it is a myth about beings

---

9 *Three Essays on the Theory of Sexuality* (1905d), *SE* 7, pp. 135–136. [*Trans.*: this passage from the *Standard Edition* has been slightly altered to reflect Laplanche's preference for translating Freud's term *Trieb* as 'drive' (Fr. *pulsion*) rather than reproducing Strachey's misleading term, 'instinct'].
10 Jean Laplanche, *Problématiques VII: Le fourvoiement biologisant de la sexualité chez Freud* (Paris: Presses Universitaires de France, 2006).
11 (1915c), *SE* 14, pp. 117–40.

that are double: four limbs, two heads, two sets of genitalia, etc.; but in Plato's version there are three kinds of double beings – man-man, woman-woman, and man-woman. I take up only the last type as this will simplify the matter for the question of instinct. So, we picture these androgynes being cut in two:

> Eventually Zeus decided to cut these men in two, "like a sorb-apple which is halved for pickling". After the division had been made, "the two parts of man, each desiring his other half, came together, and threw their arms about one another eager to grow into one".[12]

2 — For my part, I propose to use *both* notions, drive and instinct, to demonstrate their *opposition*, to show their *presence* and – a factor which often makes the terms difficult to delimit – the ways in which they are *articulated with* and *cover up* each other.

Someone is bound to say, "Look at that! Laplanche is returning to instinct and thus to the body!" Do I have to repeat myself yet again? I have never left the body and I have never opposed the body to the mind. By placing drive and instinct in opposition I am not opposing the psychical to the somatic. The mathematician is being no less 'neurobiological' when he's devouring a steak than when he's calculating an integral. Drive is no more psychical than instinct. The difference is not between the somatic and the psychical but between, on the one hand, something that is innate, atavistic and endogenous and, on the other hand, something that is acquired and epigenetic but is by no means less anchored in the body for all that.

I would remind you that when Freud abandons the seduction theory he does not say, "the psychological factor has lost its influence

---

12 *Beyond the Pleasure Principle* (1920g), SE 18, p. 58.

to the biological factor", but rather, "the factor of *hereditary* disposition [has] regain[ed] a sphere of influence".[13]

So instinct *and* drive, from both a conceptual point of view and with respect to their concrete presence in man.

I shall endeavour to be schematic. Instinct emerges as hereditary and adaptive. I shall make use of a definition of instinct, which Tinbergen proposed some time ago, as:

> a hierarchically organised nervous mechanism which is susceptible to certain priming, releasing and directing impulses of internal as well as external origin, and which responds to these impulses by coordinated movements that contribute to the maintenance of the individual and the species.[14]

I have no doubt that one could make many improvements to and criticisms of this definition of 'instinct'. Nevertheless, it is a model that is often taken up by Freud: in it, instinct is hereditary, fixed, and adaptive; it starts with somatic tension, has a 'specific *action*' and a satisfying *object*, and leads to a sustained *relaxation* of the tension. In contrast, drive in the pure sense would not be hereditary, nor necessarily adaptive. The model of source, aim, and adequate object cannot easily be applied to the drive. I have insisted more than once, notably in relation to the idea of 'source', that if one can say with any rigour that the anus is the source of the anal drive, then one must question with even greater rigour how one could ever maintain that the drive to see, voyeurism, aims at lowering something that one could call 'ocular tension'.

The economic paradox. In Freud, it is at the economic level that

---

13 Letter to Fliess, 21 September 1897, *The Complete Letters of Sigmund Freud to Wilhelm Fliess*: 1887–1904, ed. and trans. JM Masson (Harvard: Harvard UP, 1985) p. 265.
14 Nikolaas Tinbergen, *The Study of Instinct* (Oxford: Clarendon, 1951), p. 112.

the difference between drive and instinct is most pronounced and the contradiction easiest to see. Once again the contradiction is concentrated within a German term. As we just witnessed apropos of *Trieb* and *Instinkt,* German sometimes has two words for one thing or two words that can serve either for one thing or two; and we know that the difference between so-called synonyms can be enlarged to create a conceptual difference. Conversely, however, and as is the case with all languages, there are some German words which concentrate a contradiction within themselves. Such is the case with the word *Lust*. Usually translated as 'pleasure', *Lust* entails a contradiction which Freud himself takes up. First of all there are the difficulties in articulating what is called the 'pleasure principle', the *Lustprinzip*, because in Freud's formulations it is sometimes a tendency towards homeostasis (i.e. a tendency aiming at the *best possible* level of tension) and sometimes a tendency towards complete discharge (i.e. a tendency aiming at the *lowest possible* level of tension). This is the difference between on the one hand an optimum functioning and on the other what one could call a 'complete' emptying out, an utterly disordered and anti-physiological functioning.

But above all there are the ambiguities of the term *Lust* itself, which in German – and Freud raises this question twice in the *Three Essays*, in two separate notes – means both 'pleasure' (as it is usually translated) and 'desire'. *Lust* in the sense of 'pleasure' refers to discharge and the relaxation of tension; but *Lust* is sometimes used in a contrary sense to mean the 'pursuit of excitation', even to the point of complete exhaustion. Thus in the terms *Schaulust* and *Berührungslust* we have, respectively, the *Lust* to see, which is not only the pleasure of seeing but also the desire or urge to see, and *Berührungslust*, which means not so much the pleasure of touching as the desire to touch. Freud alludes to this ambiguity twice, in two notes that are quite characteristic of *Three Essays*.[15] In one of these notes he refers to

---

15 See *Three Essays* (1905d), op. cit., p. 135, n. 2 and p. 212, n. 1.

it as a fortunate contradiction that allows us to navigate in a precise way within the dialectic; then at another moment he speaks of it as an unfortunate contradiction that prevents us from finding an equivalent term for *libido* in the sense of desire. He would, he says, like to use a German rather than a Latin term for desire but cannot use the word *Lust* in place of *libido* because *Lust* means pleasure as well as desire.

Thus *Lust* is sometimes synonymous with 'drive', with 'libido', 'urge to', 'desire for' and with the 'pursuit of disequilibrium'. In this case satiety is never attained.

What we nevertheless take from this – from the point of view of substance rather than terminology – are *two radically different models*: drive, which seeks excitation at the cost of total exhaustion, and instinct, which seeks relaxation.

3 — How and where do drive and instinct exist in man? Can we locate them within those two domains which, since Freud, have become standard references and which there is no reason to renounce completely: the domains of self-preservation and of sexuality, respectively?

Self-preservation, it must be said, can scarcely – if at all – be reconciled with the variability and the drift [*dérive*] of the drives. The so-called 'primary' model of the 'primary process' is *not* a biological model. How many times have I sought acceptance for the idea that what is primary in the primary process does not come 'first' or 'before'! The primary process only becomes 'primary' secondarily, as a consequence of repression and within the domain of the unconscious. An organism that would function according to the fundamental principle of the *Project for a Scientific Psychology*[16] – I am speaking of the first few chapters of the *Project* in which the only aim of the organism is a complete evacuation of energy – would not survive for a second. So the very idea of 'self-preservation' implies homeostasis, which is to

---

16 (1950a [1895]), *SE* 1, pp. 283–387.

Drive and Instinct

say a return to a base level that is *optimal and not minimal*.[17] The notion of a satisfying object and a specific action leads us toward the idea of instinct.

In fact, at or near the conclusion of the twentieth century we have two models: the model of instinct and the model of attachment. Let us go one step at a time here. The work of Lorenz in particular introduced more flexibility into models of instinct. He established that instinct itself has much greater variability than had been thought. He introduced the notion of intercalation or alternation. The German term is *Verschränkung*, which expresses his meaning clearly. It entails a veritable braiding of instinctual threads that are innate and threads that have been acquired by training or intelligence.

But this is not the essential question. The major distinction among self-preservative behaviours is to be made between those that have no *need of the other* and those that do. The attachment model first introduced by Bowlby does indeed take up an essential aspect of instinct – I am referring to innateness – but it also introduces the notion of a *reciprocity*. I cite one definition of attachment:

> Innate behaviours that have the function of reducing distance from and establishing proximity and contact with the mother. Innate behaviours also exist within the mother and have the same function, even if learning plays some part in the expression of these behaviours.[18]

In the behaviours whose goal is to maintain life, we should thus distinguish carefully first of all those automatic, biological functions that, in a sense, have no need of the other. For example, the homeostatic function that keeps stable the amount of carbon dioxide

---

17 See *Life and Death in Psychoanalysis*, trans. Jeffrey Mehlman (Baltimore: Johns Hopkins UP, 1977), chapter 6.
[18] Hubert Montagner, "L'attachement", in *Le Carnet psy*, no. 48, October 2000, p. 13.

in the blood is a relatively autonomous one, as is the mechanism that regulates serum glucose.

And what about warmth? Well, with warmth it's not so simple. An important distinction here is the difference between 'poikilotherms' and 'homeotherms'. Poikilotherms are those creatures that do not need to maintain a specific internal temperature; homeotherms are those that are capable of doing so. But in the latter – the homeotherms – the ability is, at the outset, imperfect. That is to say that autonomous homeothermy is only established bit by bit. You are all familiar with the sudden chills and sudden fevers of nurslings. Newly hatched fishes (poikilotherms) have no need of the other, but homeothermic species (which are only imperfectly homeothermic at birth) must communicate in order to maintain warmth. I was once very struck by Jouvet's remark (I have written to him on this subject without getting a reply) that for practical purposes, the line between the species that dream and those that do not dream is the same as that between homeotherms and poikilotherms. It seems to me that this dividing line is also that between species that rely on infant/adult communication and species that do not.

But it is perhaps man who has the greatest need for interaction. Hence that statement of Freud's which I cited a moment ago: "the little human lacks the instincts necessary for survival".[19] Evidently this is only a first approximation because elsewhere he speaks of the 'self-preservative drive'. This phrase undoubtedly indicates his recognition of the deficiency of the instincts in the absence of the other's intervention. Indeed, there is an entire series of innate reactions that do not exist in the little human being; numerous experiments have confirmed Freud's assertion – for example, experiments on the fear of heights, on retreating from objects that can burn the child, etc.

Attachment theory initially emerged as a war machine against psychoanalysis, against sexuality and against the unconscious, and so

---

19 [*Editor*: See comment, note 5].

it remains. Hence the need to push things further still. First of all, by recalling that there is something in Freud that anticipates the idea of attachment, and this is the notion of *affection*. When Freud contrasts the "affectionate" relation or the "affectionate current" with the "sensual current", he is doing nothing other than contrasting attachment with sexuality.[20] The affection, which Freud places under the heading of self-preservation (at least in his first theory of the drives), corresponds to the fact that the adult nourishes and protects. Thus, from the start, there is something more than an 'attachment' in the simply literal sense of the term, i.e. the grasping reflex, the need for contact, and rooting. From birth, the 'affectionate current', the 'affectionate relation', includes many aspects of the mother-baby relation, beyond just seeking warmth. Moreover, the affectionate relation is not limited exclusively to the mother but may include many other adults; and we know that the attachment relation can exist in the absence of the mother, for instance with a nanny.

Is there an innate self-preservative relation in humans? The debate has been overrun by the opposition between the so-called baby of observation and the so-called baby of psychoanalysis. For when it comes to the observation of nurslings in particular one only really sees what one wishes to see; but in order to see it at all one must be at least able to detect it by actual observation. Think of Melanie Klein, that promoter of the priority of the 'inner world', who did not fail to write an article titled "On Observing the Behaviour of Young Infants".[21] Such observation is, however, very difficult, and while animal observation is in some ways indispensable, it is totally insufficient. It is indispensable largely because it permits us to try to identify, by means of deduction, that which is uniquely important in man. Must we say that what is uniquely important in humans is communication? Must we therefore deny the existence of communication

---

20 "On the Universal Tendency to Debasement in the Sphere of Love" (1912d), *SE* 11, p. 180 ff.
21 In *Envy and Gratitude and Other Works 1946–1963* (London: Hogarth, 1975).

in animals? Of course not – I indicated as much a moment ago apropos of homeotherms and the possibility that they dream – but animal communication is infinitely less developed. Animals have systems of communication but they do not have true language. To be sure, and as I have insisted many times, adult-baby communication is not linguistic at the outset. But it is marked from the outset in its diversity, its complexity and its ambiguities by the fact that man is a linguistic animal. In other words, the complexity of verbal language exercises a kind of contagion on pre-verbal communication.

It must be emphasised that *attachment in man* is primarily a *reciprocal* relation of communication and messages. But the second point, deductively derived from the observation of animals, is much more important: it is the presence of the sexual unconscious in the human adult. One could give up the whole theory of the drives, but could one give up the sexual unconscious? It would be doing psychoanalysis a disservice to reduce this point to the difference between the baby of observation and the psychoanalytic baby, a difference that is only constructed afterwards.[22] For if the adult unconscious is present in the primordial relationship and if, in observing that relationship, we do not see it, the reason is that we are not using the means that would enable us to see it – not so much to explore the adult unconscious directly, but at least to detect its symptoms.[23]

If I have spoken of the animal it is because attachment in man is perhaps never observable in a pure state. This is for two reasons: attachment is infiltrated by the narcissistic relation, and it is contaminated and compromised by adult sexuality. This is precisely what we refuse to see when, for example, we oppose 'secure' attachment (in which the child is made to feel secure) to 'insecure' attachment. For

---

22 Regardless of the fact that afterwardsness [*Editor*: Freud's *Nachträglichkeit*, translated in the *SE* as 'deferred action'] comes into existence very early in human beings, probably as early as the second year of life.
23 On this point cf. Herman Roiphe and Eleanor Galenson, *Infantile Origins of Sexual Identity* (Connecticut: International Universities Press, 1981), esp. chapters 13 and 14.

insecure attachment is only an aspect – the most extreme aspect, to be sure – of the *enigmatic*. If it is 'pathological' this is perhaps because the sexual – and here I am talking about the *sexual drive* – is nothing less than a deviation *itself*.

4 — Before returning to the relation between sexuality and attachment, I want to touch on two modalities of sexuality: infantile sexuality and the sexuality of adolescence.

Infantile sexuality is Freud's great discovery. It is the '*sexual*'[24] enlarged beyond the limits of the difference between the sexes and beyond sexual reproduction. It is the sexuality of the component drives, connected to erogenous zones and functioning on the model of *Vorlust* – a term in which we again encounter the word *Lust* as meaning pleasure and desire simultaneously. *Vorlust* might be called 'fore-pleasure-desire', since it is not the pleasure attendant upon the reduction of tension but on the increase of tension. Indeed, there is nothing to suggest that this infantile 'pleasure-desire' corresponds to any internal physiological tension and that it requires discharge.

Let us discuss the body for a moment, and return to endocrinology. We know that the sexual and hypophysary hormones, which are present at birth, decline very rapidly to zero within the first months of life and do not reappear until puberty or just before it. We speak of 'latency', but in my opinion there is good reason to speak of two types of latency. There is the *latency of the drive*, which is the classic type as defined by Freud. This is the latency connected to repression and the Oedipus, which occurs between the age of five or six and puberty. It is, as we know, a relative latency. And there is the *latency of the instinct*, which is in fact the latency defined by the famous 'popular view of sexuality', that is, a latency that exists between birth and puberty, an endogenous latency during which only the drive has free

---

24 [*Editor*: On Laplanche's French neologism '*sexual*' (as distinct from the normal 'sexuel'), see the Editor's note to the Forward of this volume. The term is printed here in italics to mark it off from the standard English term with the same spelling].

reign. Radio silence of the sexual instinct.

I shall take up again a few negative propositions. Nothing permits the assertion that the erogeneity of erotogenic zones is linked to an endogenous internal tension. Nothing permits the assertion that the psychoanalytic Vulgate with its succession of stages corresponds to a programmed genetic mechanism.[25] I am dismayed that there are still analytic institutes that teach Freud as one would teach the catechism, with an ordered succession of infantile stages of sexuality. Nothing allows us to see, in the always more or less chaotic evolution of the sexual drive, anything that is inscribed within a larger schema, assigned a function, with the aim of preparing the way for puberty. It is precisely such a re-inscription of the drive back into the field of instinct that Freud would eventually seek to enforce, setting out, in spite of everything, a kind of pre-programmed course of development in which infantile sexuality is continuous with pubertal and adult sexuality.

5 — Before coming to the moment of puberty, let us pose the question of the *connection* between the self-preservative, instinctual relationship – which is complicated and enriched by affection – and the sexual drive. The theory of 'leaning-on' to which I alluded earlier is one that is increasingly invoked, increasingly rediscovered and reinterpreted, and increasingly integrated into the Vulgate; but it can have a pernicious effect in this domain.

If infantile sexuality does not have an innate endogenous mechanism, how can it emerge conjointly with self-preservation? And if it corresponds to a simple representation in fantasy of bodily attachment and self-preservative functions, by what miracle would this fantasmatisation alone confer a sexual character upon somatic functions? As I have pointed out on several occasions, in Freud the putative 'experience of satisfaction' and the putative 'hallucinatory satisfaction of desire' are successful exercises in prestidigitation. They

---

[25] Melanie Klein already fought against this idea.

make the sexual emerge from the lack of satisfaction of the self-preservative instinct in the same way that that rabbit emerges from the magician's hat. But the trick depends precisely on the fact that there is someone who has put the rabbit in the hat – and it is certainly the adult who put it there.[26]

The theory of seduction, which I shall not elaborate here, proposes a model of the emergence of the sexual from within the reciprocal relation of attachment. I say 'reciprocal', but an interference or 'noise' comes to inhabit this communication like a parasite, an interference that initially *proceeds from one side only*, and that is the side of the adult. This adult is most often the mother but only insofar as she is an adult and, let me repeat, her place may be occupied by any adult. For lack of time I shall not discuss the representation or model that one could give of the process of repression, of the creation of the unconscious or of the surging up of the drive.

The source of the infantile sexual drive is the unconscious, and its characteristics are marked by that origin. The infantile sexual drive is an endless search and knows no relaxation of tension. It knows nothing of orgasm, in spite of the analogy that Freud thought he could perceive between the satisfaction of the infant who has just finished sucking and the satisfaction that follows orgasm. It knows nothing of satisfaction by means of the adapted complementary object; it always lacks sufficient binding and is ambivalent.

6 — The major attempt at binding is the Oedipus, the infantile Oedipus. Before speaking of this, however, I shall address the *sexual instinct*. Gutton suggests a model based on the notion of the 'pubertal'.[27] If I understand this correctly, a sexual instinct corresponds to genital maturation with an innate tendency to seek out what is 'complementary' (this is his term): i.e. the complementary erogenous zone, and,

---

26 The adult who, in the case of theory, is followed in this role by Freud. Once again, theoretico-genesis is modelled on ontogenesis.
27 Philippe Gutton, *Le pubertaire* (Paris: Presses Universitaires de France, 2003).

as the song goes, "the person of the opposite sex." This is precisely the 'popular opinion' that Freud rejects in the *Three Essays*, only to adopt it in *Beyond the Pleasure Principle*. Freud has nothing against this notion as long as its application is clearly delimited. I have nothing against it, on the condition that it is properly situated. To situate this instinct, or this complementarity, is not to position it as a continuation of infantile sexuality, not even as a mutation or morphing of it, but rather as a rupture. It is a qualitatively new development and not the culmination of infantile sexuality.

As regards animals, there are some things we can begin to learn about the sexual instinct at puberty, but these are very limited and slightly laughable. As regards human nature, for millennia we thought we knew that, as Mozart has it, "Mon cœur soupire".[28] But precisely those things that we think we know are, in fact, complicated by both the cultural and by infantile sexuality! What psychoanalysis teaches us – which seems utterly foreign – is that in man the sexuality of intersubjective origin, that is, drive sexuality, *the sexuality that is acquired, comes before the sexuality that is innate. Drive comes before instinct,* fantasy comes before function; and when the sexual instinct arrives, the seat is already occupied.

A case in point here is the problem of the Oedipus: 'love of the parent of the opposite sex and rivalry with, the hatred of, or the wish to destroy the parent of the same sex'. I readily admit that this formulation presents a 'homothetic' Oedipus. Rivalry on one side, attraction on the other. Homothetic because the little triangle between ego, its partner and its child would reproduce homothetically the great parental triangle of father–mother–ego. Here, the structuring appears simple. The identification is an identification with the *rival*. It is an identification that some have called 'mimetic' – I am thinking of Girard and of the success of the idea of mimetism.

---

28 [*Editor*: "My heart sighs", the French version of Cherubino's aria, "Voi che sapete" in *The Marriage of Figaro*].

However, Freud's description of the infantile Oedipus is quite different. The infantile Oedipus is always bipolar, 'positive' and 'negative' at the same time. I shall not describe the four attitudes in question, since they are obvious. So much so (and this is the essential point) that the *identifications are always replacements for love relationships*. They are internalizations of the lost object. Freud tells us explicitly that identification is either the primordial form of relationship with the object or a substitute for the relationship with the love object. Identification with the object and *not with the rival* is indispensable for any understanding of homosexuality and of heterosexuality. In one of Freud's major formulations apropos of Leonardo, the homosexual man identifies himself with the object of his love, his mother. In the same way, the heterosexual must have had a powerful and homosexual love for his father in order to identify with him. In these texts, Freud always blurs the rivalrous identifications. I have had occasion to demonstrate this in respect of the text on *Group Psychology and the Analysis of the Ego*.[29] To put it more clearly, the positive and negative attitudes are present in *every* identification.

7 — At adolescence, then, we have the confluence of two rivers bearing strongly heterogeneous waters, and there is nothing to guarantee their harmonious convergence. On one side flow the drive and the infantile fantasies, on the other the pubertal instinct. I shall pick out the points of difference, even incompatibility between them.

Firstly, there are two Oedipuses, one of which is 'complementary' while the other is irremediably bisexual and, at the same time, ambivalent – the sexuality of life and the sexuality of death. The sexual aspect of parricide – taking this term in the most general sense, i.e. the murder of the parent – cannot in itself be as easily obscured as some would have us think. Gutton speaks of the "erotic decathexis of the

---

29 *Problématiques I: L'Angoisse* (Paris: Presses Universitaires de France, 1980), pp. 341–347.

rival facilitating his being put to death",[30] but this is precisely to forget that the killing of the parent in the infantile Oedipus is an erotic act. *Secondly*, the place of the object is another point of difference or even opposition: on one side there is the complementary *object of satisfaction*; on the other side, there is the *source-object*, the designified signifiers (as I call them) in the unconscious. *Thirdly*, there are, as I indicated earlier, two distinct economic modes: the pursuit of relaxation and orgasm on one side; on the other side, the pursuit of excitation which is characteristic of the pre-genital. We must emphasise, however, that the pre-genital includes the infantile genital. To be sure, there is what is called the integration of pre-genital pleasures into fore-pleasure, but several comments need to be made on this head. It is not only the pre-genital which must be integrated into so-called genital primacy; it is the whole of the pre-genital and the para-genital or infantile genital that comes into contact with pubertal and then with adult genitality. The infantile genital, the phallic, remains in the order of the 'para-genital' and, later, of 'fore-pleasure': one need only think of how often the cult of phallic performance is the predominant element of – above all modern – adult sexuality.

On the other hand, if the drive's pursuit of excitation were completely integrated into the sexual instinct what would become of human creativity? And if the drive is not at least partially integrated we find ourselves in what Freud called 'fixation on preliminary sexual aims', we find ourselves, that is, on the ever present path towards perversion.

---

30 *Le pubertaire,* op. cit., p. 46.

Conclusion

The object of psychoanalysis is the unconscious, and the unconscious is above all the sexual in the precise Freudian sense – drive sexuality, infantile sexuality, pre-, para- or infantile-genital sexuality. It is the sexuality whose very source is fantasy itself, implanted of course within the body.

And to take up again the terms instinct and drive, I shall recapitulate in just a few words:

1. The *self-preservative instinct* exists in man, but it must be understood that (a) it is in large part affection or attachment, which is to say that it is mediated by reciprocal communication; and (b) it is from the start covered over and thus hidden by the peculiarly human and sexual phenomena of both seduction and the narcissistic reciprocity with the other.

2. In man, there is a *sexual drive* that occupies a major and decisive place from birth until puberty. It is this that constitutes the object of psychoanalysis; it is this that is lodged in the unconscious.

3. There is a *sexual instinct*, which is pubertal and adult, but it 'finds its place occupied' already by the infantile drive.

This instinct is thus very difficult to define epistemologically – and precisely to the extent that concretely and in the real it does not appear in a pure state, but only in uncertain transactions with the infantile sexuality that reigns in the unconscious.

2

SEXUALITY AND ATTACHMENT IN METAPSYCHOLOGY[1]

Daniel Widlöcher introduces his article on "Primary Love and Infantile Sexuality"[2] with a discussion of Michael Balint's 1937 lecture and article on 'primary object-love'.[3] It is difficult not to agree with this point of departure, since Michael Balint's voice emerges at a moment when the dominant position is the official Freudian doctrine of 'primary narcissism' as an objectless state. The dogma of the 'monad', a state from which the little human being would, somehow, have to exit in order to join up with the 'object', is vigorously, even definitively, swept away.

It is yet more remarkable that in just a few lines Daniel Widlöcher is able to characterise this discussion as an "eternal debate" and as a "debate that did not take place",[4] evidence that Michael Balint (and his Hungarian entourage) had probably not sufficiently

---

1 First published in *Sexualité infantile et attachement* ed. Daniel Widlöcher (Paris: Presses Universitaires de France, 2000).
2 Daniel Widlöcher, "Primary Love and Infantile Sexuality: An Eternal Debate", trans. Susan Fairfield, in *Infantile Sexuality and Attachment* (London: Karnac, 2002).
3 Michael Balint, "Early Developmental States of the Ego. Primary Object Love", in *Primary Love and Psychoanalytic Technique* (London: The Hogarth Press, 1952), pp. 90–108.
4 op. cit. p.1.

established his theses and had not, in the first instance, sufficiently cleared the ground on which he based his arguments. This is not the place to take up Balint's thought as it emerges, in all its complexity, in his collection *Primary Love and Psychoanalytic Technique*. The main point of our reservations would probably concentrate on the term 'love' itself, which is used to characterise the first mother-child relation. It is a term that brings together all the ambiguities present in Freud's late theorisation, ambiguities which Balint, in spite of himself, was to inherit.

The Freudian theory that Balint criticises is that of narcissism as the primary state of the human being. But in addition, Freud states that the key aspect of 'autoerotism' is no longer to be distinguished as a separate moment: it simply becomes "the sexual activity of the narcissistic stage of allocation of the libido".[5] As we know, in this *last Freudian theory* the world of the drives is entirely subsumed within the opposition between 'life drives' (Eros) and 'death drives'. But given the fact that the death drive will be rejected by the majority of authors cited by Daniel Widlöcher, and that Balint himself expressly criticises this hypothesis,[6] we end up with an extremely simplified view in which the entire world of the drives is submitted to the hegemony of the life drive, of love, or of Eros.[7] Under the heading of the latter are gathered not only sexuality but love in its narcissistic forms, and ultimately the self-preservative drives as well: "The contrast between the drives of self-preservation and the preservation of the species, as well

---

5 Sigmund Freud, "Lecture 26: The Libido Theory and Narcissism", *Introductory Lectures on Psychoanalysis* (1916–17), *SE* 16, p. 416.

6 Cf. for example, "On Love and Hate" (1951) in *Primary Love and Psychoanalytic Technique*, op. cit., pp. 121–135.

7 It is precisely so as to provide a counterweight to this hegemony of the narcissistic Eros that Freud introduced the death drive, which, according to my interpretation, is a means of reintroducing the destructive and 'unbinding' aspects of sexuality itself. Cf. in particular Jean Laplanche, *Life and Death in Psychoanalysis*, trans. Jeffrey Mehlman (Baltimore: Johns Hopkins 1977), chapter 6, "Why the Death Drive?"; and "The So-Called Death Drive: A Sexual Drive", in *The British Journal of Psychotherapy*, vol. 20, no. 4, 2006, pp. 455–471.

as the contrast between ego-love and object-love, falls within Eros".[8]

Balint is doubtless aware that there are different points of view in Freud, and this is something that distinguishes him from the later authors Widlöcher cites.[9] What we have often tried to show is that in Freud it is not a question of "fluctuating" views, as Widlöcher puts it, but of an entire line of thought which Freud himself attempts to re-absorb within his subsequent elaboration, yet which remains extremely stimulating.[10] It is worth recalling certain distinctions, some of which are explicit, some of which are implicit.

Explicit distinctions. First of all there is the essential idea that neither narcissism nor perhaps autoerotism is a primary state. Far from being practically innate *a priori*s they only appear in the course of the adult-child relation. This is the case for autoerotism, which in 1905 Freud believes succeeds a primary phase of relation to the object:

> At a time at which the first beginnings of sexual satisfaction are still linked with the taking of nourishment [J.L.: *this is the moment of leaning-on*], the sexual drive has a sexual object outside the infant's own body in the shape of the mother's breast. It is only later that the drive loses that object, just at the time, perhaps, when the child is able to form a total idea of the person to whom the organ that is giving him satisfaction belongs. As a rule the sexual drive

---

8 Sigmund Freud, *An Outline of Psychoanalysis* (1940a), SE 23, p. 148 [*Trans.*: James Strachey's translation of Freud has been altered here and throughout, where appropriate, to reflect Laplanche's preference for rendering Freud's German term *Trieb* as 'drive' (Fr. *pulsion*) rather than the more familiar but misleading 'instinct'].
9 Cf. in particular "Critical Notes on the Theory of the Pregenital Organisations of the Libido" (1935), in *Primary Love and Psychoanalytic Technique*, p. 46 (on autoerotism) and pp. 56–57 (on narcissism).
10 Cf. in particular Jean Laplanche, *New Foundations for Psychoanalysis*, trans. David Macey (Oxford: Blackwell, 1989) "2.7 A major instance of confusion: the 'objectless' state", pp. 68–81. The idea here is that Balint replaces the confusion of the 'objectless' state with that of primary 'love'.

then becomes autoerotic.[11]

I concluded in 1970 that the above text

> has an entirely different ring to it from that vast fable of autoerotism as a state of the primary and total absence of an object: a state which one leaves in order to *find* an object. A loss of the 'partial' object, it should be noted, since it is a loss of the breast which is being considered, and Freud introduces at this point the precious observation that perhaps the partial object is lost at the moment in which the total object – the mother as person – begins to emerge. But above all, if such a text is to be taken seriously, it means that *on the one hand there is from the beginning an object, but that on the other hand sexuality does not have, from the beginning, a real object.*[12]

In order to describe this *second* moment I have proposed the term 'auto-time', a phase in which sexuality is turned back upon the internal fantasmatic object.[13]

Now, the same thing occurs with respect to narcissism, which when Freud first advances it in "On Narcissism: An Introduction" also appears as *second* in relation to autoerotism: "What is the relation of the narcissism of which we are now speaking to auto-erotism, which we have described as an early state of the libido?" The response is given in two short sentences, which probably contain Freud's most acute and most distilled view on this question:

---

11 Sigmund Freud, *Three Essays on the Theory of Sexuality* (1905d), SE 7, p. 222. Bracketed remarks are mine.
12 *Life and Death in Psychoanalysis*, op.cit., p. 19.
13 *Life and Death in Psychoanalysis*, op.cit., pp. 85–102. [*Trans.* Laplanche's term *'temps auto'* is translated by Jeffrey Mehlman as 'self-phase'].

> [W]e are bound to suppose that a unity comparable to the ego cannot exist in the individual from the start; the ego has to be developed ... so there must be something added to auto-erotism – a new psychical action – in order to bring about narcissism.[14]

This line of thought will of course be rapidly covered over by the notion of 'primary objectless narcissism'. It does persist, however, and especially in the work of Federn. It does so to the extent that Freud was led to say he didn't understand Federn at all, as though he no longer wanted to understand anything of the position that he had initially elaborated.[15] I have for my part enlarged the furrow that was dug and then abandoned by Freud (i.e. the notion of a sequence: sexual satisfaction linked to need — autoerotism — narcissism), while rejecting the idea of successive 'stages' in favour of "moments that are, to a greater or lesser extent, both *punctual* and *reiterated*".[16]

Another explicit distinction, which Freud will be led to flatten out, not to say integrate into his all-encompassing Eros, is that between the self-preservative drives and the sexual drives. This is a major distinction, for it already outlines what will be the relation between sexuality and attachment. We shall discuss their connection further on. Let us simply mention that for Freud the self-preservative functions are not objectless: "[they] are never capable of auto-erotic satisfaction".[17] However shaky this expression may be (referring, as it does, to an autoerotism of self-preservation!) the idea is clear enough: from the beginning, the self-preservative drives are oriented towards the good-enough object. Moreover, it is precisely to this extent that they are capable of showing the way to the sexual drives.

---

14 "On Narcissism: An Introduction" (1914c), *SE* 14, pp. 76–77.
15 Cf. *Life and Death*, op. cit., chapter 4, "The Ego and Narcissism"; and Maria Teresa de Melo Carvalho, *Paul Federn, une autre voie pour la théorie du moi* (Paris: Presses Universitaires de France, 1996).
16 *New Foundations for Psychoanalysis*, op. cit., p. 73.
17 Sigmund Freud, "Instincts and their Vicissitudes" (1915c), *SE* 14, p. 134, n. 2.

But we cannot discuss this further without making reference to other *distinctions and conceptualisations* that are *implicit* in Freud's work. They are implicit in the sense that they are not the object of any thematic exposition in Freud and have gone on to be completely neglected in the entire course of a long tradition. This omission is, to be sure, already notable in the German literature but it becomes complete with the passage into English. First of all there is the total blindness concerning the distinction within the Freudian text itself between the notions of *drive* (*Trieb*) and *instinct* (*Instinkt*).[18] The difference between them is certainly never thematised by Freud, but this does not preclude there being a very clear distinction in the use of these terms, just as there is for that other pairing of 'drive' and 'need'. Yet in the English translations of Freud the two terms are collapsed into one another. In addition – a serious phenomenon – the authors who passed from German to English in their own output crossed this frontier without taking any account of it: the frontier, that is, dividing an *instinctual* conception, which for Freud is primarily applicable to self-preservation and to 'instinct in animals', from his conception of the *drive*. Instinct is relatively fixed within the species, is largely innate, and corresponds to adaptive aims; whereas drive, the model for which remains the sexual drive, is variable from one individual to another, is contingent with regard to its aims and objects, and is emphatically 'polymorphous perverse', at least in proximity to its origins. It was not until 1967 that this distinction within the Freudian usage was truly revealed.[19]

It is from the same date too that the notion of 'leaning-on' rediscovered not only its meaning and its importance but its very existence. Indeed, however important it may be, the concept of *Anlehnung* is only used sporadically by Freud. It was never given a systematic exposition. Moreover, the notion would be crushed in

---

18 Cf. "Drive and Instinct" in the present volume.
19 Jean Laplanche and Jean-Bertrand Pontalis, "Instinct (or Drive)", in *The Language of Psychoanalysis*, trans. Donald Nicholson-Smith (London: Karnac, 1973).

Strachey's translation by the invention of the barbaric and pseudo-scientific term 'anaclisis'. From that point on, and rapidly, the notion of *a genesis, in which the sexual drive leans for support upon self-preservative instinctual functioning*, would be utterly eclipsed by the entirely different notions of 'anaclitic relation' (the child deriving support from the mother) and even 'anaclitic depression', which was created by Spitz to describe states in which the child is deprived of the mother. Need it be emphasised that it was not until the 'French' reading of Freud and the selection of the word *étayage* that all the attention was drawn to this concept?[20]

Without going into detail, let us say that the very notion of leaning-on presupposes the distinction between an instinctual mode of functioning that is self-preservative and oriented towards the object, and an erotic mode of functioning that begins by deriving support from the former and then detaches itself and 'becomes autoerotic'.

In my view, it would therefore be anachronistic to align Balint in any way with a conception of leaning-on of which he knows nothing, just as he ultimately neglects its Freudian premise, i.e. the self-preservation/sexuality dualism.

Must we reproach Balint, who joined the Freudian bandwagon while it was in full swing, for taking the 'myth of the amoeba' as his starting point, thus neglecting the entire development anterior to it and everything in Freud's own thought which authorises a totally different view? Need we reproach him for a reading of Freud that neglects the very different strata of the *Three Essays*? Perhaps not. But we are justified in reproaching those authors who came after him, right up to Jeremy Holmes,[21] for having completely neglected what French Freudian and psychoanalytic research has been empha-

---

20 Cf. Jean Laplanche and Jean-Bertrand Pontalis, "Anaclisis" in *The Language of Psychoanalysis*, op. cit.; and Jean Laplanche, *Life and Death*, op. cit., chapter 1, "The Vital Order and the Genesis of Human Sexuality".
21 *Attachment, Intimacy, Autonomy: Using Attachment Theory in Adult Psychotherapy* (New York: Jason Aronson, 1996), p. 2.

sising since 1967–1970: the difference between self-preservation and sexuality, the opening of self-preservation onto the external object, and the articulation of two types of functioning within the relation of leaning-on.

Here I must note that even Michel Renard and Pierre Lab,[22] the French authors whom Widlöcher describes as coming to the rescue of this 'monadological' point of view (which is 'Freudian' only in the most restricted sense of the term), were writing in 1969 without taking account of either the theory of leaning-on or the following, pertinent points of view already developed by Daniel Lagache in 1961:

> It is to deny the evidence to claim that the newborn has no conscious experiences while it alternates between sleeping and waking. Its conscious experiences are above all experiences of bodily states and bodily acts, which means that they depend primarily upon intero- and proprioceptive receptions. The child is not, however, enclosed within its subjectivity. It is difficult to conceive of the relation between the newborn and the breast other than as the relation of a subject to an object: without existing as a cognitive structure, the subject functions and is successively actualised in the needs which awaken him and motivate him, in the acts of orientation and then consumption which appease him and put him to sleep. Similarly, the breast and the milk fulfil their function as object long before there is any positional consciousness of objects.[23]

---

22 Michel Renard, "La narcissisme", and Pierre Lab, "La conflit intra-psychique", in *La théorie psychanalytique*, ed. Sacha Nacht (Paris: Presses Universitaires de France, 1969).

23 Daniel Lagache, "La psychanalyse et la structure de la personnalité" (1961), in *Œuvres IV* (Paris : Presses Universitaires de France 1986), p. 201.

Thus for years a certain, predominantly Anglo-Saxon tradition continued to wrestle with the myth of the originary monad, or with the false problem raised by Fairbairn of the pleasure-seeking drive and the object-seeking drive, and without taking account of the fact that the double opposition between self-preservation and sexuality on the one hand, and drive and instinct on the other, would perhaps open onto new perspectives. There thus remained a mutual estrangement between, on the one hand, a French line of thought related to the thoroughgoing re-examination of the presuppositions, the implicit concepts, the historical evolution and even the 'goings astray' of Freudian thought, and, on the other hand, a debate within the Anglophone literature which congealed around a static, even ahistorical conception of Freudianism,[24] the latter being accepted or refused *without* benefit of inventory.

A striking example would be Mahlerian thought, which for years dominated entire sectors of Anglo-Saxon thinking and did so, as Lagache put it, by "denying the evidence". The idea that every child passes through an autistic phase and then through a phase of symbiosis with the mother before acquiring its 'separation-individuation' secondarily, is unable to flourish except within the framework of the theory of 'primary narcissism' conceived as a first state from which the 'monad' would somehow have to exit.

Margaret Mahler's theory has really prospered very little on French soil. Lagache's thought opposes it in a very precise fashion. For my part, ever since *Life and Death in Psychoanalysis* I have argued vigorously against the theory of the 'primitive monad', in whatever forms it may take. Finally, a richly researched and argued article by Jean Gortais did justice to a realist conception of symbiosis: "in our view it is essentially on the register of illusion, of the fantasmatic, and

---

[24] The evidence for this pervasive Anglo-Saxon ahistoricism is the authors' citations, which refer largely to the dates of the latest published edition consulted. Who would guess that the citation 'Freud (1987)' refers to the *Three Essays*, in the successive versions of 1905, 1910, 1915 and 1924?

also of definitive regression and delusion that the concept of symbiosis can be meaningful. For this reason, it is fundamentally related to dedifferentiation and not to non-differentiation".[25]

As the latest and radically desexualised avatar of originary narcissism, Mahlerism has in fact been swept away on the international level by all the data of child observation, which can currently be gathered together under the general heading of 'attachment theory'. The refutation is unconditional, and its fullest expression can be found in Martin Dornes' article, "La théorie de Margaret Mahler reconsidérée".[26] But here the danger ultimately remains the same as it did with Balint's first critique: the return to 'intersubjectivity' effected under the sign of a motivation-based monism (in this case, attachment; in Balint, it was love) in which ultimately the great loser is infantile *sexuality*, in the Freudian sense of the term.[27] We should add that the same disaster could well cause the disappearance of the Freudian unconscious, along with the major function of fantasy.

*
* *

This means that, in our view, owing to the hegemony of attachment theory there is a risk that the debate over attachment and sexuality may never in fact take place, unless attachment can be *accommodated* within the framework of a *rigorous metapsychology*. This would be a metapsychology that certainly has its origins in Freud, but which, as the outcome of a working through, does not hesitate to make choices and propose important reconfigurations.

---

25 Jean Gortais, "Le concept de symbiose en psychanalyse", in *Psychanalyse à la Université*, vol. 12, no. 46, pp. 201–257, p. 251.
26 In *Psyche*, vol. 50, no. 11, 1996. Reprinted in Martin Dornes, *Psychanalyse et psychologie du première âge* (Paris: Presses Universitaires de France, 2002).
27 Let us recall again the following passage from Balint: "In contrast to the pregenital relation, this genital or adult relation is always sexual ... whereas the pregenital object-relation is usually non-sexual (sexually not dimorphous)". "On Love and Hate", op. cit., p. 126.

In order to set out very succinctly such a *metapsychology on new foundations*, we shall take our point of departure from the double distinction already invoked above: that between instinctual functioning and drive functioning, and that between self-preservation and sexuality. First of all, it is crucial that we treat these two oppositions separately, since they only slightly overlap.

I. The opposition between *drive* and *instinct* is fundamental, and we can only regret the decades of futile debate occasioned by the confusion of one with the other: among the chief factors responsible for this confusion, although not the only one, would be the migration of Freudian thought into the English language (and not only Strachey's translation). Let us mark the points of difference on three registers: instinct appears as adaptive, genetically programmed and economically aimed at equilibrium. The drive, as we conceive it, is non- and even anti-adaptive.[28] Although it is inscribed within the body and within biology, it is not genetic in origin but owes its emergence to the specificity of the adult-child relation. Finally, it functions according to a principle other than that of a reduction of tensions.

Let us take up these points in a schematic fashion. As to instinct, it emerges as hereditary and as adaptive. I recall one definition – Tinbergen's, from a long time ago – of instinct as:

> a hierarchically organised nervous mechanism which is susceptible to certain priming, releasing and directing impulses of internal as well as external origin, and which responds to these impulses by coordinated movements that contribute to the maintenance of the individual and the species.[29]

---

[28] Primarily in the Freudian lineage of the *Three Essays* of 1905, but this is not to deny that we are making choices which 'put Freud to work'.
[29] Nikolaas Tinbergen, *The Study of Instinct* (Oxford: Oxford University Press, 1951), p. 112.

Subsequently, this fixed aspect of instinct has been rendered noticeably more supple, but without undermining its genetically programmed basis. It was chiefly Lorenz who established that in terms of its development within the individual, instinct is much more variable than was believed. He speaks of an 'intercalation' (*Verschränkung*) whereby innate instinctual elements are plaited with elements that are acquired by training or intelligence.[30] It is this increased suppleness in the notion of instinct which has enabled its opening onto the more recently explored domain of attachment.

The drive, which is unveiled in magisterial fashion in the *Three Essays* of 1905, is quite different. Here, the points of view of heredity and adaptation are closely connected and in this they are jointly refutable. Adaptation is immediately undermined by the notion of 'polymorphous perversity', which is placed at the beginning of the entire elaboration. The contingency of objects and the variability of aims, which are often interchangeable, undermine the 'popular idea' of a subordination of the drives to the biological finality of procreation. As to what Freud calls the somatic 'source', it is difficult enough to assign in the case of the 'oral' drive (the lips?) or the 'anal' drive (the anus?), and it is altogether lacking in such cases as the voyeuristic drive: how could we make sense of the idea of a 'reduction of tension at its source' here? One would not risk the absurdity of speaking of 'a reduction of ocular tension'.

Freud (and perhaps even more so his disciples, such as Abraham or, in a different way, Ferenczi) doubtless finds himself seized with vertigo when confronted with an evolution that lacks any pre-established finality, and will strive to describe a sort of normative evolution, oriented towards 'genitality'. But the purported succession of libidinal stages, even if it survives within the Vulgate of the teachings of 'psychoanalytic psychology' has been endlessly discredited, as much by clinical observation as by theoretical critique (Melanie Klein

---

30 Konrad Lorenz, *Studies in Animal and Human Behaviour*, 2 vols. (Cambridge Mass.: Harvard University Press, 1970 and 1971).

was doubtless at the forefront of this critique). To be sure, the vague succession of 'libidinal stages' can be correlated in a certain way with the progress of rearing (itself determined socially as much as physiologically). But this also means that nothing permits the postulation of a genetic programming of infantile *libidinal* evolution *as such*.

Let us also add the following point, whose full impact will emerge later on: genetic programming, in the sexual domain above all, presupposes mediation by means of a neuro-hormonal relay. This is clearly the case, and in a precise way, when it comes to the evolution and the metamorphoses of adult sexuality. However, it has never occurred to anyone to search for the presence of hormones at the level of the purported somatic 'sources' of the infantile partial drives!

But it is probably at the level of *functioning* and of the 'economy' of pleasure that drive and instinct can be radically distinguished. We have for a long time recognised the difficulties Freud has in giving a univocal formulation of the pleasure principle. We had in fact proposed distinguishing two very different modes of functioning: a homeostatic functioning governed by the 'constancy principle' and tending to restore the level to an optimum; and a functioning oriented towards pure discharge (the primary process), which leads to a total exhaustion of the excitation.[31]

'Constancy principle' and 'zero principle': in order to complete the opposition we must add a distinction that is internal to the German term *Lust*, and which Freud himself reveals: *Lust* is at once *pleasure* as a relaxation of tension (the classical meaning of the 'pleasure principle'), and the 'desire' or 'pleasure-desire' related to the increase of tension.[32]

---

31 Jean Laplanche and Jean-Bertrand Pontalis, "Constancy principle", "Nirvana principle" and "Pleasure principle", in *The Language of Psychoanalysis*, op. cit.; and Jean Laplanche, *Life and Death in Psychoanalysis*, op. cit., p. 113 ff.
32 See the two notes in the *Three Essays*, op. cit. p. 135 n. 2 and p. 212 n. 1, as well as my commentary in *Traduire Freud*, eds. André Bourguignon, Pierre Cotet, Jean Laplanche and François Robert (Paris: Universitaires de France, 1989) pp. 125–126, and "The Freud Museum Seminar", in *Jean Laplanche: Seduction, Translation, Drives*, ed. John Fletcher and Martin Stanton (London: ICA, 1992) p. 54.

If we are prepared to take some distance from the Freudian formulations, which are frequently ambiguous and tend to collapse drive and instinct into one another,[33] we can distinguish between a functioning of the instinctual type, which always tends towards relaxation by obtaining the best possible level, and a drive functioning which defies and transgresses the line of the homeostatic level – the principle of excitation or desire tending sometimes towards an excitation beyond all limit, sometimes, and perhaps at the end of the process, towards total exhaustion

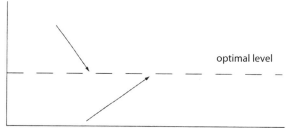

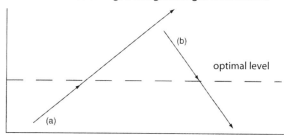

This radical repositioning, moreover, enables us better to situate the question of aim, object and pleasure than the clarification Fairbairn offered, for the real opposition is not that between 'object-seeking' and 'pleasure-seeking'. From his earliest writings Freud

---

33 Cf. for example, Jean Laplanche, *Problematiques III: La Sublimation* (Paris: Presses Universitaires de France, 1980), p. 37 ff.

clearly demonstrates that these two searches are strictly correlated: the good-enough *object* is procured by means of the specific action ('aim') and leads to a lasting relaxation of tension ('pleasure'). But these are a matter of behaviours that we encompass with the broad term 'instinct'. However, what is opposed to this *joint* pursuit of the object and of satisfaction is most certainly the drive-based quest, which, for its part, is the *pursuit of excitation* to the point of exhaustion, regardless of both the real object and the relaxation of tension.

This also entails a complete reversal as regards the type of 'object' and its position. The object of the instinct is the real object, which is situated at the end of the process, even if it is pre-intuited in the form of a 'value'.[34] The object of the drive is to be situated within unconscious fantasy; it is the exciting object, the 'source-object', of which the real can offer nothing but *unsatisfying*, though in their turn *exciting*, effigies.

II. Drive and instinct are general categories. It is important not to tack their opposition onto the different types of motivation and/or behaviour in question. From this second point of view we come to the terms of the first Freudian dualism (while reserving the right to nuance and update it): self-preservation/sexuality.[35] But why do we not simply align self-preservation with the 'instinctual' on the one hand, and sexuality with the 'drive' on the other?

On the one hand, 'self-preservation' – the totality of forces that tend towards the preservation of the individual – is, by its very definition, adaptive and innately based, and tends towards a state of vital equilibrium. 'Self-preservation' is by nature, then, 'instinctual'; but it

---

[34] In the sense that Lagache speaks of hunger as the intuition of the value of food.
[35] It seems to me that the 'second dualism', life and death, must be subsumed under the term 'sexuality' (Cf. *Life and Death* and *New Foundations*):

is important to apply some nuances here, owing to the introduction of the notion of 'attachment'. Attachment, which had already been discovered by Freud under the name of 'affection', has been considerably extended by the recent work done in infant observation. After Bowlby came Zazzo, Brazelton, Stern, Dornes, Montagner etc. Schematically, the following points should be underlined:

1) Attachment emerges from a domain that is broadly understood as that of *self-preservation* and instinct. The majority of authors insist on the innate and 'attuned' basis of inter-relations between the adult and the child. This does not mean that one should neglect the way in which this relation is enriched in the course of its development. But this enrichment (where narcissism and the narcissistic relation will play a major role) remains, despite everything, oriented by the self-preservative aim.
2) Attachment is only *one part of instinctual self-preservative behaviour*: it is that part in which the individual essentially needs the other to ensure his survival, his 'homeostasis'. The proportion of non-relational homeostatic mechanisms (for example, the maintenance of blood constants) to mechanisms that immediately require the intervention of the other, varies according to species. As such, in certain species the provision of nourishment is necessarily mediated by the congeneric adult, whereas for others it is not. (Roughly speaking, we may assume that the dividing line is that which lies between homeothermic and poikilothermic species).[36]
3) One final point is essential for our purposes: the attachment relation is supported by a *communication*, an exchange of messages between adult and child. These messages are not initially linguistic, even though they may become so later on. For the most part they derive from an innate origin, which is in sharp contrast to

---

36 [*Trans*: the terms 'homeothermic' and 'poikilothermic' refer to warm- and cold-blooded animals respectively].

Freud's supposition that it is the mechanical path of discharge (that is, the uncoordinated cries of the thirsty infant) which acquires the function of "mutual understanding" in a "secondary" fashion.[37]

Let us turn to sexuality in respect of our distinction between drive and instinct. Here it must be affirmed that in man sexuality is double, and profoundly split. The immense Freudian discovery merits being properly situated within this duality.

1) It is not a matter of denying the existence – within the animal, of course, but also within man – of an instinctual sexuality connected to the maturation of the organism and involving neuro-hormonal relays, the complexity of which is now beginning to be recognised. As Freud had already emphasised, this sexuality pushes human beings towards sexual behaviours that are more or less pre-programmed and that are aimed, without this aim being consciously posed, at the self-preservation of the species. But the *problem* is that this sexuality, which is hormonal in origin, is *absent in man* from birth to the pre-pubertal period.
2) It is precisely between birth and puberty that *human drive sexuality* is situated – the infantile sexuality that Freud discovered and which continues to scandalise today.

    This sexuality is an *enlarged* sexuality and is not, at first, connected to any one erotogenic zone; nor is it connected, in any absolute way, to the difference of the sexes.

    This sexuality is not *innate*, which does not, however, justify the objection that we are returning to the notion of the

---

37 [*Trans.*: Laplanche is quoting Freud's *Project for a Scientific Psychology*. Freud's German term is *Übereinstimmung*, which Strachey simply translates as "communication" ((1950a [1895]), *SE* 1, p. 318). We render it as 'mutual understanding' in order to distinguish it from Laplanche's own use of "communication" earlier in the paragraph and so as to acknowledge Laplanche's own more faithful translation of Freud's term: "*compréhension mutuelle*"].

'innocent child'. The child is a 'genetic-sexual-innocent', if one wishes to put it that way, which does not prevent the child from becoming sexual in the first hours of its life.

This drive sexuality is indissociably connected to *fantasy*, as its cause. Repressed, it is what constitutes the contents of the unconscious and is the very object of psychoanalysis.

3) What, then, is the relation between drive sexuality and instinctual sexuality within the human being?

It is not one of collaboration or of harmonious blending, but a deeply conflictual relation, which at first glance looks like a temporal succession. Instinctual sexuality arrives in the pubertal or pre-pubertal period, *after* infantile sexuality. But nevertheless, it is in no sense infantile sexuality's *legitimate heir*: the sequence of infantile stages described by Freud is a barely credible fiction. Infantile sexuality before puberty is largely repressed and unconscious, rendering it all the more toxic. Finally, the two respective modes of functioning – 'the pursuit of excitation' and 'the pursuit of pleasure in the object' – are and will remain most difficult to reconcile.

Ultimately, our idea is that with respect to his sexuality man is subject to the greatest of paradoxes: *acquired* drive sexuality *precedes* innate instinctual sexuality within him, such that when it surges forth, adaptive instinctual sexuality finds its place 'occupied', as it were, by the infantile drives, already and always present within the unconscious.

III. We shall not advance onto the issues that follow from this: problems concerning sublimation; problems concerning the integration of desire into the pursuit of pleasure; the persistence of infantile sexuality within the adult, etc. We shall, however, return to this long period in which *attachment and infantile sexuality seem to coexist*. What is their original relation? Is there a connection or relation between them of support? Of genesis?

Here, the notion of *leaning-on* remains indispensible, at least as a stage in, or support for, our thinking, in order to grasp what is at stake. Having developed and examined this notion for a long time,[38] we shall recall what is at stake in just a few words. Infantile sexuality first emerges in the exercise of the great functions, in the satisfaction of the great needs of self-preservation. Initially conjoint with the satisfaction of need (feeding, defecation, etc), sexual pleasure detaches itself secondarily, becoming autonomous with autoerotism and its relation to fantasy.

This process, which is barely outlined by Freud, requires interpretation. We have proposed to distinguish three versions of it:[39]

1) an impoverished interpretation that proposes a mechanistic parallelism;
2) an interpretation that makes it into a process of emergence;
3) a contrary interpretation, made in terms of seduction.

The mechanistic interpretation is rejected by Widlöcher, as it is by me. It presupposes an homogeneous conception of instinctual self-preservative functioning on the one hand and drive sexuality on the other, which I have never stopped rebutting. A single source for two instincts? And what source? What parallel aims? What 'object' common to both?

The interpretation by emergence, of the kind I have proposed as a way to save the Freudian hypothesis.[40] In this schema we not only have the notion of support ('leaning-on') but simultaneously that of a time-lag and a borrowing by one from the other. Conjunction followed by emergence, by means of a sort of metabolisation and symbolisation of aims and objects. In this positive and saving interpretation of lean-

---

38 *The Language of Psychoanalysis* (1967), *Life and Death in Psychoanalysis* (1970), *Problématiques III* (1975–76), *Le fourvoiement biologisant de la sexualité chez Freud* (1991).
39 *Problématiques VII: Le fourvoiement biologisant de la sexualité chez Freud* (Paris: Presses Universitaires de France, 2006), p. 55 ff.
40 One of the most recent discussions of this appears in *Problématiques VII*, ibid., p. 60 ff.

ing-on, the object of self-preservation is the milk, while the breast is the sexual object. With leaning-on there is thus a 'metonymisation' of the object at the same time as a turning around within fantasy. For its part, the aim undergoes 'metaphorisation' in passing from the domain of self-preservation to the sexual – anal expulsion or projection, for example, being the metaphorisation of the excretion of *faeces*.[41]

This type of solution, which is ultimately *endogenous*, seems to me to be that retained by Widlöcher: it is an action on the part of the subject which, taking up self-preservative functioning in a second moment, transforms it into sexuality by making it pass into fantasy. Where I speak of 'metaphorisation', Widlöcher uses the terms "early psychic creativity", "pure subjectivity proper to fantasmatic activity",[42] "treatment of scenes on the level of illusion",[43] "a resumption within the imaginary which ... confers new meaning". According to Widlöcher, "infantile sexuality [would be the] hallucinatory resumption of a physical and relational experience of satisfaction which has another origin".[44]

I have frequently, and for a long time, criticised such a 'creativist' and 'illusionist' conception of human sexuality. In Freud these conceptions find their apogee in the theory of the 'hallucinatory satisfaction of desire', which I reject. Indeed, the first real satisfaction can only be the satisfaction of a *need* (an alimentary need in the Freudian example); and *its reproduction* – be it within a memory, a fantasy or even an hallucination – can only be the reproduction of an *alimentary* satisfaction. There is in Freud and in his successors, right up to the most developed version by Widlöcher, a veritable sleight of hand: if the sexual is not present *within* the original, *real experience* it will never be rediscovered in the fantasmatic reproduction or the symbolic elaboration of that experience.

---

41 [*Editor*: For this derivation of psychical entities according to relations of contiguity as distinct from relations of similarity, see "Derivation of Psychoanalytic Entities", *Life and Death*, op.cit., pp. 127–139].
42 Widlöcher, "Primary Love and Infantile Sexuality", p. 19.
43 Ibid., translation altered.
44 Ibid., p. 20, translation altered.

But the 'creativity' by which Widlöcher sets so much store does not in fact go so far as to create sexuality: this is in reality introduced from the earliest intersubjective experience, and introduced by the activity of the adult rather than the infant.

You can see how it may be said that "seduction is the truth of 'leaning-on'".[45] Not that I deny the active role of the infant in terms of symbolisation and the creation of fantasy, and within the process of *afterwardsness*. But this activity is brought to bear upon messages that are *already* compromised by the sexual on the part of the adult other. It is precisely by virtue of this enigmatic aspect of the adult message that the child is stimulated to develop an unusual activity of 'translation'. An exchange of messages that remain purely self-preservative benefits from an 'attunement', since the codes used between the adult and the child are largely pre-established. However, the child's creativity, asserted by Widlöcher, is kindled by the 'drive to translate', which comes to the child from the adult message 'to be translated' – an enigmatic message since it is compromised by the sexuality of the adult.

To return to attachment, we can see why the 'communication' aspect, the exchange of messages and responses, is essential to the theory of seduction. It is only because the adult's messages are compromised by his sexual unconscious that, secondarily, the child's attempts at symbolisation are set in motion, where the child actively works on material that is *already* sexual.

[46]

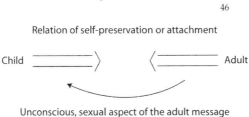

Relation of self-preservation or attachment

Child ⎯⎯⎯⎯⎯> <⎯⎯⎯⎯⎯ Adult

Unconscious, sexual aspect of the adult message

---

45 *New Foundations for Psychoanalysis*, op. cit.pp.144–5.
46 Diagram taken from "Les forces en jeu dans le conflit psychique" (1995), in *Entre séduction et inspiration: l'homme* (Paris: Presses Universitaires de France, 1999).

We shall not pursue here the process of repression resulting from these attempts at translation, which always partially fail.[47]

However, apropos of 'the general theory of seduction', I shall take the occasion of the present article to respond to objections made by Widlöcher.

Widlöcher's earlier objection had been that the mother-child relation is not sufficiently universal, even among humans, to account for the appearance of infantile sexuality in all cases. I responded to this by saying that I have doubtless been misread, for what I call the 'Fundamental Anthropological Situation' is the truly universal relation *between a child* who has no genetically programmed unconscious ('genetically innocent') and *an adult* (not necessarily the mother) who, psychoanalysis tells us, is inhabited by an unconscious. It is a situation that is absolutely ineluctable, even if the infant has no parents, and even if he is . . . a clone!

In his present article, Widlöcher's objection is very different: he willingly accepts the mechanism of seduction but wishes to leave a space for a more spontaneous and less interpersonal emergence of autoeroticism. To tell the truth, the objection is valid not only for my thought but for his own conception of a secondary elaboration of sexuality within hallucinatory 'creativity'. Indeed, I think that we both admit that a somatic reactivity, a general organic excitability must certainly be pre-existent, but that something else is needed in order to make it a *drive*. This is something that has already been said by Lichtenstein:

> [T]here is an innate body responsiveness, a capacity
> ... to respond to contact with another person with
> a specific kind of somatic excitation which is not a
> drive, because it has no direction, but which is the

---

[47] The fullest account of this appears in "Short Treatise on the Unconscious" (1993), in *Essays on Otherness*, ed. John Fletcher (London: Routledge, 1999).

innate prerequisite for the later development of a drive.[48]

For the other's message to be *implanted* we must acknowledge the existence of a primary somatic receptivity.[49]

To resume my debate with Widlöcher briefly, our points of view are largely convergent when it comes to the nature of the infantile sexual drive (its connection to fantasy) and its mode of functioning being wholly different from instinct. However, as to the articulation between self-preservation and the drives, and as to the genesis of the sexual, our points of view are close but do not coincide: his adherence to the fiction of hallucinatory satisfaction (of need? of desire?) – which is still too often considered to be beyond criticism – remains as a point of dispute between us.

*
* *

Having attempted to situate clearly attachment and sexuality, in terms of their essence, their relationship and their genesis, we shall say a few words about the errors that lead to the epistemological hegemony of one over the other.

Attachment has become the privileged domain of those who *observe childhood*. Even so, must infantile sexuality – as well as adult sexuality – therefore disappear from the field of observation? I do not think so; and nor do we find among the best child observers the sort of epistemological blindness with which they are credited by André Green.

It is, however, true that infantile sexuality, connected as it is

---

[48] Heinz Lichtenstein, "Identity and Sexuality", in the *Journal of the American Psychoanalytic Association*, vol. 9, 1961, p. 250.

[49] Cf. Gérard Mendel, *La psychanalyse revisitée* (Paris: Le Découverte, 1988), p. 113 ff. Mendel thinks that this reactivity is not sexual. Lichtenstein thinks that it is 'already' sexual. A quibble over words? Not at all. The fact that sexuality, in Freud's sense of the term, only appears with fantasy would rather confirm Mendel's view.

to the appearance of fantasy and to repression, is by definition left poorly identified in any direct way. Child observers such as Roiphe and Galenson demonstrate that these two aspects – a sexuality that is in the process of being repressed and parental sexuality – are nonetheless discernable, at the heart of observation itself, if one wishes to take the trouble.[50] The path remains open from this observation to a more concrete identification of the connection between attachment and infantile sexuality.

On the side of analysis, and essentially the analysis of the adult, the point of view is the opposite. Here, drive sexuality is on the way towards monopolising all our attention (and with good reason!):

1) Within individual evolution, sexuality has a tendency to cover over like a net and to co-opt the totality of inter-human relations. This is what I have sometimes called 'pansexualism in action'[51].
2) The analytic rule that privileges 'saying everything', even what is considered improper, necessarily promotes the 'sexual' within communication.
3) The transference situation itself supports this hegemony of the sexual. The two previous factors are constitutive of what I once named the 'tub' of psychoanalysis.[52]

Coming back to transference, in our view it is 'provoked', created by the analytic situation, which confronts the analysand with the enigma: his internal enigma but also the enigma of the other. In this sense, the analytic transference has in essence nothing to do with a simple transference of habits. It places the subject back within the originary situation, that of the genesis of infantile sexuality.

---

50 Herman Roiphe and Eleanor Galenson, *The Infantile Origins of Sexual Identity* (New York: International Universities Press, 1981), chapters 13 and 14.
51 "Sublimation and/or Inspiration", *New Formations*, no 48, 2002–3, p.35.
52 Cf. *Problématiques IV. Le baquet. Transcendance du transfert* (Paris: Presses Universitaires de France, 1987).

We can see to what extent abstract metapsychological considerations are alone capable of focusing adequately on the essence of psychoanalytic *practice*, Freud's primary and inaugural invention.

3

DREAM AND COMMUNICATION: SHOULD CHAPTER VII BE REWRITTEN?[1]

The theme that is my point of departure today is the relation between the dream and communication. This issue is much larger than that of the relation between the dream and language, to which it has frequently been reduced – especially since Lacan. There are communications without verbal language, and conversely there are elements of language that have lost all relation to communication.

However, the question is in reality much older than Freud, even though it has been revived by the discovery of psychoanalysis and the role played by dreams within our practice. One might even say that curiosity about this subject is coextensive in human beings with the enigma that is posed to us by dreams – those astonishing fragments of our life which appear to be both meaningful and yet radically removed from our will to communicate and even from our will as such.

For the sake of clarity, I shall divide the question into two: on the one hand, the communication *of* the dream, chiefly

---

[1] Lecture delivered in Metz on June 23rd, 24th and 25th, 2000, at the congress of the Association de Recherche en Psychiatrie et Psychanalyse de l'Enfant, on "Le rêve cent ans après". First published in *Le rêve dans la pratique analytique* (Paris: Dunod, 2003), pp. 51–73.

within the treatment;

on the other hand, the dream *as* communication; or, more generally, the relation between the phenomenon of the dream and interhuman communication. They are related but distinct.

The Problem of the Communication of the Dream

Evidently, this is a problem that has to be posed in connection with the communication constituted by *analysis* itself. Indeed, our practice has considerably expanded what we might call the quantum of verbalisation with respect to dreams as dreamed, and above all it has radically expanded the ways of 'treating' this material.

One hundred years have passed since the publication of *The Interpretation of Dreams* and many developments have occurred – purposeful and theoretically justified changes as well as surreptitious changes in our practice. These days one can distinguish two major attitudes among analysts, which can be contrasted in the following, somewhat caricatured way:

the purely subjectivist or intersubjective attitude;

the purely objectivist attitude.

I say 'caricatured' because one does encounter many positions that are more nuanced.

The Intersubjective Attitude

On the intersubjective view, everything happens within the analytic dialogue, in the here and now.

By way of introduction, I should like to offer a personal recollection of an entirely commonplace situation. During a conference or a congress, I was invited to participate as a discussant of a presentation by an analyst in training. The work had been well prepared and posed precisely the question of how to interpret dreams today. Unfortunately, the answer came before the question. The young analyst had barely begun recounting his patient's dream when my neighbouring panellists, this candidate's elders, began to interrupt in order to teach him a thing or two. He had not understood what the patient was saying to him *by the very act of recounting* the dream. The transference and even his counter-transference were obvious. In short, the problem of the interpretation of the dream had vanished and had been replaced with what is sometimes called the intersubjective dynamic.

This stance is commonly taken. One sticks with the manifest content. More precisely, the manifest content is considered solely in terms of its value as an utterance. *Not*: what is the meaning of this dream? *Nor even*: why did this analysand have this dream at this moment in the analysis? Rather: what is the analysand saying to me *by recounting* this dream?

These on-the-spot interpretations are well known to all of us who attend analytic meetings: most often they rely on symbolism of a very general kind.

The manifest content is not considered to conceal anything of a fundamentally heterogeneous nature. It is taken in the same way as all other discourse, even if a few simple modifications apply: transformation into the opposite, denial, puns.

It is difficult to exaggerate the devastation created by the Lacanian method of listening to signifiers when this method is adopted in an exclusive way. For ultimately, this kind of listening is only 'authorised' by the listener himself.[2] It is the listener, and the listener alone, who decides that the expression 'prendre sur soi' contains an allusion to sexual intercourse.[3] It is the listener, and the listener alone, who chooses to hear "ah! que c'est difficile à dire" as "ah! queue c'est diffi-

---

2 [*Trans.*: an allusion to Jacques Lacan's claim that 'l'analyste ne s'autorise que de lui-même' ('the analyst is only authorised by himself')].
3 [*Trans.*: 'Prendre sur soi' (literally: 'to take [something] upon oneself) is a common French idiom meaning 'to face up to', 'to accept responsibility for'].

cile à dire".[4] Here one cannot rely unconditionally on Freud's example and his frequent recourse to more or less 'good' jokes to support his interpretations. For Freud's interpretations – and we shall return to this point – are very far from endorsing the sovereignty that our master interpreters often proclaim. When this putative sovereignty is really backed into a corner, the single recourse available to its supporters is the claim that the only unconscious is the one hidden within common language, an unconscious that is independent of the individual's attempt to make language serve him, since he himself is in fact at the service of language. Thus we have a collective unconscious – collective and specific to each language.

In sum, within a certain conception of the analytic dialogue, the analysis of dreams appears utterly outdated. Freud was wrong to believe he was talking about the dream when in reality he was only talking about "the spoken account that the dreamer gives of his dream" (ibid., p.294). The analysis of dreams has brought to light mechanisms that can now be recognised as being universal and specific to language:

> Listening to the dream as a discourse has enabled analysts to understand discourse as a dream, which is to say as being subject to the same grammar of unconscious discourse (ibid.).

A moment ago I mentioned Lacan, but this warrants qualification. It seems to me that Lacan never advocated the reintegration of the dream into general discourse, or the abandonment of those rules specific to the interpretation of dreams. What is more, in the analytic world, scorn for the famous 'royal road' is in no way restricted to

---

4 [*Trans.*: These two homonymic phrases may be translated respectively as "Ah, that {*que*} is difficult to say" and "Ah, cock {*queue*: means tail and is slang for 'penis'} is difficult to say"]. The examples are borrowed from Jean-Claude Lavie, "Parler à l'analyste", *La Nouvelle Revue de Psychanalyse*, vol. 5, 1972.

Lacanian circles. It seems to me that such scorn goes hand in hand with the decline of reference to the individual unconscious, both in clinical practice and in the theory of the treatment.

It remains true, nonetheless, that Lacan was no stranger to this drift, especially in his pure and simple assimilation of the mechanisms of the dream-work – displacement and condensation – to universal modes of language functioning: metonymy and metaphor. It is an assimilation that, despite a thousand critiques with supporting arguments,[5] has given weight to the rumour according to which the dream is a discourse like any other.

Now, to this factor we must add another: the assimilation of the fundamental analytic rule – free association on the side of the analysand, evenly suspended attention on the side of the analyst – to a sort of putting-into-parentheses of reality, after the fashion of a 'phenomenological reduction', a suspension of the entire referential dimension of discourse, with which one should no longer be concerned. From this perspective it is a matter of indifference whether the discourse of the analysand concerns a dream, a fantasy, an event from everyday life, the words of a third party, etc.

Winnicott says somewhere that in the presence of the patient the analyst cannot reasonably feign ignorance of the fact that King George died that day. However, according to those Winnicott is implicitly criticizing, the statement "King George is dead" is nothing but a part of the enunciation of the analysand, and the mental asceticism of the analyst would be such that, for him, the utterance alone is what occupies the psychic field.

If psychoanalysis entails the total suspension of reality, then the 'dream referent' certainly loses all privilege. However, consider this little experience, which is not rare and which I call the 'the first minute distraction'. During the first seconds of a session, the men-

---

[5] Among many other critiques, cf. Jean-François Lyotard, *Discours, Figure* (Paris: Klincksieck, 1971), pp. 250–260.

tal state of the analyst sometimes lags behind the discourse of the patient, having been distracted by some external or internal circumstance. As the analyst regains his concentration he hears the patient say: "…so the car lightly bumped the guy on the bicycle, etc." I would challenge any one of our colleagues not to ask himself, at the very least: is this a dream that the patient is telling me, or something that really happened? And I would challenge any colleague to deny having inwardly tried to pick up clues that would enable him, as it were, to jump aboard the patient's discourse when it is already in motion.

Let us draw things together. The subjectivist point of view, which suspends all reference to anything external to the discourse of the session – even reference to the unconscious and to that privileged phenomenon, the dream – makes almost three quarters of Freud's work obsolete. Not only the interpretation of dreams, but also the work on the psychopathology of everyday life, jokes, etc.; and indeed his works of what is called 'applied' psychoanalysis, if it is true, as Viderman sometimes declares, that here too the suspension of reference should be the rule: "What does it matter what Leonardo saw? … What does it matter what Leonardo said? … What is important is that the analyst … makes it exist by saying it."[6]

The Objectivist Attitude

Throughout his life, Freud's point of view about dreams remained objectivist. Objectivist in that he presumed that the dream-as-dreamed exists, that the memory of the dream is something different, and that the telling of the dream is different again. One reads with interest the passages in Chapter VII on the subject of the forgetting of dreams and on the supplementary censorship that the telling of the dream can introduce. To demonstrate the point, Freud

---

6 Serge Viderman, *La construction de l'espace analytique* (Paris: Denoël, 1970), p. 164.

doesn't hesitate to have the dream repeated a second time in order to note the differences between the two narratives:

> But the parts of the dream which he describes in different terms are by that fact revealed to me as the weak spot in the dream's disguise … That is the point at which the interpretation of the dream can be started. My request to the patient to repeat his account of the dream has warned him that I was proposing to take special pains in solving it; under pressure of the resistance, therefore, he hastily covers the weak spots in the dream's disguise … In this way he draws my attention to the expression which he has dropped out.[7]

Here Freud's realism about dreams is clear. The dream has an existence distinct from its telling and distinct from what the analysis will make of it. And the best proof of this, for Freud, is that each part of the psychic phenomenon of the dream exceeds the use to which psychoanalysis puts it as the 'royal road to the unconscious'. As late as 1923, Freud argues fiercely against the objection that the dreams of the analysand are entirely shaped by the analytic situation and by the suggestions of the analyst. It is worth quoting his conclusion:

> [The patient] recollected some dreams which he had had before starting analysis and indeed before he had known anything about it; and the analysis of these dreams, which were free from all suspicion of suggestion, led to the same interpretations as the later ones.

---

7 *The Interpretation of Dreams* (1900a), SE 5, p. 515.

And Freud concludes:

> I think that in general it is a good plan occasionally to bear in mind the fact that people were in the habit of dreaming before there was such a thing as psycho-analysis.[8]

To accept that there is a dream object, which has a revelatory capacity independent of its inclusion in the transference, is to accept the possibility of a different stance towards dreams and indeed towards all discourse within the treatment. It is a stance that, following Guy Rosolato, we could call 'technical', but with the following important qualifications. Firstly, that the term 'technique' is not to be understood as something pejorative, but is to be associated with the notion of flexibility, which implies that the activities of listening and intervening are adapted to their particular object. Secondly, that in spite of its prosaic appearance the word 'technique' refers to Freud's major discovery, when he defines psychoanalysis above all as "a procedure for the investigation of mental processes which are almost inaccessible in any other way."[9]

Here I should like to refer not only to Freud's own era but also, very briefly, to a contemporary psychoanalyst, Danielle Margueritat, whose approach in this area seems to me to be marked by the best kind of fidelity to the Freudian position. But let us first cite Ferenczi who recommends listening to dreams in a manner completely different from 'evenly suspended attention': "One should ... endeavour to observe accurately the wording of ... dreams. Complicated dreams I often have narrated to me again, in cases of necessity, even a third time".[10]

---

8 "Remarks on the Theory and Practice of Dream-Interpretation" (1923c), *SE* 19, p. 116–117.
9 "Two Encyclopedia Articles" (1923a), *SE* 18, p. 235.
10 Sàndor Ferenczi, "Attention During the Narration of Dreams", *Further Contributions to the Theory and Technique of Psychoanalysis*, trans. Jane Isabel Suttie et al. (London: The Hogarth Press, 1969), p. 238.

Now let us cite Danielle Margueritat's article "L'analyste et le rêveur":

"What happens to me when someone tells *me* a dream? Something happens to me first of all because I have a tendency to isolate dreams not from the context of the analysis but from the entirety of the discourse of the session."

And the theme returns like a leitmotiv, that of the dream-event, which is to say, fundamentally, what Freud designated as 'the other scene':

"Thus, when someone tells me a dream, an alarm goes off, my attention is mobilized." (Attention and vigilance, not abandonment pure and simple).

"Thus a dream emerges and I am prey to a disturbance in the rhythm of time …"

"Thus a dream emerges, with its associations…" [11]

"With its associations": I wish to insist upon this, which is a second essential aspect. The dream cannot be reduced to its associations. This is so important that as late as 1923, in the previously cited "Two Encyclopedia Articles", Freud lists the different possible rules, the different means by which associations may be elicited and obtained. Indeed in Danielle Margueritat we have this astonishing sequence regarding a dream that concerns contact lenses [*verres de contact*]:

> I no longer knew if we were in the account of the dream or in the associations, and when I asked her, she replied, "it was in the dream, but in the dream it was *lentilles* [*Trans.*: meaning both 'lenses' and 'lentils'], and I didn't want to say that word". Here again the strictly Freudian approach considers as

---

[11] Danielle Margueritat, "L'analyste et le rêveur", in *Le Fait de l'analyse*, no. 4, March 1998, pp. 172–3.

> being significant the difference between the formulation of the dream-as-dreamed (*lentilles*) and the already more censored formulation (*verres de contact*) of the dream as it is recounted (ibid., p. 186).

Let me be clear: ever since Freud, and all the more so after him, psychoanalysis has been unable to do without the dimension of enunciation or, to use other terms, the address, the transference. On the other hand, however, analysis cannot use this as a pretext for simply dissolving the dream into its telling – that is to say, into precisely what Freud considers to be more deceitful, more disguised, more defensive than the dream … *itself*.

We cannot, I'm afraid, go much further on the subject of the 'communication of the dream'; we'll conclude with the opposition between Freudian realism (which admits that all discourse, including that of analysis, *refers* to existing material or psychic realities) and a sort of idealism of discourse (an idealism of the discourse of clinical analysis first of all, and then of all discourses in general). This latter stance recreates and radicalizes the sophist's position in which the dream would be nothing but discourse about the dream, just as love or paternity etc. would be nothing but the words 'love', 'paternity'…

Communication and the Dream-as-Dreamed

Having allied myself unambiguously to the Freudian position on this point, I am all the more at ease in freely taking up the question of 'communication *in* the dream', a question that I would formulate as follows: does the dream itself, the dream-as-dreamed, have anything to do with interhuman communication?

Here we come up against two of Freud's peremptory propositions, shocking and revelatory in the abruptness with which they are formulated.

On the 'efferent' or output side of the process: "A dream does not want to say anything to anyone. It is not a vehicle for communication".[12]

On the 'afferent' or input side: "the remarks made by the physician ... operate like somatic stimuli which impinge on the sleeper during his sleep" (ibid., p. 238).

The latter affirmation, taken in an absolute sense, means that the dream does not take account of any message or, what amounts to the same thing, that it treats all messages as purely material stimuli.

The term 'message' (*Botschaft*) is relatively rare in Freud, which makes it all the more instructive to identify the passages where it does occur: primarily in passages concerning telepathy. Let me briefly summarize what is involved. In the 1920s Freud, chiefly influenced by Ferenczi, became interested in two kinds of occult phenomena: clairvoyance and thought transmission. These two phenomena could obviously be translated into *premonitory* dreams on the one hand and *telepathic* dreams on the other. Freud's position on this subject will hardly vary at all:[13] Premonition is inadmissible in theory, quite simply because it would invert the arrow of time, and because it has never been demonstrated by experiment. By contrast, and chiefly on the basis of personal experiences, Freud accepts categorically the possibility of the transmission or 'transference' of thoughts or of memories that carry a strong affective investment.

We are not interested here in taking a position on telepathy itself. We are concerned with the connection between the telepathic message and the dream in which it may re-emerge. Would this not be a case in which the dream is the receiver of a certain speech, whatever the means of its arrival? Well, Freud is going to be radical here.

---

12 "Lecture 15: Uncertainties and Criticisms", *Introductory Lectures on Psychoanalysis* (1916–17), SE 15, p. 231.
13 This position is already the subject of the final paragraph of *The Interpretation of Dreams*. For a short account see: 'Some Additional Notes on Dream-Interpretation as a Whole', part (C), "The Occult Significance of Dreams" (1925i), SE 19, pp. 135–138.

According to him, the theory of dreams need not change one iota to account for this possibility. Indeed, *exactly as is the case for all other messages,* the telepathic message does not reach the dream as speech; it is treated like any other *material* stimulus: "A telepathic message will be treated as a portion of the material that goes to the formation of a dream, like any other external or internal stimulus, like a disturbing noise in the street..."[14]

This assimilation of the message to a *noise* is obviously something we shall have to question. To do so, it is indispensible to enter a little way into Freud's conception of the psychic machinery, the 'apparatus of the soul', as he describes it in Chapter VII of *The Interpretation of Dreams.*

Here, then, is the apparatus as Freud describes it and makes it develop before our eyes:

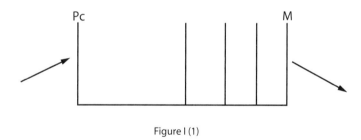

Figure I (1)

This is not a somatic apparatus, although the body may be said to be represented by the two arrows: afferent and efferent.

This is not a neurological apparatus. The systems are virtual systems, psychic systems. They may be produced by neurological functioning but they do not have any direct correspondence with it.

Let us accept, then, that this is the 'psychical apparatus'.

A further nuance: this image is a two-dimensional slice of a three-dimensional apparatus, one that is a sort of parallel-piped tub, in which

---

14 "Dreams and Telepathy" (1922a), *SE* 18, p. 207.

the systems of memories are suspended like photographic plates:

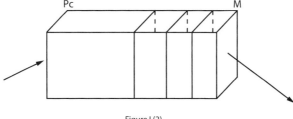

Figure I (2)

For our purposes, let us pause to consider the two ends of the model:
  perception: the afferent arrow;
  motility: the efferent arrow.

According to Freud, there is no communication, no message, either at the entrance or at the exit. At the entrance and at the exit there are only material actions. Thus we have here a purely behaviourist apparatus for which, according to Freud, the model is the reflex: "Reflex processes remain the model of every psychical function".[15]

Let us come immediately to the state of sleep. Here, inputs and outputs are – *almost* – totally abolished.

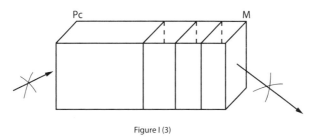

Figure I (3)

But it is precisely here that a distinction would be instructive: namely, the distinction that must be established between, on the one hand, what is of the order of perception but carries no signification, and, on the other, what is of the order of the message. In this connection André Bourguignon reports numerous experiments demonstrating

---
15 *The Interpretation of Dreams*, op. cit., p. 538.

that signifying stimuli – words, for example – are much more readily perceived by the sleeper than are physical stimuli, whether or not they wake the sleeper or are integrated into the dream thoughts.[16]

These remarks leave us perplexed about the Freudian diagram. If the human psychical apparatus cannot be inserted, as Freud wished, between the two poles of stimulus and reaction, but must rather be inserted between the pole of messages received and that of messages sent, then perhaps it would be wise to leave this schema on hold until we can take it up on the basis of other data.

The Interpretation of Dreams is an immense work. The essential parts of Chapters II to VI are devoted to two trajectories that are considered to be reciprocal even if they are not identical: the interpretative trajectory, which traces the account of the dream back to its original elements, and, conversely, the trajectory of the dream-work, which is supposed to account for the genesis both of the dream-as-dreamed and of the dream-as-recounted. As for Chapter VII, it develops two or even three major theses, which are, moreover, interlinked:

> the dream is the fulfilment of a wish;
> the dream is hallucinatory (a point that requires explanation);
> the dream is the guardian of sleep.

On the second of these theses, hallucination, Freud remained to the end unsatisfied with his formulations, proposing varying explanations of these revived creations. The 'wish fulfilment' thesis, however, is fundamental. *Its very phrasing* gives us material for reflection. It is not that the dream expresses a wish, nor even that the dream represents a wish as fulfilled, but rather the dream *is* a fulfilment of a wish without any distance between the wish and its fulfilment.

---

16 André Bourguignon, "Neurophysiologie du rêve et théorie psychanalytique", *La Psychiatrie de l'enfant*, vol. 11, no. 1, 1968, p. 6.

Dreams, Freud also says, are expressed in the present and not in the optative (we shall ignore the apparent inaccuracy of opposing a 'tense' – the present – with a 'mood' – the optative.) In fact, according to Freud, the dream is always expressed in the present indicative.

Ultimately, Freud always refers this wish back to an archaic wish that, in spite of certain denials, is sexual and, according to the well known metaphor, is always the 'capitalist' of the dream. Yet the basis of this entire argument refers to a theory, a model of the origin of the infantile wish or desire: namely, 'the experience of satisfaction'. This *'Befriedigungserlebnis'* is itself taken up in the *Project for a Scientific Psychology* and we must linger over it for a moment.

The infant experiences an internal tension, that of need. Here the need in question is explicitly hunger, which is of course associated with the experience of suckling.

The need for food is conceived, in a plausible enough manner, as a continuous mounting up of tension, which the organism cannot escape. Despite the triviality of the image, imagine a pot of water on the stove. The water boils, the lid rattles. If no one intervenes the caloric energy will continue to escape in a disordered fashion. "A hungry baby screams or kicks helplessly".[17] But this series of actions is not capable of halting the stimulus. The alternative possibility is what Freud called the specific action: "outside help" (ibid.), a curious phrase to designate the mother who, alerted by the cries, will bring food that will, for a significant period of time, halt the excitation.[18]

Now here is how Freud explains the birth of the *wish*: a psychical connection is created which from then on associates the memory of the food with the memory of the excitation of hunger. Then any reoccurrence of the state of tension, of hunger, will revive the image of food and, if real food does not appear, its image will be invested with so much force as to acquire the intensity of an hallucination.

---

17 *The Interpretation of Dreams*, op.cit., p.565.
18 "Helpful person" is the term Freud uses in the *Project for a Scientific Psychology* (1950a [1895]), op. cit., p. 318.

> An impulse of this kind is what we call a wish; the reappearance of the perception is the fulfilment of the wish; and the shortest path to the fulfilment of the wish is a path leading direct from the excitation produced by the need to a complete cathexis of the perception ... wishing ended in hallucinating.[19]

This model is well known, even a bit worn out. There is even an attempt to see in it the very birth of infantile sexuality; but to do this it would be necessary to deal with two major deficiencies.

First of all, in Freud's account there is practically no role for communication, and even less for dialogue, between mother and infant. The message of the infant is reduced to purely mechanical movements; and as for the message coming from the mother, in Freud one reads only of a *purely material provision of food*.

Secondly and most importantly, the action takes place solely on the level of a single need, in this case the *alimentary* need. The object that is given is food, milk. It is hard to see how the mnemic trace of the perception could be anything other than an *alimentary* image.

The so-called 'experience of satisfaction' is certainly a fertile model that could be developed in relation to the emergence of the sexual from a self-preservative relation. But first we must *refuse to believe in the illusion that Freud proposes*. From the hat of hunger, from a self-preservative instinct, Freud the illusionist claims to produce the rabbit of sexuality, as if by magic. This is only possible if sexuality has been hidden somewhere from the start. The image of the breast can easily be derived from the image of milk by association. But such a breast would be purely instrumental, the means and the symbol of alimentary satisfaction and nothing else.

The experience of satisfaction cannot split apart and open onto sexuality unless there is something sexual that is there from the

---

19 *The Interpretation of Dreams*, op. cit., pp. 565-566.

start. That is, unless from the very beginning the experience of satisfaction was double, ambiguous, and in a word, enigmatic.

Consequently there are only two ways to understand the emergence of the sexuality/self-preservation dualism. Firstly, one may presuppose that, from the very beginning, there are two original internal needs acting within the child: the one alimentary, the other sexual; this, in its simplest form, is what is called the theory of 'leaning on'. Infantile sexuality is present from the start, is endogenous; but, in order to establish itself, it needs to lean on the alimentary function. I have frequently pointed out how unsatisfactory this theory is, for it relies on the presupposition of an *innate*, sexual oral drive for which there is no basis at all in the psychology of the child.

The second interpretation seems much more plausible to me and permits us to preserve the experience of satisfaction as a basis. Yes, this experience does initially take place in the realm of self-preservation. However, it is an experience that is much more complex, much more intensely charged with meaning and affect than is suggested by the simplistic model of the kettle: it is the commencement of reciprocal communication, which is established from the first moments of life, probably on the basis of certain innate organisations that develop rapidly (*Attachment, Bindung* i.e. *binding*).

For the psychoanalyst, however, this is not the essential point. What matters is the introduction of the sexual element, not from the side of the physiology of the infant but from the side of the messages coming from the adult. To put it concretely, these messages are located on the side of the breast, the *sexual breast of the woman*, the inseparable companion of the milk of 'self-preservation'.

I have thus tried to provide a model of the genesis both of the unconscious and of the drive, the source of which is furnished by the unconscious thing-presentations. I shall not spend much time on this model of repression, the 'translational' model, which entails both an attempt by the infant to translate the mother's double, enigmatic messages and the partial failure of this translation, the untranslated remainders of which are precisely what constitute the elements of the unconscious. I would only add, without being able to develop the point here, that it is no longer possible to hold onto a conception of the birth of the sexual drive that is limited to a single time (which is precisely the case in the simple model of the experience of satisfaction).[20] For Freud himself taught us that every inscription in the unconscious requires at least *two moments*: the experience itself and its signifying *resumption*, which I call 'translation' (a necessarily imperfect translation). Thus, to complete the model of the experience of satisfaction, it must be modified profoundly: we must substitute the notion of the message for the notion of perception; introduce the duality, the compromise between the sexual and the 'self-preservative' on the side of the adult's message; and finally, we must make full use of the notion of afterwardsness.[21]

At this point, I should like to note that the introduction of the notions of the message and the signifier has an effect on the problem of what is called 'the identity of perception' and on the problem of hallucination. From the Freudian perspective it is the perceptual remainders relating to the satisfying object that are reproduced, and with such force that they even become hallucinations – to such an extent, in fact, that one wonders how the infant is able to escape from an hallucination that fully satisfies the need, and why he would continue to seek food when he possesses it so completely as an hallucination. However,

---

20 "As a result of the link that has thus been established, next time this need [for food] arises, a psychical impulse will at once emerge which will seek to re-cathect the mnemic image of the perception and to re-evoke the perception itself, that is to say, to re-establish the situation of the original satisfaction. An impulse of this kind is what we call a wish; the reappearance of the perception is the fulfillment of the wish ...", *The Interpretation of Dreams*, op. cit., pp. 565–566. The words "for food", which I have added in square brackets, come directly from the text itself, two lines above the passage quoted.
21 [*Editor*: 'l'après coup,' Freud's *Nachträglichkeit*, translated in *SE* as 'deferred action'.]

once we introduce the notion of the message, and specifically the messages of the adult, we see that what are expelled into the unconscious are not accidental, inert perceptions lacking any intersubjective meaning or significance. The elements of the unconscious are fragments of message, signifiers that, having been extracted from their context, acquire a 'thing-like' consistency. These 'designified signifiers' are entirely different from memories; having lost their links with meaning, their contextual relations in time and space, they quite naturally impose themselves with the force of psychical reality. Consequently, there is no need to look for a mechanism by which some additional intensity may be added to a perception to transform it into an hallucination – a problem that never stopped haunting Freud and to which he gave the most diverse and contradictory answers from the *Project for a Scientific Psychology* to the "Metapsychological Supplement to the Theory of Dreams". In the latter text it seems that Freud finally runs aground on the objection he himself raises: a very powerful regression can produce "very clear visual mnemic images, though we do not on that account, for a single moment, take them for real perceptions ..."[22]

Without claiming to solve the problem, I should like to point out an approach that may be productive: the question of the dream *considered as hallucination* cannot be detached from that of hallucination in the clinical sense. Yet here Freud will content himself with a supposedly clinical model called 'Meynert's amentia', an entity that disappeared almost as soon as it had been described.[23] On the other hand, there is now a consensus within psychiatry that considers hallucinations as being primarily of the order of speech, heard or re-voiced. Clinically, visual hallucinations are relatively rare and above all very localized phenomena.

Furthermore, the question here is not exactly that of the 'sensorium' involved (sight or hearing) but the presence or absence of

---

22 (1917d), *SE* 14, p. 231.
23 See Christine Lévy-Friesacher, *Meynert-Freud, 'l'amentia'* (Paris: Presses Universitaires de France, 1983).

a message. Visual percepts, like auditory ones, can carry a message. Since Clérambault, since Freud's writings on Schreber, since Lacan and his seminar on the psychoses, the old notion of 'perception without object' has been pushed aside by the much more fertile notion of a *message without a sender or with an indeterminate sender*.

With that key in hand, research about the dream as hallucination ought to be oriented towards a more elaborated, even a more phenomenological description, demarcating, for example, what truly belongs to the visual from that which belongs to the auditory (as spoken words) and, above all, to conviction and interior discourse: what clinically is called a verbal psychic hallucination: "*I was telling myself*[24] that my friend Pierre was in the room".

Moreover, it would be essential to rethink the articulation between two factors mentioned by Freud which are far from being equivalent: on the one hand, hallucinations per se, and on the other, the fact that dreams only have a 'present indicative', thus leaving no distance whatsoever between the expression of the wish and its fulfilment. Perhaps it would be useful to pursue the analogy that Freud establishes between the grammatical present ('my father dies') in comparison with the infinitive ('my father to die') and with the subjunctive ('that my father die').[25]

Let us note only this: if we accept the idea that the unconscious is characterized by the disappearance of all the links of discourse, then the various modalities of enunciation (grammatical moods) must also be absent. As such, the unconscious would always be in the 'present', which is to say always *presenting* its contents as fulfilled. It would hardly be forcing things to say that, by virtue of its thing-like consistency, the unconscious is 'hallucinatory' *in itself*, except that it

---

24 [*Editor*: The French idiom 'je me disais' means literally 'I was telling / said to myself' but can also mean 'it seemed to me'].
25 Freud, "Notes Upon a Case of Obsessional Neurosis" (1909d), *SE* 10, pp. 151–318. Cf. the discussion of this point in connection with "The Rat Man" in *Problématiques I: L'angoisse* (Paris: Presses Universitaires de France, 1980), pp. 273–80.

remains ... unconscious.

All this is to make it clear that the very idea of the hallucinatory fulfilment of an unconscious wish involves something of a tautology. Fulfilment – as actuation, as abolition of the distance between signifier and signified – is *in itself* an hallucinatory presentation; and this is so precisely when what is in question is an unconscious wish.

It is for this reason that I have always considered it clinically superfluous to attribute psychical reality to the so-called hallucination of the nursling. It is only a question of a metaphor that gives an intuition of the constitution of a timeless unconscious, an unconscious that is always present and current, which is, we might say, always actuated.

I shall be returning to my principal question of whether or not the *dream* is a *communication*. But first, I shall briefly try to approach a specific problem that is linked to the Freudian model of what, in Chapter VII, is called the psychic apparatus.[26] In the different versions that he gives of this model, Freud slightly varies the position of the letters at the right-hand end. Here is a two-dimensional version of the diagram:

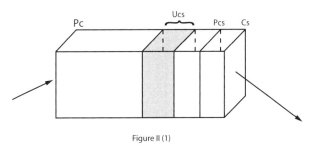

Figure II (1)

The advantage of this diagram is that it poses a problem: consciousness is found at both ends of the apparatus: on the left-hand side as

---

26 For a more detailed elaboration see *Problématiques V: Le baquet: Transcendance du transfert*. (Paris: Presses Universitaires de France, 1987), pp. 34–83

the conscious perception (Pc) of the exterior world, and on the right-hand side, immediately after the censorship of the Preconscious (Pcs), as the consciousness of internal processes. Yet, for Freud, these two types of consciousness are one, and both are linked to a perception. It is here that he introduces a note, composed in 1919:

> If we attempted to proceed further with this schematic picture, in which the systems are unrolled in linear succession [*Ed. linear aufgerollt*], we should have to reckon with the fact that the system next beyond the Pcs. [*Ed.* Preconscious] is the one to which consciousness must be ascribed—in other words, that Pcpt. = Cs [*Ed.* perception = consciousness].[27]

In spite of appearances, this note is clear. It points out that the schema of the tub is only linear because it has been *unrolled*. It needs to be rolled back up again so that the two ends – i.e. the two modalities of consciousness – coincide.

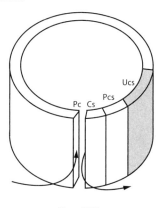

Figure II (2)

---

27 *The Interpretation of Dreams*, op. cit., p. 541, n. 1. [*Editor*: This passage from the *Standard Edition* has been modified here, since Strachey translates Freud's German phrase '*linear aufgerollt*' as 'set out', thus erasing the metaphor of 'unrolling', which Laplanche's reading restores and develops].

This is a model. In spite of what he promises in the note, Freud never went on to develop it. Almost no one has noticed this 'rolling up'. Since January, 1972 (*Problématiques*, I: "L'angoisse dans la topique") and again in 1980, I have never stopped insisting on it.

It is a *model*, and as such, one should not rush to apply it to a single reality. It is richer and more polyvalent.

It is not a model of a body, nor is it a model of a neuronal system, nor even is it a model of a psychic apparatus (it lacks everything needed to make a psychology: emotions, affects, reasoning, etc.); nor again is it a model of the unconscious, for the latter constitutes only a part of it.

This diagram can be depicted from above, which has the particular advantage of highlighting a crucial aspect, namely the tangency of two circuits. It is difficult to imagine that they are anything other than language-like circuits.

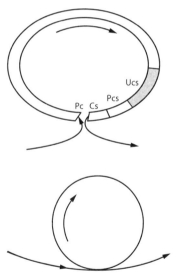

Figure III (1 e 2)

It should be noted that the idea of tangency corresponds exactly to the idea of marginality (the prefix *neben*), which Freud always uses to designate the emergence of the sexual and/or the unconscious as a by-product (*Nebenprodukt*).

Although this is a polyvalent model, it applies first and foremost to the emergence of what one might call, following Lacan, the 'formations of the unconscious'. Thus it is, among others things, a model of the dream. But we must also acknowledge that the afferent arrows of the external circuit could be reversed in a subtler manner than the simple 'all or nothing' of deep sleep.

In relation to all of these formations, the external circuit should be conceived of as the totality of the everyday, self-preservative messages. At the point of tangency the two circuits touch for an instant but the internal, sexual circuit begins to function on its own, and it does so in reverse, in the opposite direction. The formations of the unconscious – dreams, parapraxes, etc. and *without doubt analytic sessions as well* – do not constitute an 'other thing' that purely and simply *excludes* everyday discourse, but are rather something produced, something launched, so to speak, at the point of tangency and which is marginalised and thus becomes autonomous.

What is more, a paradox merges from this rolling back up of Freud's model. The previous model, unrolled in 'linear succession' was a model of closure, a black box functioning according to the behaviourist principle of stimulus-response. With the rolling up suggested by Freud, the model that would appear to close up on itself, paradoxically becomes a *model of opening* by means of the tangency between the two circuits.

Returning again to what is called the experience of satisfaction and the criticisms we have brought to bear on it, one could show that our model would be fully capable of depicting what I shall now call *'the experience of seduction'*. The external circuit, the adult's enigmatic message, self-preservative but contaminated by the sexual, is inscribed at the point of contact and then subject to repression. What we see here is the veritable *neogenesis of sexuality* in the child, which is not the hatching out of something endogenous. In this version of the model, nothing prevents us from representing the body precisely at the point of tangency.

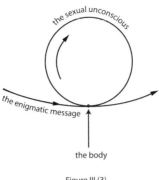

Figure III (3)

I now return to my question of the dream as communication, or as the embryo or initiator of communication. It is here that the phrase 'royal road to the unconscious' must not lead us to confuse the two things: the unconscious and the dream. To say that dreams have no communicative intention, as Freud sometimes says, may be putting it too strongly. At a pinch the formula is only really valid for the unconscious, for the id itself. When, in 1923, Freud re-examines the question in "Remarks on the Theory and Practice of Dream-Interpretation", he is much less categorical. No doubt, he says, "the employment of dreams in analysis is something very remote from their original purpose"; but he willingly concedes that "within an analysis far more of the repressed is brought to light in connection with dreams than by any other method", which reflects "some motive power, some unconscious force."[28]

That he attributes this force to suggestion is not satisfactory from our point of view; we are more comfortable when he invokes the term transference. Once again we must understand the word!

Do dreams obey a communicative aim during analysis? Certainly. But however unprecedented, however inaugural the psychoanalytic situation may be, we cannot ignore the fact that it is

---

28 op. cit., p. 117.

prefigured to some degree in other interpersonal situations. It cannot be denied that, *always and everywhere*, dreams have contained a certain allocutionary opening. Assuredly, the dream does not speak directly to anyone. It is fully functioning even if it is forgotten. A multitude of dreams sink into oblivion. But one cannot deny that there has always existed a certain compulsion to recount one's dreams, to open them up to others.

Ferenczi – again Ferenczi – wrote a short fragment, "To Whom Does One Relate One's Dreams?", which is worth citing in its entirety:

> We analysts know that one feels impelled to relate one's dreams to the very person to whom the content relates. Lessing seems to have had an inkling of this, for he writes the following epigram:
>
> Alba mihi semper narrat sua somnia mane,
> Alba sibi dormit; somniat Alba mihi.[29]

But we have to go further, which is to say beyond the notion of an addressee who is a *simple receiver* astonished by a fantastic story. The poetic understanding of dreams, whether it be that of the German Romantics or the surrealists, far from satisfying us risks misleading us. The art of divination has always *required* the telling of dreams *for it to interpret*, and it is difficult not to suppose that the soothsayer, and the *enigma* that he embodies, is the provoking element in some dreams.[30]

'Provocation by the analyst' is a phrase I once used apropos of transference. If the transference in analysis is indeed provoked by the

---

[29] [*Trans.*: "Alba always tells me her dreams in the morning, / Alba sleeps by herself; but Alba dreams for me"]. "To Whom does one Relate one's Dream?", *Further Contributions*, op. cit., p. 349.

[30] Cf. Alexander's dream about the taking of Tyre, and my commentary in *Problématiques V*, op. cit., pp. 217–18.

enigma embodied by the analyst, why wouldn't the same be true for dreams during an analysis? The diagram of tangency applies equally well in each case: for the transference in the dream and for the transference in the analysis. In both cases, it is the address of the analyst – real or supposed, but always enigmatic – that incites the transference and provokes the sort of libidinal neogenesis that is linked to it.

To give the primacy of the other its due as inherent in the constitution of our unconscious, I have sought to privilege the verbs and the actions for which *the subject of the verb is the other*, as opposed to those mechanisms that originate in the subject. Thus, to the central term seduction, we can add that of provocation – or even inspiration (the other seduces, provokes, inspires, etc.). Today it occurs to me that we might add to this list the notion of 'looking for it' [*chercher*] in the popular sense, as in the phrase, "Are you looking for trouble?" ["*Tu me cherches?*"].

"He 'looks for it' from me and I find him:" a phrase in which Picasso ("I don't seek, I find") meets Freud (his 'finding' of the object (*Objektfindung*)) and even Pascal (who hears from the mouth of Christ: "You would not seek Me if you had not already found Me"). Thus, one could say that in certain circumstances the dream is looked for or provoked by a potential interlocutor; and the dream in turn will in a sense 'seek' unconscious desire.

Within the monument that is *The Interpretation of Dreams*, Chapter VII is a monumental work in its own right. In translating it, step by step and with considerable difficulties, I learned once again that Freud is not always, as he is often claimed to be, a great writer nor, *a fortiori*, an author to be read on the train, but that he is a tremendous thinker. I have, once again, sought to put him to work. But what a joy it is to discover, hidden away in a corner so to speak, the primary tool needed for such work. This three-line footnote on the rolling up of the diagram gives us a kind of door or corridor that opens on another Chapter VII, one which is virtual but no less powerful. This 'other'

Chapter VII is not the mirror image of the first. Rich with a thousand developments, if one elaborates the consequences that flow from it, it takes account of Freud's first and major discovery, even if the discovery itself gets repeatedly buried: the discovery of the primacy of the message of the other in the constitution of the sexual unconscious.

Postscript to "Should Chapter VII be Rewritten?"

To move further in the direction of 'rewriting Chapter VII', I should like to quote Freud's inaugural passage and indicate the inflection that I give it:

> Accordingly, we shall ascribe a sensory and a motor end to the apparatus. At the sensory end there lies a system which receives perceptions; at the motor end there lies another, which opens the gateway to motor activity. Psychical processes advance in general from the perceptual end to the motor end. Thus the most general schematic picture of the psychical apparatus may be represented as follows

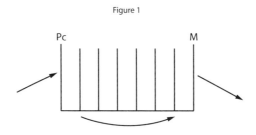

Figure 1

This, however, does no more than fulfil a requirement with which we have long been familiar, namely that the psychical apparatus must be constructed like a reflex apparatus. Reflex processes remain the model of every psychical function.[31]

On the face of it, this schema is supposed to represent a living organism (alone and having no relation with others) immersed in the material world. It receives stimuli (Pc = perception) and releases motor responses (M). The schema of the reflex arc is characteristic of this kind of functioning: it releases everything that it has received.

I propose that what we actually have is an 'apparatus of the soul' – be it in man or in social animals (homeotherms) – that is immersed not in a world of stimuli but a world of messages. It receives messages and must translate them, albeit at the risk of leaving something untranslated. It is this schema that is rolled up on itself.

---

31 *The Interpretation of Dreams*, op. cit., pp. 537–38.

4

COUNTERCURRENT[1]

To go against the current of many things that are said and done in the psychoanalytic movement – the movement taken in the most inclusive sense, beyond any reference to psychoanalytic institutions. First of all, however, it is necessary to clear up a misunderstanding: it is not a question of advocating, in a nostalgic way, a simple return to the Freud of 100 years ago. For Freud himself was against the current of his own era, although he was, more than once, swept away by that current without knowing it. To go against the current is thus to try to rediscover the first and constant exigency at work in Freud, which is in opposition to those aspects of his work I have sometimes called his 'goings astray'.[2] We must try to restore this exigency – which continues in a more or less latent way to drive the practitioners of analysis – as a live force in both theory and practice. This means that the necessity for 'new foundations' remains always present.

It was not just in 1897, nor in 1900 but as late as 1923, that Freud continued, like a 'conquistador', to assert the extraordinary

---

1 First published in, "Courants de la psychanalyse contemporaine", *Revue Française de psychanalyse*, n⁰ hors série, 2001, pp. 299–309.
2 [*Editor*: Laplanche's term here is *fourvoiement*, which he elevates to the rank of a methodological concept. See Jean Laplanche, "Exigency and going astray", *Psychoanalysis, Culture and Society*, vol. 11, 2006, pp. 185–89.]

character of his *discovery*. It is this discovery that *defines* psychoanalysis first of all, while the therapeutic and theoretical aspects are only consequences of it: "Psycho-Analysis is the name (1) of a procedure for the investigation of mental processes which are almost inaccessible in any other way"; (2) "of a method ... for the treatment of neurotic disorders"; (3) "of a collection of psychological information ... gradually being accumulated into a new scientific discipline".[3]

This passage should, by the way, serve as a notice to all those Associations that currently define themselves in their own bylaws with reference to the therapeutic aspect above all, subordinating their *truths* to the vagaries of technical 'results' and the disagreements about psychopathology.

Neither, however, is psychoanalysis a new theory to explain old facts, already appropriately identified but just badly explained.

The Object and its Point of Access

Psychoanalysis is first of all an absolutely new exploratory procedure, which reveals a *domain of being* (the 'processes of the soul') to which barely anything else gave access. Everything has been tried subsequently to banalize the 'realism of the unconscious' – the name of this *terra incognita* – by finding its precursors and equivalents. Indeed – at least, this is our thesis – the radical novelty of the Freudian unconscious consists in the fact that it does *not* bring a supplementary meaning to our conscious universe; it is not a new meaning that could be read within phenomena that are already known. It is not a code and still less a new theory. It reveals itself through the *faultlines* of consciousness, as another domain of being.[4] In spite of all attempts

---

3 "Two Encyclopaedia Articles" (1923a), *SE* 18, p. 235

4 There is nothing unusual in the fact that a new instrument should not only open up new explanations but also new realities that had not previously been recognized. Cf. the telescope, the microscope, etc. For the human being, however, there is an intense humiliation in discovering something radically other within himself.

at *rapprochement*, it has nothing at all to do with what the poets (the Romantics) or the philosophers (Schopenhauer) refer to by the same name.

It is certainly true that the tendency to 'read' the conscious 'text' for a more deeply hidden intention – hermeneutic 'decoding', in a word – makes a reappearance in Freud himself: in the powerful return of symbolism, for example, as a collective system of keys which allows an open book translation. It is as easy and as pointless to read sexual symbols everywhere as to read class struggle everywhere. Then there's the fact that psychoanalysis invents its own keys: 'Oedipus', 'castration', or Kleinian 'positions' – universal keys that are very often used *a priori*, before the subject has had a chance to say a word.

Further on we shall see what *function* to attribute to this ongoing hermeneutic translation. Here it is enough to recall just how distant it is from Freud's original discovery.

Freud's *invention* is thus the invention of a method; his *discovery* is the unconscious – real, separate, and not immanent within the conscious. As to the method, it is essentially divided into two components: the fundamental rule and the analytic situation. In the encyclopedia article cited above which *defines* 'psychoanalysis', it is the 'rule' that comes first.

One has only to note the degree to which this fundamental rule will be subsequently devalued or debased. Devalued by all those who speak 'about' psychoanalysis. Thus Lévi-Strauss limited his knowledge of Freud to those texts that are most marked by 'symbolism'.

It is also debased by a large number of clinicians. They barely mention it at the beginning of the treatment, instead taking for granted the 'free speaking' that has found acceptance in our sociological climate and which constitutes the common denominator of all the psychotherapies. How, after all, is this any different from 'confession' understood in its largest sense? How is it different from the free speaking of Alcoholics Anonymous groups or from 'debriefings' after serious accidents?

Yet, it is barely a paradox to say that the rule relating to 'freely occurring ideas' (*freie Einfälle*) is completely contrary to the notion of 'speaking freely'. For we must add to the latter injunction: 'without omitting anything that occurs to you', precisely, what is on the margins of this 'confidential' discourse, as its scoria, its dross. To *force* oneself not to omit what seems *irrelevant* – whether *trivial* or *meaningless* (the unbound), or *inappropriate* and *uncomfortable to say* (the sexual and/or aggressive) – in fact goes, very exactly, against the current of all confidential discourse, even the freest.

At the same time, the notion of resistance in the treatment disappears along with the fundamental rule. But as Freud forcefully emphasizes, resistance is bound up with any such discourse that is only apparently 'unrestricted'. Yet it is the latter that will henceforth be legitimated in common practice by being presented in a continuous and coherent manner, with all its edges smoothed.

In the same way, it is easy to see that the *analysis* of the dream is very often abandoned in favor of its *synthesis*, its narrative, its secondary revision; defensive and 'anagogic' features according to Freud, but here pompously adorned with the label and with all the virtues of 'symbolization'.

The Therapeutic Dimension

The debate about the relationship between psychoanalysis and psychotherapy has become banal and trifling, to the point where it is sometimes reduced to matters which, however important they may be, are essentially *secondary*: the number and length of sessions, whether the patient sits or lies down, etc. The debate must begin at a deeper level – that is to say, at the metapsychological level: what does it mean 'to treat'? And who is it that does the treating?

We maintain that to treat means, essentially, to confront the 'unbound' in order to give it a form, a meaning, a coherence. This coherence is achieved primarily by means of a putting into narrative; it corresponds to a temporalization, which is usually incomplete, and is carried out according to registers that may well be poorly integrated with one another. Here 'treating' assumes the complex meaning that it has in French: not only in the therapeutic sense but in the 'treatment' or processing of a text (breaking it down into its primary elements), or again, in the language of war, attacking and putting out of operation selected targets.

Who treats? No one treats anyone but himself, at least on the psychic level. It is the human being who treats and is treated, thereby constituting himself as that always more or less precarious unity that we call 'me' or 'subject'. It would seem at first glance that *what* the human being has to treat are his unconscious drives, which are sexual in the broad sense of the term (sexual death drives and sexual life drives). It should also be fully recognized that Freudianism enables us to go beyond the Platonic image of the spirit taming the passions of the body (taking the latter in the biological sense).

Here, the general theory of seduction provides a hypothesis that at the very least deserves to be examined: what from the beginning is 'to be bound', 'to be translated', does not come from the depths of an innate id but from the other human, the adult, in the essential asymmetry of our first months. The first attempts at 'treatment' are made in order to respond to the enigmatic messages (compromised by sexuality) coming from the adult other. The partial failure of these attempts at translation – by which the ego constitutes itself and begins to represent itself within a narrative – entails the exclusion of real elements, which then become the internal sources of sexual excitation against which the ego must continue to defend itself. The *socius* provides continual assistance for this defense by offering the subject rules, myths, ideologies and ideals. In a certain sense, psychotherapy (all psychotherapies, and at all times) does nothing but take up and systematize this imperious movement of binding. Its effort is at once to help 'contain' the most destructive tendencies of the drives and to make a contribution towards giving them a meaning. This is something for which therapy has never been short of narrative schemas: one thinks of shamanistic treatments and of Jungian indoctrination with its religious echoes, but also of the schemas discovered or renewed by psychoanalysis and *instrumentalized* as scenarios for a renewed symbolisation: 'castration', 'the murder of the father', 'the overcoming of the depressive position'.

Why, then, would psychoanalysis itself not be just one more form of psychotherapy among others?

But does it really have the same status as the others? This is the essential question.

When Freud opposes the idea of providing the patient with a psychosynthesis, he does not do so out of stubbornness or dogmatism. He merely affirms that the human being, 'the patient', aims at nothing other than synthesis. The entire specificity of psychoanalysis consists precisely in the movement against this current, in the movement of *analysis* – which is to say, the 'dissolution' of syntheses that have previously been accepted by the subject.

In this respect, we must not be afraid of proposing the idea that every synthesis, every attempt by the subject to represent himself within a narrative or a story, is defensive. Which certainly does not mean that we must take the 'anarchy of the drives' as our goal – something that would, in any case, be impossible, strictly speaking, even unthinkable. Some syntheses are better than others: that is to say, they are more inclusive, better able to integrate the repressed. But we shouldn't fool ourselves: even in the most harmonious life, there will always be something of the repressed, of the unconscious, of that internal 'other' that is the residue of the external other.

This is the moment to call upon the other aspect of Freud's 'methodological' invention for gaining access to the unconscious: alongside the fundamental rule is the establishment of the *analytic situation*. It is a situation of radical asymmetry that has lent itself and still lends itself to all sorts of misunderstandings. Some have spoken of professional hypocrisy (Ferenczi). Some have invoked the participant-observer situation in order to point out immediately that, in the case of an inter-human relation, the observer has no privileged position when it comes to highlighting what, in the patient's statements, arises from a projection and what arises from a realistic perception. With this critique (which is true as far as it goes) the door was thrown wide open to what has since become a kind of refrain at conferences: the so-called 'transference-countertransference dynamic'.

We can only fully understand the inspired invention of the analytic situation, however, if it is coupled with a conception of the 'fundamental anthropological situation' (adult-*infans*) as originary asymmetry, whose other name is 'seduction'.

Only infantile asymmetry can explain and justify the 'intolerable' asymmetry of analysis. 'Neutrality' is not primarily a refusal to give the other (the patient) help, advice, knowledge, etc. It can only be maintained by what must be called a 'refusal'[5] internal to the analyst: an apprehension, perhaps, of his own unconscious mechanisms, but most importantly a sense of his limitations and a respect for the other within himself. This involves a relinquishing of any aim to master or fashion the other, of a *poiesis* or making over.

Transference,[6] if we want to preserve for it an analytic specificity, can only be conceived within the framework of this situation, which fundamentally returns the subject as closely as possible to the enigmas that were presented to him in his childhood. Beyond the enigmas of the internal other (the unconscious), it is the 'treatment' of

---

5 [*Editor*: '*Refusement*' – this is a neologism invented by Laplanche to translate Freud's *Versagung*, which Strachey translates as 'frustration' in the *Standard Edition*. Where 'frustration' refers to the lack of an external object of satisfaction, '*refusement*' refers to a subject who refuses a desired object or mode of satisfaction, often to himself. Here Laplanche applies the term to the analyst, whose refusal to advise or control the analysand or to know in advance the significance of his symptoms and behaviour is sustained by a similar refusal with regard to his own internal other.]
6 If one wants to avoid the aporias masterfully described by Lagache: how could any human act otherwise than in conformity with his history, his dispositions, etc?

the enigmas of the external other (the adults – the parents) that is, in the most favorable cases, a work in progress.[7]

Thus, even if it inevitably slips back into the ruts of the *talking cure* (the chatting cure) that characterize *every* form of psychotherapy, one can recognize the degree to which the psychotherapy *immanent* to analysis takes on a new form when it is able to include within its 'narrativity' some fragment of otherness unearthed by the analysis. Without ever forgetting, however, that every new synthesis, however flexible it may be, remains defensive nonetheless.[8]

Since I have proposed a 'translational' theory of repression, let me quickly take up that model here.[9] Every translation is the translation of a message, which necessarily lets some scoria or residue, some nuances, 'drop out'. All the more so if the initial message is not transparent to itself, that is to say if it is marked by the unconscious of the sender. On the other hand, I have also likened the subject's location within a history, his constitution within a narrative form, to the translation of received originary messages (translation – mastery – treatment).

If A is the first message – for example, the New Testament, supposedly composed in Aramaic (but we do not have this original text) – B would be the Greek translation, the only one that scholars have. From A to B, some of the original signifiers have been, in part, 'allowed to drop out' for lack of an adequate equivalent. Now,

---

7 Let us merely mention that if psychoanalysis is fundamentally the 'analysis of the human condition' (Favreau), then the complete abolition of the 'training analysis' is consistent with this aim.

8 I do not feel in any way obliged to integrate here the psychotherapy of the psychoses, or rather of the psychotic part that is more or less extensive in most human beings. How can one speak of '*psycho-analysis*', in the precise sense defined by Freud, vis-à-vis psychic spaces in which repression into the unconscious seems not to have happened? Which does not mean that the metapsychological theory that arises from psychoanalysis cannot help to create other psychotherapeutic approaches.

9 Cf. "La parabole Chouraqui" in *Le Primat de l'autre* (Paris: Flammarion, 1999) pp. 228–29. This is also discussed in "The Wall and the Arcade" in *Jean Laplanche : Seduction, Translation, Drives*, ed. John Fletcher and Martin Stanton (London : Institute of Contemporary Arts, London, 1992), pp. 207–8.

to retranslate the Greek text B into a Latin text C, and then C into a French text D, is necessarily to accumulate repression upon repression. The same thing occurs in the *chatting cure*, unless it attempts to undo text C, and even text B, on the assumption that behind the latter there is a first message A (Aramaic), which reveals itself in the fault-lines, the incongruities and the incoherences of B.

This model is insufficient in relation to what happens with the child, in that for the child the first messages are *by their nature* inhabited by otherness – not the alterity inherent in the signifier as postulated by Lacan, but the concrete otherness of the sexual unconscious of the other. Certainly this model is imperfect, as are all models; but it does make clear that every narrativization of our own history is constituted as a defense, and that each one leaves out and always will leave out something of the other.

The Theoretical Dimension

The topic proposed for this series of contributions to the *Revue française de psychanalyse* sets out, in just a few lines, a diagnosis that is indisputable: the generalized fragmentation, the juxtaposing of points of view, the absence of references to other authors or contributions, the selective citation – poorly understood, poorly integrated, purely eclectic – of those authors whom one 'must' mention. The immense congresses where each participant only waits to sing his theme song during the ten or twenty minutes that he is allocated. The supposed 'roundtables' during which no one engages anyone else in dialogue, and which are a sort of ragbag of surplus interventions. In the past, the journals were not thematically organised but did sometimes publish an article worth thinking about; today the journals are supposedly thematic but they lack any coordination, except the 'headings' that a talented editor-in-chief can artificially introduce. Even the best journals are not exempt from this.

It really does seem as though we are reduced to the notion that "Everything has been said ... since there have been men who have been thinking."[10] Would Freud's audacious claim – *to say something different* – be at least accepted by those who claim to refer to him? One might well doubt it when one sees the 'psychoanalytic' invoked to justify the 'anything goes' that is called postmodernism. 'Allude to the topic in passing' is the only rule.[11]

"Neither laugh, nor weep, but understand".[12] Let us propose a path towards an understanding of this state of things. We maintain that the human being is an interpreter by nature: the only originary hermeneut; a hermeneut by virtue of his condition, according to Heidegger. From the very beginning, an interpreter of the enigmatic messages of the human adult other: this is what we propose with the general theory of seduction.

The codes he employs to understand these messages do not come from nowhere; they are themselves supplied by the social universe. It is a fact of modern culture that these codes (or ideologies) circulate, become universal, and wear themselves out more and more quickly.

Psychoanalysis, for its part, has provided two things: on the one hand, a strict method and a strict theory, which are not easily understood and not particularly inviting; on the other, interpretive schemas that it *rediscovered* within the human being, and which it remodeled as supposedly universal myths (universal keys). It was inevitable that this second aspect was the only one retained and given prominence, not only by public opinion but by psychoanalytic thinkers themselves (by *everyone*). Without this clear distinction, analytic

---

10 [*Trans*.: "Everything has been said, and we come more than seven thousand years too late – seven thousand years since there have been men who have been thinking – to say anything that has not been said already". La Bruyère, "Des ouvrages de l'esprit", *Les Caractères* (Paris: Flammarion, 1965), p. 82.]

11 "My paradigm is as valid as yours; stop being intolerant!" A phrase of this type from the mouth of a 'Lacanian' resounded one day across a congress: a curious statement, if one considers the scientific pretensions of 'the matheme'.

12 [*Trans*.: A paraphrase of a statement by Spinoza].

theory has been poorly defined in terms of its specificity and has itself been bundled up with the numerous models by means of which the human being represents itself metaphorically: it is here that the spontaneous hermeneutics of the human being offers a helping hand to postmodernism and epistemological relativism.

So, we propose rigorously to distinguish between two fields:

1) That of myths, narrative schemas, frameworks for symbolization and narration, some but not all of which were 'discovered' by psychoanalysis: e.g. the Oedipus. It makes no sense to describe such schemas as being true or false. This doesn't mean (quite the contrary) that they should be considered as *a priori* axioms or that they cannot be studied – studied as to their genesis, their greater or lesser capacity to symbolize, as to what constitutes their core (e.g. does 'thirdness' explain the power of the Oedipus?), or, finally, as to their 'universality'. Concerning this last point: on the eve of the appearance of cloned human beings, is it reasonable to continue to hang the Oedipus on biological parenthood[13] or on the equation mother = nature, father = culture and spirituality?[14]

2) *Psychoanalytic theory.* This is metapsychology; even if it is necessarily articulated with psychology, it makes no claim to encompass or to conquer it. The extension of 'psychoanalytic psychology' is one of the grave errors of our era, the cost of which has been the 'cognitivist' reaction.

Metapsychology is not the theory of clinical work. It is the theory of the human being insofar as he is affected by an unconscious. A theory, therefore, of the unconscious, of its nature, its genesis, its returns, its effects etc. As such it is fundamentally a theory of repression, of its failures and even its absences (which thus opens onto the theory of psychosis).

---

13 Freud contented himself with saying to those who denied the Oedipus: "Don't you have a father and a mother?"

14 As I recall, the reason for this was *pater semper incertus*: it is always uncertain who the father is. In this age of genetics, who would dare to maintain the Latin adage?

One of the major tasks of metapsychology must be to prove its capacity to account for the *function of myths* and therefore of hermeneutics, as much within the human being as such as in the effects of psychotherapy.

A theory that explicitly aims to account for hermeneutics cannot itself be a hermeneutics! It must aim at rationality, that is to say, at articulating truths and refuting errors.

Rationality within psychoanalysis, such as Freud practiced it throughout his work, has nothing to learn from the sciences of physical nature. The ideal of mathematisation is in any case a trap, as is that of experimental reproducibility: how many of the physical sciences are situated explicitly outside of these two criteria? As for the appeal to statistics, the latter has never been anything but a poor relation of rationality.

It is here that psychoanalytic rationality must try to rid itself of the *vulgar* pragmatism that infests it at the present moment. Besides, the expression 'truth is what works' is not univocal but has at least two meanings: (1) what succeeds as 'cure', which implies a utilitarian definition of practice and a reduction of theory to the level of a recipe; (2) what succeeds as explanation, which implies the dimension of truth, of success – at least provisionally – at the level of thought. In a word, the theory of gravitation does not work *because* it provides methods for constructing bridges. It is verified just as much by bridges that fall down as by bridges that stay up.

But it must be said that at many psychoanalytic and/or psychotherapeutic conferences these days, the only question is: "how does it help?" It becomes inconceivable that Freud's own confession of failure to cure the psychoses might be coupled with the affirmation of a success in understanding them! As far as the physical sciences are concerned, our impotence is confirmed by a great number of cases; but as to human nature one doesn't admit that it cannot be changed with just a nudge in the right direction: these criminals, these maniacs, these suicides, why don't you cure them? And if you can't, please leave the premises immediately![15]

Freudian rationalism

In our view, Freudian rationalism is marked by the missed encounter between Freud and Popper. In his critique of psychoanalysis, Popper superficially retains only the most ideological aspects of it, such as were being propagated at the time by Adler and Jung. It is precisely those aspects that I have placed under the heading of myth and hermeneutics. Popper was scarcely informed about the real complexity of psychoanalysis, and was scarcely aware of the profound discussions that Freud conducted, most often by taking himself as a demanding and contrarian interlocutor.

We are not unaware of the criticisms and modifications that have been made to 'Popperism', and which have forced the abandonment of the model of abrupt transformation in science, the model of *localized* 'falsifications' leading to *complete* upheavals. Nevertheless, *The Logic of Scientific Discovery*[16] remains an important moment in epistemological thought, and one that is not bound to a particular type of scientific reasoning, nor, as a result, to the sciences of physical nature alone. The basic idea is that scientific models are never derived on the basis of arduous induction – which could never prove anything absolutely – but are rather *invented*, so as to account in the best

---

15 In place of these two criteria – of success in 'modifying' nature and success in providing rational explanations – a certain sociologicalizing epistemology has sought to substitute a third: success in rallying the policy makers and obtaining research grants. One could ask which of these three criteria our epistemological theories would wish to have applied to *themselves*. Have they renounced, in their own domain, the question of what is true and what is false? Is it the case that in epistemology, as elsewhere, *anything goes*?
16 Karl Popper, *The Logic of Scientific Discovery* (London and New York: Routledge, 2002 [orig. 1935]).

possible way for the facts that have been identified so far.

These models are henceforth put at risk of 'falsification' or, more generally, *refutation*. A model that cannot, on any point, be confronted by a refutation is precisely of the order of myth, not of science. 'Nature never says 'yes'; it only expresses itself with 'no': this maxim was already adopted by Freud, both in his search for the 'negative case' that would show the absence of the sexual factor and in his famous discussion of "A Case of Paranoia *Running Counter* to the Psychoanalytic Theory of the Disease".[17]

To maintain a *minimal positivism* is, in my view, to maintain three requirements:

1) To agree on the terms used and be ready to change them if they lead to persistent ambiguity. For instance, what purpose does it serve to debate 'metaphor' and 'metonymy', when the meaning of these terms is extremely varied from Quintillian to Du Marsais, through to Fontanier, Jakobson, Lacan, Rosolato and Hock. I fully realize that this demand, like others, runs counter to the current tendency to deify language and its infinite polysemy (or should we say 'poetry'?).

2) To be capable of saying which domain of 'facts' corresponds to the theory one is propounding. Where in experience can one find points of contact with the theory? Take, for example, 'the paternal metaphor'. In what circumstances of life, in what period of childhood, at what moment in the treatment, etc. can one identify its effects? In what domain of experience is it to be found: verbal language, meanings, affects, actions?

3) To be able at least to imagine circumstances (of fact or reasoning) in which what one affirms could be called into question. This does not entail any rigid application of the notion of falsification. The 'letter of the equinox' (21 September 1897) clearly shows the flexibility and the variety of the bundle of No's with which Freud objects to his own theory of seduction.

---

17 (1915f), *SE* 14, pp. 263–272.

The rationality of psychoanalysis has always been open to multiple sorts of arguments, drawn from the most varied domains. One has only to read any ordinary text by Freud to see that he never limits himself to the closed universe of the analytic relation, in order to define a sacrosanct domain of the 'psychoanalytic' from which those who are not in the inner circle are permanently excluded.[18] In *Beyond the Pleasure Principle* Freud just as easily evokes biological experiments and biological theories as child observation, cosmological speculation, etc. How, in the era of genetics, can we continue to speak in the same way as before of 'phylogenesis'?

The argument proposed by this issue of the *Revue* has not managed to escape the following contradiction: it denounces, with great pertinence, the simultaneous fragmentation and lack of communication that reign in the analytic milieu. At the same time, it can only propose a juxtaposition of contributions: 'featured side by side but assembled into a single space of writing'.

However, we shall have to go much further if psychoanalysis is not to become a corpse. There is an urgent need to restore debate among those who want to debate. It is time for texts and theses to reply to each other, and with a rigour that does not exclude tolerance; rigour with respect to ideas, tolerance with respect to others. Do we not all too often see the opposite: a laxity of thinking, but bitter and narcissistic polemic *vis-à-vis* individuals?

---

18 A universe that is often combined with another bias, that of skepticism and of postmodern montage.

5

STARTING FROM THE FUNDAMENTAL ANTHROPOLOGICAL SITUATION[1]

My "starting from" refers to a real point of departure, which underscores the term *fundamental* anthropology. This does not mean that as psychoanalysts we take it as our starting point. We start out from an experience. This experience is the *ratio cognoscendi*, a way of gaining access to knowledge, whereas the fundamental anthropological situation might be considered – if you'll pardon the somewhat pedantic term – to be the *ratio essendi*. It is a conjecture to be confirmed, and possibly to be falsified; it is inferred from our particular paths of approach, which does not imply that it cannot be corroborated by experience. It is a historical conjecture, to be situated within the history of the individual, of any individual we call 'human'.

The theory of seduction is not a metaphysical hypothesis. Throughout the length of its trajectory in Freud, it is supported by facts of observation. Nevertheless, I shall quickly come to the *ratio cognoscendi*, which is to say, to our path of approach in psychoanalysis: the analytic experience, the Freudian experience as the experience

---

[1] Lecture delivered at the Societé Psychanalytique de Paris on September 20, 2002. The discussant was André Green. First published in *Penser les limites. Ecrits en l'honneur d'André Green*, ed. César Botella, Champs psychanalytiques series (Neuchâtel: Delachaux & Niestlé, 2002).

of a radical alterity; and also to the double register that this experience implies: the experience of the unconscious and the experience/invention of the analytic situation, which is to say the experience/invention of the treatment.

The experience of the unconscious in dreams and symptoms underlines its alien-ness [*étrangèreté*].[2] Our experience of the dream is never exhausted. From this emerges a sort of negative metapsychology of the unconscious (negative in the sense of negative theology): the absence of time, of coordination, of negation – all attributes which, in a word, show the difficulty we have in grasping the unconscious in itself. The unconscious is explained, however, by the theory of repression – which is itself 'alien', since within that theory, if one reads Freud's texts carefully, the downward movement of repression does not follow the same paths by which the repressed returns. Repression is a loss, which will never be compensated by a complete return. It used to be said that communism was a journey without a return ticket. Well, repression is something a little like that – a journey without a return ticket. The unconscious is not an 'ancient consciousness'; it is not a memory that one could hope to recover completely. The unconscious is something that has dropped out of conscious experience, that has escaped the domain of ordered memories. The unconscious is not a memory, as Freud's earliest terms clearly indicate: it is a 'reminiscence'[3], which is something completely different from a memory.

The alterity of the analytic situation is Freud's extraordinary invention – an asymmetry whose *raisons d'être* and the full extent of

---

2 [*Trans.* Laplanche's noun *étrangèreté* is a neologism in French, not *etrangété* – 'strangeness' – but 'strangerness'. Our hyphenated term seeks to capture this abstract substantive by preserving the connection with 'stranger' and 'alien' as nouns rather than 'strange' or 'alien' as adjectives.]
3 [*Editor*: "The return to mind of an image that is not recognized as a memory … an influence more or less unconscious … a vague, imprecise memory, where the affective tonality dominates", *Le Nouveau Petit Robert* (Paris: le Robert, 2010), p. 2182. While the English term 'reminiscence' has kept the emphasis on emotional tonality, it has become virtually synonymous with conscious memory.].

whose consequences we have yet to draw out. However, I think that the first theory of seduction, the Freudian theory, was perhaps the best suited theory possible (given the means Freud had at his disposal) for giving an account of this double alterity. There was an extraordinary conjunction of the alterity described in the situation of seduction and this double alterity of the experience of the unconscious within us and the experience of the analytic situation. Freud's stroke of genius is to trace back the alterity of the unconscious and the alterity of the transference to the alterity of the originary situation of seduction. This alterity is a radical asymmetry. With the philosophers, we remain stuck in the adult-adult relation, the adult other being faced by another adult; and in phenomenology, as we know, within this adult-adult situation, the one is supposed to be 'reduced', as in the technical sense of the term in phenomenology, by the constitution of the other. In the post-phenomenology of the Lévinasian type, the other is indeed irreducible in the face-to-face relation. But Lévinas does not take account of what produces the irreducible, that is to say, the unconscious, the sexual unconscious, the infantile sexual unconscious.

What makes for the irreducible? What is Freud's hypothesis about seduction? It is the hypothesis of the adult-*infans* asymmetry – the asymmetry which we find in major texts such as "The Aetiology of Hysteria",[4] and, much later, in the well known paper by Ferenczi.[5] It is the asymmetry between what the latter calls two types of language. The theory of seduction is the hypothesis best suited to the discovery of the irreducible unconscious. I have tried to say in what respects it was, in Freud, a restricted theory, a restricted theory of seduction. Restricted because it limited itself to the domain of psychopathology; to use an instant formula: 'neurotic daughter, perverse father'. Freud lacks various elements, which he would have needed in order

---

4 (1896c) *SE* 3, pp. 189–221.
5 "Confusion of Tongues between Adult and the Child: The Language of Tenderness and of Passion", in *Sandor Ferenczi: Selected Writings*, ed. Julia Borossa (Harmondsworth: Penguin Books, 1999), pp. 293–303.

to reform and generalize it, instead of abandoning it, as he did in the famous letter of 21 September 1897. What he lacks, beyond the notion of psychopathological perversion, is the notion of polymorphous perversity such as he will describe in the *Three Essays* which were to follow; what he lacks is the notion of early communication, the notion of the message; what he lacks, although he had, nevertheless, sketched it out more than once, is a fully theorized notion of repression as being related to translation. What I am emphasizing today, however, is something else again. Seduction is not a relation that is contingent, pathological (even though it can be) and episodic. It is grounded in a situation from which no human being is exempt: the 'fundamental anthropological situation', as I call it. This fundamental anthropological situation is the adult-*infans* relation. It consists of the *adult*, who has an unconscious such as psychoanalysis has revealed it, i.e. a sexual unconscious that is essentially made up of infantile residues, an unconscious that is perverse in the sense defined in the *Three Essays*; and the *infant*, who is not equipped with any genetic sexual organisation or any hormonal activators of sexuality. The idea of an endogenous infantile sexuality has been profoundly criticized, and not only by me: I refer you to one of the best critiques that could be made, that by Gérard Mendel.[6] The major danger, of course, is moving from a critique of *endogenous* infantile sexuality to a denial of infantile sexuality as such. As we know, infantile sexuality is what is most easily denied and Freud even made this point one of its characteristics: the fact that the adult does not want to see it. Might this be because it derives from the adult himself?

How can the contributions of the modern psychology of the first years of life be situated in relation to this notion? There is indeed a great deal to be added here thanks to recent observation. There is the considerable development of what Freud formerly called *self-preservation* – something which, incidentally, he forgot about in his second

---

6 Gérard Mendel, *La psychanalyse revisitée* (Paris: La Découverte, 1988).

theory of the drives, and which I nonetheless strive to put back on the agenda, although in a greatly expanded way. Self-preservation now has made a return with the notion of attachment, together with all the developments and all the observations around this theme. Very early on – perhaps immediately – a dialogue, an adult-*infans* communication, develops upon a manifestly genetic and instinctual foundation. The old theory of symbiosis (a state from which one is supposed to exit – who knows how?) vanishes thanks to the observation of early relations which are organized, differentiated and immediately reciprocal, and in which the 'not-me' is distinguished at the outset from 'me-possessions'. But what is lacking, both in attachment theory and attachment observation, is a consideration of the asymmetry on the unconscious level. What is lacking in all the observations, among even the best observers, is an insistence on the fact that the adult-*infans* dialogue, as reciprocal as it may be, is nevertheless parasited by something else, from the beginning. One does sometimes encounter an allusion to this – I am thinking of observers such as Roiphe and Galenson, for example, or even Martin Dornes[7] – but it is little more than a clue. The adult message is scrambled. On the side of the adult, and in a unilateral direction, there is the intervention of the unconscious. I would even say 'of the *infantile* unconscious of the adult', insofar as the adult-*infans* situation is a situation that reactivates those unconscious infantile drives.

To give things some emphasis, I would say the following: why speak of the adult and the 'fundamental anthropological situation'? Why not speak of the fundamental familial situation, or even Oedipal situation? Because in its generality, in its universality, the adult-*infans* relation seems to me to go beyond the relation between parents and child. The fundamental anthropological situation can exist between a child without a family and an entirely non-familial rearing environ-

---

7 Martin Dornes, *Psychanalyse et psychologie du première âge* (Paris: Presses Universitaires de France, 2002).

ment. A long time ago I planned a small volume, which was to have been titled, *A Clone on the Couch*. A clone, emerging from some laboratory in the Far East, goes successively to see several specialists who treat him as a 'crime against humanity' incarnate. He then visits Professor Freud who says (and this is something Freud actually wrote): "You claim not to have an Oedipus complex; but don't you have a father and a mother?" Yet this clone is a human being who can be put on the couch, because he has no more escaped the fundamental anthropological situation than has anyone else. For the adult-*infans* relationship is simultaneously one of attachment and unilateral sexuality, and is characteristic of all human rearing, including the rearing of a clone. This may all have been a fantasy; but who knows, it could happen one day! – though don't suppose that I want it to!

In this fundamental anthropological situation the important terms are 'communication' and 'message' – together with the following idea, on which I want to insist: I am *not* speaking of an unconscious message; for me every message is a message produced on the conscious-preconscious level. When I speak of the enigmatic message, I am speaking of a message compromised by the unconscious. There is never an unconscious message in a pure state. The character of the message is, therefore, compromised from the start, from a single direction, even if reciprocity establishes itself very quickly there as well, i.e. on the sexual level. In this situation, what matters is what the receiver makes of the message, that is to say, precisely, the attempt at translation and the necessary failure of translation.

I would like to add three preliminary remarks to what I have said so far:

First of all, the question of *the biological option*. The general theory of seduction and the fundamental anthropological situation are absolutely *not* a way of taking a stance against biology. For me, every human process is indissociably biological and psychical. Even the most abstract mathematical reasoning is inconceivable without a neuro-biological corporeal correlate. When Freud abandons the theory of seduction in the famous letter, he does not say: "I am returning to the biological", but "I am returning to the innate, to the hereditary". I can give the exact wording of this little text: "with [the abandonment of the seduction theory] the factor of an hereditary disposition regains a sphere of influence from which I had made it my task to dislodge it – in the interest of illuminating neurosis."[8] At no point does he say: "the biological factor regains its sphere of influence", for there is nothing whatsoever for it to regain. The biological is always present as the other side of the psychological. This resurgence of heredity announced by Freud, the return of the hereditary factor, covers the entire history of Freudianism and through several stages, of which I shall mention only three: the 'primal fantasies', *Totem and Taboo* (1913), and *Moses and Monotheism* (1939).

To return to the biological, this factor may be acquired as well as innate. Thus, as regards infantile sexuality, it is the primacy of heredity that I oppose. I say *sexuality* and *infantile*, by which I mean that there is certainly something innate in what is not sexual, and also something innate in the sexuality that is not infantile. To my mind there exists a fundamental difference between the sexual drive of childhood and what surfaces at the moment of adolescence, which is effectively the emergence of the sexual instinct. The sexual instinct then catches up with the drive, which has developed over many years, and there is between the two a serious problem of coherence and cohesion and, most importantly, of content.

The second point, on which I can give a few indications and which seems to me to be very important, is the question of *afterwardsness*. Since Freud articulated it (in German as *Nachträglichkeit*), and since Lacan underlined the term (proposing the French translation *après coup* but without really giving it a theory), afterwardsness

---

8 Letter to Fliess, September 21st., 1897, *The Complete Letters of Sigmund Freud to Wilhelm Fliess, 1887–1904*. Trans. and ed. Jeffrey M. Masson (Cambridge: Belknap Press of Harvard University Press, 1985), p. 265

obviously has flourished. These days it is invoked on all sides, and in contemporary thought – including psychoanalytic thought, but even more so in an entire philosophy based on psychoanalysis – it seems irremediably wedded to the hermeneutic interpretation. In other words, afterwardsness is systematically interpreted as a retroactive conferral of meaning. This interpretation of afterwardsness seems to have prevailed for decades; one could point to Spence, one could equally well cite Viderman, who was its most eloquent apostle in France. Even if he does not situate his theory under the banner of afterwardsness, Viderman's conception is clearly that of a retroactive conferral of meaning.

In what way does Freud's conception of afterwardsness leave a way open to the purely retroactive interpretation? I am fond of citing the brief passage in which Freud gives an anecdote to illustrate the notion of *Nachträglichkeit*. Let me cite it again: "Love and hunger ... meet at a woman's breast. A young man who was a great admirer of feminine beauty was talking once – so the story went – of the good-looking wet-nurse who had suckled him when he was a baby: 'I'm sorry,' he remarked, 'that I didn't make a better use of my opportunity.' I was in the habit of quoting this anecdote to explain the factor of afterwardsness in the mechanism of the psychoneuroses."[9] In what way, then, does Freud's conception leave itself open to the purely retroactive or, conversely, the purely progressive interpretation of afterwardsness? In this anecdote, and in the form of a composite image, he present us with the same subject who is, successively, an *infans* and a young man. It is evidently the same subject who sees himself retrospectively, held at the breast of his wet-nurse. We are thereby enclosed within a 'one-body psychology' – that is to say, a psychology centred upon a single protagonist. The single protagonist is the subject X, whether *infans* or adult. Some will say that the *infans* already

---

9 *The Interpretation of Dreams* (1900a), *SE* 4, pp. 204–5. [*Trans.*: Strachey's translation of *Nachträglichkeit* as 'deferred action' has been altered to reflect Laplanche's preference for 'afterwardsness'].

possessed an oral sexuality that will develop in the young man. Others will say, "Not at all!; it is as an adolescent or as a young man that he fantasizes, in a purely retrospective way, the sexual pleasure that he could have taken at the breast of his wet-nurse". You thus have two possible interpretations. First there is what formerly prevailed in Strachey's translation with the idea of 'deferred action' – which in fact refers to the development within the adult of something placed in the child like a seed. Then we have the modern, or even postmodern interpretation, which is completely inverted by means of a reversal of time's arrow: it is the adult who afterwards reinterprets an infantile experience. Whether he does it himself or aided by an analyst is of no importance. Thus, in the end, 'retroactive attribution' approximates to the 'retrospective fantasizing' advocated by Jung, against which Freud had so much trouble arguing – that purely retroactive interpretation of fantasy which he discusses at length for many pages in the Wolf Man case.

What does the theory of seduction contribute to this image, so well devised by Freud, to this anecdote illustrating afterwardsness? What it contributes, alongside the unilinear child-adult succession (which is condemned to run either in one direction or the other: either in the direction of the arrow of time or in the reverse direction), is the presence of the other of the subject. That is to say, quite simply, what is completely forgotten in Freud's anecdote: the presence of the *wet-nurse*, i.e. the presence of the other for the child, who is subsequently the other for the young man. Once her presence is taken into account, we are no longer faced with a sequence composed of a succession of pure facts devoid of meaning, infantile facts to be interpreted subsequently. What is to be interpreted by the young man is not pure fact, or even pure trauma; *it is already a message* awaiting translation, awaiting delivery, so to speak; it is already a message from the nurse to the nursling. Furthermore, before this 'afterwardsness', which is situated in the long period separating the young man from the infant, there is already a kind of afterwardsness in the quasi-simultaneity of the adult other with the child who registers and then translates the message. In the end, this conception of afterwardsness, which has been little understood, is I think essential if we are to escape the dilemma of time's arrow in which we are trapped, and in which the hermeneuts, and even a philosopher of history such as Raymond Aron, find themselves trapped. We can only escape this unilinear vision of time's arrow by invoking the simultaneous other and the message of the other. What is interpreted is already the bearer of meaning. It is never pure fact.

My third point is, in a certain way, the *rehabilitation of child observation*. The richness of the observations of modern psychologists no longer needs to be demonstrated. It is enormous. It remains to be seen whether they are capable of extracting the full quintessence of what they observe. One could say that there is an obvious blind spot among those who make these observations as well as among those who criticize them: namely, the negligible consideration, or total absence, of the fundamental anthropological situation; that is to say, the intervention of the sexuality of the adult, and most of all of his unconscious infantile sexuality, which is awakened by the relation with the child. One can take as an example Roiphe and Galenson's very interesting book on the *Infantile Origins of Sexual Identity*, published in 1981.[10] It contains very finely described observations and yet does not take into account the role of adult sexuality in the situation, or does so only in the final analysis, with regret and at the end. Here, Roiphe and Galenson have to admit that it would be indispensible for the observation itself to grasp the action of the parental unconscious.

I am convinced that these three points, *heredity and/or biology*, *afterwardsness*, and *the psychoanalytic child*, could nourish discussion considerably. However, I would not want to stop here without

---

10 Herman Roiphe and Eleanor Galenson, *Infantile Origins of Sexual Identity* (New York: International Universities Press, 1981).

alluding to some more recent attempts to advance matters. The essential thing in the general theory of seduction and in the fundamental anthropological situation is an exchange of messages on the conscious-preconscious level, messages that, on the side of the adult, are parasited by his unconscious. On the other hand, it is the imperfect attempt at translation by the recipient, an attempt that leads to a repression of a part of the message. Yet the conscious-preconscious code, to which I have, up to now, principally referred, is the code, both acquired and innate, of attachment: let's say the care given to the child by the adult, taking the notion of 'care' in the broadest sense.

But there are other codes and other messages. The problem that I lingered over for several years in a Seminar, and which gave birth to a text, now published in this volume (see essay 9), is that of *gender* and *gender choice*. In other words, I consider 'gender identity' primarily as a message. The problem is that of the birth of gender identity. Why use the notion of gender? Clearly, it must be used only on the condition that it doesn't erase either sex or sexuality. In my view, Freud's use of the opposition between 'masculinity' and 'femininity' demonstrates that gender does have an obvious if rare presence in his thought. This opposition, he says, does not correspond to the oppositions between active and passive or phallic and castrated. In Freud, gender is present at two ends of the chain of existence. It is present at the definitive configuration of human existence, he says, because masculinity and femininity are two complex syntheses made up of psychological, biological and sociological elements; but it is also present at the beginning, if one recalls the fable that he offers us concerning infantile sexual theories. A traveller from Sirius arriving on Earth would be struck by a certain number of enigmas, and among them the major enigma he would encounter would be the separation of the human species into two . . . (he does not say 'genders' as German does not have this term at its disposal; but in the end it is precisely gender that is at issue, and not sex). In short, the traveller from Sirius sees the difference in habitus without, at first, necessarily discerning the different genital organs. Human beings are separated into two genders by means of many other things than their genitals.[11]

In my opinion, it is possible to think in terms of a sort of triad, the triad made of the terms *gender*, *sex* (which sends us back to the category of sexuation, and to what Freud calls the phallic-castrated pair), and finally what, a bit provocatively, I like to call the *sexual*,[12] that is to say, enlarged sexuality, which is essentially based on infantile sexuality.

In what way can the general theory of sexuality be called to the rescue here? It allows us to see that gender is first of all a message, an assignment (an enigmatic one, as we will see), an assignment *within the social*, in the most general sense of that term, by the *socius* – that is, by a close relative, a parent, or a friend or a group of people: "you, little Henry, are a boy". But frequently there are other modalities: if one says: "you, little Leslie, are a boy", things are already more difficult because the name itself is more ambiguous.

However it might be inflected, the assignment comes from the other, and this seems to me capable of challenging Freud's famous notion of 'primary identification', a primary identification, which he initially tells us is "with the father of [one's] own personal prehistory",[13] only to modify this assertion to "identification with the parents" (ibid., p. 31 n1), because the distinction between masculine and feminine does not yet exist during this period of life. Here I suggest a radical inversion of the notion of identification by proposing the following path: it is not an 'identifying of oneself with', but a 'being

---

11 "When you meet a human being, the first distinction you make is 'male or female?' and you are accustomed to make the distinction with unhesitating certainty. ... what constitutes masculinity or femininity is an unknown characteristic which anatomy cannot lay hold of." "Lecture 33: Femininity", *New Introductory Lectures on Psycho-Analysis* (1933a), *SE* 22, pp. 113–114.
12 [*Editor*: On Laplanche's French neologism 'sexual' (as distinct from the normal 'sexuel'), see the Editor's note to the Forward of this volume. The term is printed here in italics to mark it off from the standard English term with the same spelling].
13 *The Ego and the Id* (1923b), *SE* 19, p. 31.

identified by'. In this way, the subject *is identified* by the assignment to a certain gender. This notion of *identification by* would certainly enrich the question of the ego ideal.

All observers – and Stoller first and foremost – have emphasized the meaningful impact of gender assignment, however it may be inflected, and even if it diverges profoundly from the anatomy and physiology of the subject. But what I have just added is that this identification is not only meaningful; it is, at the same time, *enigmatic*. I have referred to the particular case of first names; but it is clear that any assignment carries along with it the unconscious desire of the parents, the most baroque and the most incredible desires, which may be in conflict with the manifest assignment. In other words, the language of gender is compromised by sexual difference and even more by the infantile sexuality of the parents and, more generally, of adults.

Thus alterity is at the heart of the assignment of gender and takes shape not as difference, two terms that exclude a third one, but as diversity. Gender is by rights multiple: why are there two genders, why not any number of genders? That is what the traveller coming from Sirius might have asked himself. Blue and pink, those two colours emblematic of the little boy and the little girl, have a relation of diversity, not oppositionality. So why not three or four genders to go with green and yellow? Why not the *'mauvais genre'* as well?[14]

Yet the child must master and reduce diversity. This is what I have named *phallic logic*, whose best possible summary is the following, by Jacques André: "the primacy of the phallus is the pillar of a synthesis rather than the last word of analysis. It is a synthesis which the child effects within his or her sexual theories long before the psychoanalyst".[15] The function of the castration reaction, 'the early

---

14 [*Trans.*: 'genre' is French for 'gender'. 'Mauvais genre' is an idiom that, literally translated, would be 'bad kind/type (of person)' and is equivalent to the English idioms 'bad sort' or 'bad seed'.
15 Jacques André, *Aux origines féminines de la sexualité* (Paris: Presses Universitaires de France, 1995), p.67.

castration reaction', is to reduce the diverse to the same, to the more/less, or in any case to the plus/minus opposition. A moment ago, I referred to Roiphe and Galenson whose observations are interesting in that they tend to dissociate this castration reaction from the Oedipus complex, viewing the former as emerging earlier than the latter. The early castration reaction is a reaction to diversity that resorts to difference and a response to that difference that resorts to the theory of castration.

Speaking anthropologically, I should like to insist again upon the following point: it is claimed that with castration we have reached the 'biological bedrock', and certain Freudian formulations suggest precisely this. But it is, in fact, an *anatomical* bedrock of which we should speak, and what's more a *false or deceptive anatomy*. The castration complex is based upon a perceived anatomy, one which is illusory and peculiar to the human species. From the moment that humans assumed the upright posture, only one of the two sets of genital organs remained visible. The bedrock of the biological is the bedrock of the anatomical. "Destiny is anatomy",[16] says Freud, and it is a completely contingent and illusory anatomy, one which is connected to the evolution of the human animal. Be that as it may, this *anatomical difference* furnishes a sort of translation code, which is the most elementary and the most restrictive possible: either phallic or castrated. Here we have the contingent origin of something that will take on extraordinary dimensions in modern civilization: the rapid growth of the 'digital'. It is hardly surprising that this translation into presence/absence, which is so rigid and so minimal, lets almost everything escape, lets the *sexual*, infantile sexuality, slip through the net.

To conclude, infantile sexuality is the heart of the unconscious. It is the irreducible alterity constituted in the very movement of its attempted domestication by difference and phallic logic, and

---

16 [*Trans*: Laplanche's apparently inverted rendering of this familiar Freudian claim is explained in essay 9 in this volume.]

in the failure of that domestication. To underline matters once again: gender will be domesticated, symbolized by the oversimplified code of presence/absence, phallic/castrated, the 1/0 of computers. It is doubtless as a function of the rigidity of the phallic/castrated pair that the essence of the infantile *sexual* escapes that type of symbolization. This infantile sexuality is what constitutes the object of our psychoanalytic experience.

6

FAILURES OF TRANSLATION[1]

Yves Manela: Our thanks to Professor Laplanche for coming to the Bibliothèque de Lamoignon, where we are very honoured to receive him.

Jean Laplanche: Thank you. This will be more of a talk than a lecture. *Man who speaks* is the phrase you use to introduce this series. One might also have said *man who communicates*, which is a little different, for human beings have modes of communication governed by codes that are not simply verbal but are profoundly influenced, retroactively, by spoken language. What I mean is that the mother/child code, or, more generally, the non-verbal adult/child codes, cannot be equated with the codes that obtain between an animal and its young, on account of the very fact that the human adult speaks. There are thus forms of communication other than verbal forms, as we shall see during the course of what I shall try to say to you.

I have chosen translation, or rather the failures of translation, as today's theme. We must distinguish among these failures or difficulties; and I have the most extreme reservations about the idea of a

[1] Delivered at the Association des psychiatres français, January 21, 2002. First published in "Les conférences de Lamoignon: Le langue – 1", *Psychiatrie française*, vol. 33, no.3/4, 2002.

general or quasi-metaphysical failure of translation. I have chosen this theme because it is on the horizon of two of my current major activities: the translation of Freud and a longstanding metapsychological elaboration that is formulated in terms of a 'translational theory of the unconscious'. In order to prepare the present talk I re-read Jakobson's article "On the Linguistic Aspects of Translation"[2] – a useful, if questionable article, and one that leaves room for improvement. I shall take up, while also modifying, the three forms of translation he distinguishes:

1. *intralingual* translation, of which little is generally made, and which refers to reformulation or paraphrase within a single language;
2. *interlingual* translation, such as the translation with which we are concerned when, for example, we translate Freud into French; thus, translation from one verbal language to another;
3. *intersemiotic* translation, i.e. interpretation that passes from a non-linguistic system to a linguistic one; but one can also imagine an intersemiotic translation that would go from one semiotic system to another.

It is important, then, that Jakobson, like Saussure, introduces the term 'non-linguistic system', and the term 'semiotic system' which encompasses linguistic systems as well as non-verbal languages. We can also enlarge the Jakobsonian categories that I have just recalled by saying that what he calls intralingual translation, i.e. reformulation, could even be understood to take place within a single non-verbal semiotic system. A reformulation could take place within a single non-verbal code, such that intralingual translation would not only be intralingual but perhaps intrasemiotic. This point will be clarified in the second and third parts of my talk. So, here are the three areas I shall cover:

---

2 Roman Jakobson, "On the Linguistic Aspects of Translation", in *The Translation Studies Reader*, ed. Lawrence Venuti (New York & London: Routledge 2000).

1. some reflections as an interlingual translator;
2. the legitimacy of the concept of translation within metapsychology;
3. failures of translation as a metapsychological concept.

1. My reflections as an interlingual translator will be confidences, confessions of a translator of Freud. Let me say immediately that I am not an unhappy translator. I do not lament each day over the failure or the difficulty of translation. I am perhaps a masochistic translator, but, as you know, one can be a happy masochist. Thus I am chained to Freud, as some among you know, for at least two afternoons per week in arduous editorial sessions involving discussions whose primary and secondary gains are of the utmost importance. On the other hand, there is a 'masochism', if you will, involved in the fact that along with my partners I am attacked, not to say flogged, with the sarcasm of those who, for the most part, don't know the first word of German and certainly don't know the first word of Freud, which is a different matter. Ignorance of one does not preclude ignorance of the other. The rule is to respond only to intelligent critics, to those who understand the issue and who believe that the project merits a certain loyal and informed discussion. So, I am not an unhappy translator: which is precisely to say that I am not centred on failure. I do not harp on that fine, if now slightly tarnished expression that Freud recalled: *traduttore, traditore* – a fine expression that is itself untranslatable but which can nevertheless be transposed in an intralingual fashion, that is to say by paraphrase and commentary. Were it not for the fact that the expression is a pun, I don't think that a commentary would necessarily lose anything of it.

I am not an unhappy translator, because I think that for every difficult passage the best possible translation – to an asymptote of 99% or 99.9% – does exist. One must weigh up what is possible and what is impossible, not harp on about failure. Without going as far as Wittgenstein's "what we cannot speak about, we must pass over in silence",[3] we can nonetheless imagine something like, "what we cannot translate…" not "…we must leave untranslated", but "we must explain why". Thus merely to say why one cannot translate something seems to me to be very important. When we come up against a problem of translation we must, therefore, distinguish the 'why' in each case, for problems can range from the most obvious examples to the most uncertain or, if you like, from impossibility to failure. After all, one cannot bathe in the sea in Paris; one cannot transport cities to the countryside: these are absurdities and impossibilities, not failures.

We must demarcate what is impossible to translate. And we must point out first of all that one can only translate utterances [*la parole*], and not a language. For example, one patently cannot translate a dictionary. Everything that makes up the very fabric of a language is untranslatable. It can only be transported as it is. What about a grammar, as distinct from a dictionary? The metalinguistic discourse within a grammar is easily translated; language as an object is not. The following phrase is more or less invented but it might well be found in any German grammar: "*Unsere Sprache hat ein Neutrum, 'Mädchen' zum Beispiel ist ein Neutrum*". This translates as: "*notre langue a un neutre, 'jeune fille' par exemple est un neutre*" ["our language has a neuter: 'young girl', for example, is a neuter"]. The absurdity here obviously consists in the words "our language" (which language? those reading the grammar are French). We must be absolutely precise: "our German language has a neuter"; and it is equally absurd to say that *jeune fille* is neuter:[4] we have to write "*Mädchen*" and place it in quotation marks. I do not see any failure of translation in all this, only one of the limits of translation.

Now here is a famous passage from Freud which was discussed

---

3 Ludwig Wittgenstein, *Tractatus Logico-Philosophicus*, trans. Brian McGuiness and David Pears (New York & London: Routledge, 2001), p. 89.
4 [*Trans: jeune fille* is feminine in French].

again recently by Janine Altounian. In "Mourning and Melancholia" Freud demonstrates that the self-accusations of the melancholic are in fact directed against someone else. He dedicates a long clinical passage to the description of the melancholic's complaints in order to demonstrate that in fact they are addressed to others, to a spouse for example; and he finishes as follows (forgive me for having to speak German, but it's simple German): *"Seine Klagen sind Anklagen"*, which means that the melancholic's complaints are *Anklagen*, that's to say complaints expressed towards someone, directed against someone.[5] We find this difference between the simple verb and the verb with the prefix *an* within another distinction that, as a rule, we maintain scrupulously when we are translating Freud; this is the difference between *Drohung* (threat) and *Androhung* (a threat that is uttered or expressed). For example, it's obvious that when the castration threat is uttered – by the father, according to Freudian ideology – it is an *Androhung*. I return to my example *"Seine Klagen sind Anklagen"*. Here is a translation that I came up with a long time ago and which we adopted for the *Œuvres complètes*: *"Ses plaints sont des plaints portées contre"* ["His complaints are complaints against"]. Which is not, after all, a bad translation since it clearly renders the directional implication of *an*: to *complain against* and not the simple fact of *complaining*. These complaints are thus complaints that are brought against someone. But then, between parentheses I believe, Freud adds the metalinguistic remark, "in the old sense of the word", to explain that he is referring to the old, slightly obsolete word *"Anklagen"*. Obviously this remark – "in the old sense of the word" – is not valid for our translation: *"plainte portée contre"* is no more an old word in French than *jeune fille* is a neuter in French. We must therefore either not translate Freud's remark or supplement this metalinguistic remark by writing some-

---

5 [*Trans*: The sentence to which Laplanche is alluding, and of which he will go on to offer his own translation, is translated by James Strachey in the *Standard Edition* as follows: "[The melancholic's] complaints are really 'plaints' in the old sense of the word", "Mourning and Melancholia" (1917e), *SE* 14, p. 248.]

thing like, "in the old sense of the German word *Anklagen*". I've no wish to make a meal of it, after all. I don't consider this to be a failure; I am demarcating and circumventing an impossibility.

By way of a parenthesis, and this is a discussion that continues with Janine Altounian in particular, I don't think one can consider Freud's aphoristic formulas as evidence of the fact that he would try to reach the signified by starting from the signifier. I take the all too famous example from Lacan: *les noms du père* / *'les non-dupes errent'*.[6] Lacan begins to ramble about this play on words; elsewhere he relies on that term *une-bévue*,[7] where there is even a back-and-forth play on words between German and French, since the *une-bévue* is the *'unbewusst'*, which is to say the unconscious. Lacan claims to let himself be guided by the signifier and even by the purely phonic form of puns. He has no interest at all in etymology, for example. It is obvious that in the *une-bévue* or *les non-dupes errent* there's no reference whatsoever to etymology. Compare the difference from what we find in Freud: when he refers to language he refers to the etymological fabric of language itself. Thus, in Freud things are always anchored in language, even in etymology. Moreover, Freud only rarely departs from the *singular usage of the language ('Sprachgebrauch')*. He does sometimes rely upon it, but as a rule his aphoristic formulations are accompanied by a long development, such as we have just seen in the case of the melancholic's complaints. There is an obvious limit case – the central formula of the entire Freudian oeuvre, which I won't labour. This limit case is *'Wo Es war, soll Ich werden.'* Entire pages have been dedicated to this sentence. Yet it must not be forgotten that *Ich* and

---

6 [*Trans*: These phrases, which are virtually homophones in French, mean 'the names of the father' and 'the non-dupes wander' respectively. *Les noms du père* was the title of Lacan's abandoned 1963 seminar, the introduction to which is available in English, trans. Jeffrey Mehlman, in *October*, vol. 40, 1987, pp. 81–95. *Les non dupes errant* was the title of Lacan's seminar during 1973–4].

7 [*Trans*: A blunder or slip, and hence a parapraxis. See Jacques Lacan, "Le Séminaire, Livre XXIV: L'insu que sait de l'une bévue s'aile à mourre, 1976–1977", in *Ornicar?* Vol. 17, 1979].

Es are not unknown categories that emerged for this formula alone; these are terms that appear in complete texts by Freud and which are extensively explained by him. Doubtless, one can get carried away by the language and isolate this phrase from the whole context of the oeuvre. Many authors have done just that with this formula. But all the same, one cannot make of it whatever one wants, precisely because Freud doesn't make just anything of *das Ich* and *das Es*, and least of all in the text where he introduces the formula. But this is a limit case where one can, in a somewhat dangerous way in my view, risk venturing beyond what Freud says. This is, for example, what Lacan did, attempting to derive from the formula a sort of philosophy of the 'subject' (*das Ich* = I), which in my opinion is profoundly alien to Freud's thought. But ultimately one does have the right to try.

A limit case, I said, between two extremes; these two extremes being, for me, a poetic work on the one hand and an intellectual work on the other. To say that the one is centred on the signifier and the other on the signified is insufficient, if not simply false. What, for example, would a poem be which did not seek to communicate something? And what would an intellectual work be which did not at some point or other rely upon the signifier? The real issue is knowing in what way the work relies upon it. In this connection I am very fond of the metaphor of *dwelling* – *dwelling* in the sense that Hölderlin says we dwell poetically upon this earth. In any event, I would say that the author of an intellectual work dwells within his language. He makes a home of it and within this home – to pursue the metaphor in a trivial, spatial way – within this home he prefers to dwell in certain parts, he prefers to traverse certain corridors, he favours the fact that this part is split into two smaller rooms, or that certain others have been joined together as a large drawing room. In a word, he constitutes within the very interior of this home his own code, his own dialect. As to poetic works, I would not say that they are absolutely coextensive with the language in which they are written, but they certainly tend toward being so. The poet is inhabited by language. By definition, then, the more poetic poetry is, the more untranslatable it is. But once again there are differently untranslatable texts: the dictionary that we cited a moment ago, or certain types of joke – what Freud calls 'verbal jokes' rather than 'conceptual jokes' etc.

I could recount a thousand stories from Freud's book on jokes that are *conceptual* jokes, perfectly translatable and able to make the hearer laugh whether he is French or German. But verbal jokes specifically are untranslatable, and in my view all translations that endeavour exactly to transpose *German verbal jokes* into *French verbal jokes* have fairly pitiful results. But one can perfectly well gloss *verbal jokes*. It should be added, moreover, that a pure verbal joke is a pun in the sense Victor Hugo was so scathing about, although he did not favour conceptual jokes either.

With poetry things are different. In contrast to verbal jokes no commentary can realise poetic effect, which is coextensive with the language itself. The translation can only ever be an allusion, an incitement to consult the original. I thought of this recently while watching a very fine film by Al Pacino called *Looking for Richard*. The film explores Shakespeare's *Richard III* and adds to it the extraordinary character of Al Pacino himself; but this isn't exactly the issue. I thought about the role of the subtitles; obviously this is a film that only works in English, even if one's own English is a little impoverished. And yet the New York English of Al Pacino and the English of Shakespeare make it a delightfully rich linguistic performance. And the subtitling, which isn't too bad, helps us savour the extraordinary English that is the language of Shakespeare. So, go and see it. But there are various ways of saying *go and see it*. In the worst case – although even this might be of some use – there's the tourist guide; at best, there's the superb photograph album. Best because, after all it was Malraux – with what, many years ago, he already called the 'imaginary museum' – who inaugurated and instilled within us the idea that a splendid album of well-taken, sumptuous photographs was perhaps just as interesting, if not more so, than the original. Which is better? A beautiful album of photographs of Petra, or to be taken there guided by a tour operator?

The height of untranslatability in poetry, it seems to me, is the famous Haiku to which most of us have no access except by way of French, by way of French transpositions, which incidentally are often very beautiful in themselves; and who, after all, is to say that these transpositions are not more beautiful than the originals? All of this is to underline the fact that I do not weep over the incommunicability of languages any more than over that of consciousnesses. It is sometimes said that when the terms *Weib* and *Frau* appear in German we are at the heart of the incommunicable, and that the mystery of the feminine is entirely contained within it. I don't think that the mystery of the feminine is contained within the German language, least of all in the opposition between *Weib* and *Frau*. In a very prosaic and slightly quibbling fashion I respond by offering instances where the opposite is the case: with *Weib* and *Frau* we have two words for a single, impoverished French word (*la femme*); but in other cases things are otherwise: the richness lies on the French side, and the poverty on the German side. If we take *Berührung*, there is a single word in German, whereas in French we have the very precise difference between *contact* ['contact'] and *toucher* ['touch']. *Contact* is not the same thing as *toucher*, but when you translate the German word *Berührung* you are constantly forced to choose between them because the German knows nothing of this difference that is, nevertheless, essential.

Let us, then, hold to the difference we have suggested, even if the borders are a little blurred: poetry is inhabited by language, its message tending to be coextensive with the language (*tending*, of course, because there is always something of a message nonetheless). On the other hand, intellectual work inhabits its language. Freud, even if he has an internal, intimate relationship with his native tongue, inhabits it in his own way. He does not allow his thought to be led by the language. He uses and arranges certain rooms within it, certain routes through it; he drops others. There are explicit concepts that Freud names technical terms, '*unsere Termini*', and there is an implicit conceptuality that falls to the attentive translator to emphasise. I am thinking, for example, of the French term *étayage*, which for a very long time has covered an implicit concept in Freudian thought, that of *Anlehnung*.[8] But this distinction between implicit and explicit concepts doesn't presume that every German term, even those that recur in Freud, 'constitutes' a concept. There are different levels of conceptuality; there is a 'Freudian German', about which I once remarked that it is necessary to translate it into a 'Freudian French' and not a Germanic French. You see that with this idea of a 'Freudian German' we return to something I alluded to a moment ago: a sub-code, a species of idiolect. Freud does not allow his thought to be dominated by the German language. If he did we would be led to an automatic translation, to a sacredness of the language and a sacredness of the text.

I could of course say much more, for these remarks relate only to my present concerns. I could have tackled the question using many other examples that have occupied me and my companions for years and which have given us the privilege, if not of being immortal, at least of pushing back our expiry date by at least ten years: Freud, our torturer, will support us for a good decade or so; which is not, in the final analysis, a disagreeable situation.

2. My second point, then, is the metaphor, or the exporting of the model of translation, in which connection I refer in a certain way to Jakobson and Saussure so as to propose two extensions in line with them. Firstly, the extension of the model of language to other systems of communication, and thus the idea of a *semiotic* system that is broader than the *linguistic* system; and secondly, the extension of the model of translation within the very systems themselves: be they semiotic, interlingual or even intrasemiotic. Examined closely, this implies sub-codes and idiolects, and you can see that in a certain

---

8 [*Trans*: Laplanche has for many years been critical of James Strachey's choice to translate Freud's *Anlehnung* as 'anaclisis'. The English translation he proposes is 'leaning-on'].

way this returns us to the idea of the 'Freudian' as an idiolect within the German language. At the beginning of his article – and it is truly shocking to say such things – Jakobson claims: "Any representative of a cheese-less culinary culture will understand the English word 'cheese' if he is aware that in this language it means 'food made of pressed curds'"[9]. In any case, this is an example of intralingual translation, the full responsibility for which I leave to him. Here the idiolect would be the technical, not to say scientific language. It is also worth pointing out that in the French anthology of Jakobson's writings, *Essais de linguistique générale*, the first article is titled "Le langage commun des linguistes et des anthropologues" ["The Common Language of Linguists and Anthropologists"]. You can see how the notion of language is displaced here. It is not a question of languages – German, French, Polish, etc. – but of a kind of possible idiolect that is common to two kinds of specialist. In order to develop this, then, we must combine the idea of communication systems (which include non-linguistic systems: semiotics) and the possibility of translation within a single type of communication (thus the idea of sub-systems at the semiotic level as well). After all, in psychoanalysis a number of indications point in this direction. One often hears mention of Freud's remark about the 'language' of the oral drive.[10] There is also the famous letter to Fliess of December 6th 1896, where he forms the hypothesis of a system of successive inscriptions and tries to define precisely what defines each of these systems: simultaneous association in some cases, rational association in others etc.[11] With this idea of successive inscriptions Freud thus uses the notion of systems in an enlarged sense, and in particular he enlarges the notion of a non-verbal sign system. What he describes are successive modes of organisation of signs, which are what I characterised a moment ago as idiolects.

---

9 "On the Linguistic Aspects of Translation", op. cit., p. 138.
10 'Negation" (1925h), *SE* 19, p. 237.
11 See, *The Complete Letters of Sigmund Freud to Wilhelm Fliess: 1887–1904*, trans. Jeffrey M. Masson (Cambridge Mass..: Harvard UP, 1985).

One text that it is good to return to from time to time is Ferenczi's article on "The Confusion of Tongues between Adults and the Child".[12] The content is a little disappointing in places, but the title alone should catch our attention, if we are willing to notice that it doesn't refer to the confusion of tongues between parents and children. The Oedipus complex is completely dispensed with and replaced by the fundamental relation between adults and the child. It is a question of adults because adults have drives that the child does not, a 'language' other than that of the child. We can therefore understand why Freud would have wished, on the basis of its title alone, to sweep the article under the carpet. There is, to be sure, a certain imprecision in the article itself, and it would seem to me that replacing the notion of confusion with the notion of translation would be a critical step forward.

I am often asked, "Why do you speak of translation rather than interpretation?" I have answered this objection from time to time, and it was put to me again recently. My answer is that interpretation seems to me to be centred, by the one who interprets, upon an object. One can interpret a natural phenomenon just as well as anything else; and one can interpret a text, but without referring to the fact that this text carries a message. This, I would say, shows precisely the direction in which hermeneutics has drifted over the centuries. In the eighteenth and nineteenth centuries, hermeneutics became a hermeneutics of human phenomena and thus became a methodology within the human sciences. If we go back in time, it has long been a hermeneutics of texts, but originally it was a *hermeneutics of the message*. The hermeneutics of the message, as distinct from the hermeneutics of human phenomena or even of texts, is a *translation* that contrasts with these derivative forms. Its source does not lie in the hermeneut, or in his curiosity, but in the message itself and the ques-

---

12 "The Confusion of Tongues between Adults and the Child: The Language of Tenderness and the Language of Passion" (1933) in *Sándor Ferenczi: Selected Writings* ed. and trans. Julia Borossa (Harmondsworth: Penguin, 1999).

tion it poses. In my view, it is therefore necessary to revisit Ferenczi bearing in mind the 'translation letter' cited above, and perhaps to revisit that letter by way of the notion of the message, which is always a message 'addressed to'.

In the translational model as applied to metapsychology, we do not have two languages that are foreign to each other, such as Bantu and High German, as the title of Ferenczi's article would perhaps suggest. What do we have? First of all there is a common language, or rather a common semiotic system, shared in this instance by adults and the child. There is a common semiotic system (indeed there are perhaps several of them). The principal system, which has of late been developed with increasing thoroughness by psychologists, is the communication system of *attachment*. Yet given that this is a common system, whence arises the compulsion to translate? What is it that compels a *rewording*, as the English say? What is it that ultimately compels the creation of an idiolect? Well, it is the fact that this message, even though it is formulated in a common language, is parasited by another thing, another thing that is hardly a language and which is quite simply the unconscious of the other. Although Ferenczi speaks about adults and the child, he does not endeavour to ask why the adults and the child have two different 'languages', which in my opinion is a rather approximate way to define things. He fails at that point to refer to the great Freudian discovery: that adults have an unconscious and children do not, as a direct result of which their dialogue takes place on different levels and the language of the adult is enigmatic. The language of the adult is not enigmatic owing to confusion or absolute foreignness, or owing to polysemy (for in respect of the latter, all messages would be enigmatic); it is enigmatic by virtue of a unilateral excess that introduces a disequilibrium into the very heart of the message. Excess, disequilibrium, the need for translation: there is – to take up Ferenczi's two terms – an intrusion of signifiers of 'passion' into the common language of 'tenderness'.

As you are aware I have used this 'translational' model, as

it's known, to give an account of the genesis of the unconscious and of repression – primary repression, in particular. What better *in vivo* example could there be than the text in which Freud describes the genesis of unconscious fantasy. I am referring to "A Child is Being Beaten".[13] Freud goes so far as to call this unconscious fantasy a primal fantasy, which clearly undercuts the idea of phylogenetically inherited primal fantasies. For Freud will demonstrate *the individual genesis of this primal fantasy*. This unconscious fantasy is, as you know, the second phase in a sequence that Freud describes with great precision, and it is formulated as follows: *"My father is beating me."* Let me rapidly recall that Freud discerns a first phase, which is real and perceived, in which *"My father is beating the child [little brother or sister]"*. The second phase is the fantasy, which is entirely unconscious and which itself remains inaccessible to consciousness and can only be reconstructed in analysis: *"My father is beating me"*. The third phase is a conscious fantasy, *"A child is being beaten"*, which returns symptomatically and is usually accompanied by sexual pleasure and masturbation. Let us develop phase 1 a little: *"My father is beating the child [little brother or sister] in front of me."* He is obviously showing me this spectacle; it is a message. And Freud adds: *"He is beating in front of me the child [little brother or sister] whom I hate."* "Whom I hate", is obviously a contextual element, and one that gives the message its entire meaning; it is also a common element, a secret or a piece of common knowledge between my father and me. "We two, he and I, know I hate this little brother or sister." To the formulation *"He is beating in front of me the child [the little brother or sister] whom I hate"*, Freud suddenly adds: *"He loves only me."* "He beats the one I hate, he loves only me", is a conclusion but also a kind of illumination, and a kind of translation. Freud introduces it elsewhere with these words, *das heisst*: 'it means'. Another code, another idiolect appears here, which is invented so as to translate this extraordinary scene: it is a code of love. The father thus says more

---

13 Sigmund Freud, "A Child is Being Beaten" (1919e), *SE* 14, pp. 175–204.

than he intends. He might, for example, intend to educate, to set an example; but something else is intuited, and this intuited surplus is translated into love. Why doesn't it work? Why does it fail? Because underneath is something that finds expression in the common French saying: *'Qui aime bien châtie bien'* ['Who loves well, punishes well']. To love is to punish, says the proverb. But for the translator, to love and to punish are opposites. "He punishes the other, he loves only me, so how can to love possibly be to punish?" Because to love and to punish are confused in the infantile unconscious of the adult, in the sadistic unconscious of the parent, since for the parent who does the beating to love is also and necessarily to copulate (with the mother, for example), to sodomize (you, for example). In the translation "he loves only me" there is thus a failure of translation. It is this repression, this partial failure of the translation, which leads to precisely the most sexual part of the message falling into the unconscious: the equivalence between "My father is beating me" and "My father loves me".

To summarize: the message is a conscious-preconscious message; there is no such thing as an 'unconscious message', a term that in my opinion is meaningless. There is thus a conscious-preconscious message compromised by the unconscious of the transmitter. There is then an attempt at translation by the recipient, a translation that we shall call intra-semiotic, for it is done by drawing upon codes or idiolects, or by the attempted creation of new ones. I say "by drawing upon" because the child often does not create every part of this idiolect of the translation; it is offered to him by the social world. Only after this attempt at translation does the splitting occur between a preconscious and a repressed unconscious element: the preconscious element is the translation, "he loves only me". It bears the scar of the failure. Our hope – our good fortune from a clinical point of view – is to find, again and again, other partially translatable elements, and that ultimately the scar will enable us to reconstitute something of the initial message, and lead us to a new translation that is a little better able to encompass the total message.

Our other fundamental hope is that there has been a message, a compromised message; that there was this interplay between two levels, even if the message sometimes appears to be brutally sexual. Ferenczi's text, which one can reread in its entirety, insists on *confusion* rather than translation, on the confusion that provokes within the child, and within ourselves, the possibility that a message might be radically untranslatable or, what may be worse, that there might be no message at all. Both Freud (in his earliest period, at the moment when he was concerned with the facts of sexual abuse) and Ferenczi open up the question of the untranslatable. The untranslatable that dumbfounds us, whose horror – which in Freud and in Ferenczi is overtly paedophilic and sadistic – obsesses us; the horror too, we would add, of the serial killer. Monsters are making a return nowadays and, with them, the all too easy phenomenon of the scapegoat: we reject into the outside the monstrosity that we do not want to see within ourselves. How many more or less unconscious paedophiles are assembled within the ranks of the long processions of public protest condemning sexual abuse?

3. If we want to begin to understand, we must try to use the concept of translation and this thing that we are attempting to approach: a radical failure *to* translate; not a partial but a radical failure of translation. This seems to me to be a fruitful path. There are some who are already engaged in asking what conditions make such a failure possible. I am thinking in particular of Tarelho's book, *Paranoïa et la théorie de la séduction généralisée*.[14] What are the conditions of this failure? It is a failure that may, in particular, result in an intergenerational transmission of the message as such, without any metabolisation. I think that the question of the intergenerational needs to be taken up again, asking what are the conditions of failure from the point of view

---

14 Luiz Carlos Tarelho, *Paranoïa et la théorie de la séduction généralisée* (Paris: Presses Universitaires de France, 1999).

of communication and of the very structure of the message, and from the point of view of the recipient of this transmission. Several authors are already engaged in this: the path and the theoretical framework have been proposed, and specifically for psychiatrists who, it seems to me, are being increasingly confronted with these problems. Is there a message when it is something no longer compromised by the unconscious but inhabited absolutely by it? Is such a thing even possible? Is there a message when it is something that conveys and imposes its own code, when it is something that thus imposes a translation that is nothing other than the message itself? Or when the message is paradoxical, perhaps? What possible uses are there for the concept of the paradox, if it is employed with rigor?

I have for years proposed a metapsychological theory founded on this concept of translation and the failure of translation – a theory that bears primarily upon the neuroses. I am tempted to say that this theorization could be used as a basis for widening psychopathological investigation in fields that have become increasingly significant and urgent; but the urgency here risks preventing thought, shocking thought, replicating within the psychiatrist the very shock that is present in the reality of patients.

'Man who speaks', man who is exposed to messages; thus, man who is spoken to, man who must imperatively translate those messages, make them his own, man who translates. When he fails to translate them, in what ways is he possessed by them? This is the line of questioning that must be pursued in your own field. Thank you for listening . . .

7

DISPLACEMENT AND CONDENSATION IN FREUD[1]

This nimbly written book contains rigorous and detailed information on the question it illuminates: metaphor and metonymy. It is a question that has been endlessly embroiled, first of all by Lacan – who tried in vain to make a formalist point of view prevail, with scant regard for any relation to semantics – and then by a number of his disciples, who were very uncomfortable in this yoke. The critiques formulated by Alain Costes are relevant and supported by evidence and documentation. The model he proposes is sound and enables us to find our bearings clearly. So, rather than reprise or paraphrase what he develops, I offer in what follows a short text that has been in my files for some time. It does not address the linguistic problem but something altogether different: what Freud calls condensation and displacement.

The Associative Chains

These chains connect (word- and thing-) representations. A, B, C, D, etc. They thus consist of the links, that is to say the connections, between two consecutive elements: A–B.

---

[1] Preface to Alain Costes, *Lacan: Le fourvoiement linguistique* (Paris: Presses Universitaires de France, 2003).

The connection of A to B is made according to the major types of association that have been emphasised since at least the eighteenth century: analogy, contiguity, contrast.

> *analogy*:   if A is wine
>   B is the sun

(Like wine, the sun warms the body and the heart. As the song goes: "wine, it is sunshine in a bottle"). Heat constitutes what is called: *tertium comparationis*; it is the common element linking the two representations.

Contiguity: contiguity may comprise quite diverse modalities: container-contained / part-whole / cause-effect / etc.

>   if A is wine
>   B is the glass (container)

As to association by *contrast*, its autonomy is debated, and it is often reduced to the first two or to analogy alone.

Remarks:

a) All of this is thoroughly classical and constantly taken for granted by Freud

b) Freud does not employ the words 'metaphor' and 'metonymy'. He frequently speaks of *Gleichniss* to mean comparison, fable, allegory. He also employs the words *Kontiguität* and *Kontinuität*.

c) Metaphor and metonymy are tropes of classical rhetoric, that is to say, figures of speech, 'ways of saying' that involve the *replacement* of A by B. It is therefore only by a certain impropriety that these words are sometimes used to refer to the *type of connection* according to which the substitution is made.

Displacement and Condensation

These words appear very early in Freud's work,[2] but they are most emphatically foregrounded in *The Interpretation of Dreams* as characterizing the primary process.

Displacement and condensation are two processes that are supported by the associative chains defined above, and this is so whatever the type of association linking the elements to each other.

A. Displacement

In an associative link A–B, the representation B receives the entire investment that was originally assigned to A. Thus B is finally substituted for A.

If the link A–B is one of analogy, the *displacement would be analogical* (metaphorical according to post-Freudian terminology):

$$\text{wine} \rightarrow \text{sun}$$

The sun, in my discourse or in my dream, replaces the wine.

If the link A–B is one of contiguity, the *displacement would be 'by contiguity'* (metonymic according to the post-Freudian terminology):

$$\text{wine} \rightarrow \text{glass}$$

The glass, in my discourse or in my dream, replaces the wine.

Metonymy and metaphor are thus two types of substitution whose only difference consists in the modality of the connection A–B (contiguity or analogy).

---

[2] See the relevant entries in Jean Laplanche and Jean-Bertrand Pontalis in *The Language of Psychoanalysis*, trans. Donald Nicholson-Smith (London: Karnac, 1973).

B. Condensation

It frequently happens that associative chains intersect at a common element; thus, if D is the same representation as M, the chains A–B–C–D and J–K–L–M will cross at the element D = M.

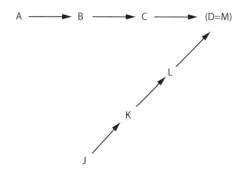

It is a matter of condensation because the element (D = M) *condenses* in itself the entire investment of the two chains. (D = M) comes to represent simultaneously J and A. The energies that have been displaced along the two associative chains will be added together at the junction of the representations.

NB
a) Each of the connections of each of the chains can be either 'metaphorical' or 'metonymic'. Condensation is no more closely related to metonymy than to metaphor; it comprises both metonymies *and* metaphors.

Displacement and Condensation

Example of condensation:

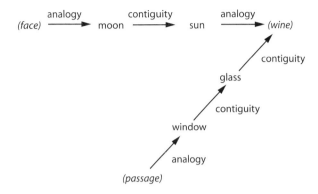

The dream image (wine) condenses the latent representations: (face) and (passage).

b) A double connection – of contiguity and resemblance simultaneously – may exist between two terms. Suppose, for instance, that Robert is a carpenter. He becomes known, by contiguity, as The Plank. But it may also be the case that Robert is very thin. He becomes known as Plank by analogy.

There is no reason why Robert might not be both a carpenter and very thin. The determination of his nickname would thus be double.

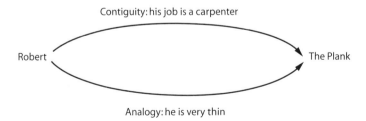

Displacement and Condensation

In Conclusion

This entire development is strictly Freudian. The only new contributions are the *words* metaphor and metonymy. But if they seem to create a problem, *one can omit them and only speak of analogy and contiguity, following the associationist tradition.*

8

SEXUAL CRIME[1]

"Sexual Crime": now there's a title that sounds like something of a challenge, if only by virtue of the scope it contains. Inevitably, the result will not entirely live up to expectations, or cover the full expanse of the theme. But this is a challenge to myself, above all, and to my own trajectory in attempting to think or rethink psychoanalysis and the Freudian discovery in a certain way. For, from the moment one maintains, as I do, that infantile sexuality is not innate but that, like fantasy, it emerges within a dialogue, an exchange between adult and infant in which the sexual initiative comes from the adult, one must completely invert one's perspective on sexual crime.

I shall quote a short excerpt from Freud that can be found in the *Minutes of the Vienna Psychoanalytic Society* – the proceedings of the meetings of the Vienna Society in the historic period. It is a text that is perhaps not often read, and since it is not always well translated I have retranslated it for you. On January 24, 1912, Freud makes the following intervention concerning the fantasy of seduction by the father:

---

1 First published in *Adolescence*, Spring, 2003, 21, 1, pp. 163–78.

> The grain of truth contained in this fantasy lies in the fact that the father, by way of his innocent caresses in earliest childhood, has actually awakened the little girl's sexuality … It is these same affectionate fathers that are the ones who then endeavour to break the child of the habit of masturbation, of which they themselves had by that time become the innocent cause.[2]

The word "innocent" occurs twice. In the German, two different words are used, but this is of little importance: Freud clearly says that the father is "innocent", that he awakens the little girl's sexuality with "innocent" caresses. Notice what a complete inversion this is of *Ferenczi's theses* (which we shall have cause to return to), since *for Freud* tenderness is on the side of the adult, and it is the language of tenderness which, so to speak, encounters the language of passion or sexuality in the child.

Of course, Freud does not always forget, as he does here, about the sexuality of the parents in this relation, but all the same, in the official doctrine at least, the perspective is generally an inverted one. In the 'Oedipus complex' the criminal is Oedipus, which is to say, ultimately, the child. An inversion of culpability is also precisely what we find in this little excerpt, since in the end the father punishes the child for the masturbation that he himself has provoked. We thus have an inversion of culpability. One might even speak of a kind of injection of culpability into the child.

It should be emphasized, then, that Freud does not (far from it) completely follow the ancient myth of Oedipus, in which things happen quite differently. First of all, Jocasta hangs herself, which

---

2 *Minutes of the Vienna Psychoanalytic Society*, eds. Herman Nunberg and Ernst Federn, trans. Margaret Nunberg with the assistance of H. Collins (New York: International Universities Press, 1962–1975), vol. 4, p. 24; translation altered.

might lead one to suppose she also considers herself to be guilty. Then there is Laius. Beyond the famous Oedipal triangle and beyond the 'murder of the father' (which is somewhat overworked), there is the full story of Laius, and it is a story of paedophilia: in the prehistory or preamble to the Oedipus complex, Laius is the seducer of a pubescent boy named Chrysippus. To further complicate things, one version of the myth even indicates that Oedipus himself was Laius' rival for the young Chrysippus, and that they both seduced him.

To return to my personal motive for addressing this theme, it is a kind of responsibility, as though something calls me, saying this: "You, who return the initiative of sexuality to the adult message, who believe that the adult message is essentially impregnated with sexuality, how do you distinguish this sexual initiative on the part of the adult from criminal sexual assault?" There is perhaps one principal means of approaching this question: to acknowledge the presence, or the various *modalities* of the presence of infantile sexuality within the adult, within every adult – parent or criminal – and especially when in the presence of a child. Here I shall again quote from the *Minutes* (January 11, 1911) where Freud, expressing himself a little more freely than he does in his writings, says:

> [T]he chief effect that the sight of the child produces consists in the revival of the mother's own infantile sexuality.
>
> On the one hand, sexual envy is awakened; on the other hand, the sexual repression that often enough has been carried through and maintained only with great effort takes place again. And thus it could be that the hostile impulses that express themselves in the maltreatment of children are also connected with the reawakening of the mother's childhood sexuality.

I shall continue because this passage is extremely interesting:

> The gratification of certain erotogenic zones (suckling, coprophilic inclinations) in the care of the child is accompanied by a retrograde character formation, by some regression; this often expresses itself clearly enough in many a young mother in the form of sloppiness.³

Here, it is the mother who is in question; a moment ago it was the father – and you can see how Freud tends to exonerate the father and place responsibility onto the mother. What remains clear, nonetheless, is Freud's preoccupation with the presence, in the adult-child relation, of the *adult's infantile sexuality*.

In order to take this step of speaking about adult infantile sexuality it is once again essential not to forget Freud and one of his central discoveries: i.e. precisely, infantile sexuality, which is to say 'enlarged' sexuality as Freud understands this term. That is: 1. a sexuality that absolutely goes beyond genitality, and even beyond sexual difference; 2. a sexuality that is related to fantasy; 3. a sexuality that is extremely mobile as to its aim and its object; and 4. (a point on which I myself lay great emphasis) a sexuality that has its own 'economic' regime in the Freudian sense of the term, its own principle of functioning, which is not a systematic tendency towards discharge, but a specific tendency towards the increase of tension and the pursuit of excitation. In short, it is a sexuality that exists before or beyond sex or the sexed, and which may perhaps encompass genitality but only under the very specific modality of the phallic.⁴

Rare are those theoreticians of incest, and even of sexual crime

---

3 *Minutes of the Vienna Psychoanalytic Society*, vol. 3, ibid., pp. 119–120.
4 These points are developed in two essays included in this volume: "Drive and Instinct" and "Sexuality and Attachment in Metapsychology".

– rare even among psychoanalysts! – who face up to the fact that incest is a matter of sexual practice in this Freudian sense of the word 'sexual'. Anthropologists and jurists often blithely forget this point. Irène Théry, whose research is considered to be authoritative, gave a seminar a short while ago on "the normative order in sexual matters". I have here the bibliography she gave out at the seminar. The major references are to texts about matrimonial prohibitions, which means that the question of the sexual aspect of incest vanishes the moment it is evoked, since in the literature "the normative order in sexual matters" is reduced to prohibitions in the field of marriage. One sometimes hears quoted a comment made by the anthropologist Robin Fox: "Every teenager knows [sex and marriage] are different".[5] It is a point that a number of anthropologists seem to have forgotten. This redounds against many anthropological theories, beginning with those of the monumental Lévi-Strauss, who only ever treats modalities of marriage, i.e. marriage as distinct from the sexual. If we are to make any advance, and perhaps to invoke the difference between coitus and sexuality – 'sexuality' in the enlarged sense in which Freud understood it – we must take the reverse direction along all the paths, and dismantle all the structures, which have led to the denial of sexuality in the Freudian sense of the term. Some happily sidestep the Freudian corpus in order to forget the presence of infantile sexuality, not only within the child but, in a repressed form, within each of us.

To return to the subject of sexual crime more directly, three types of motivation are frequently invoked which end up desexualizing it: sadomasochism, narcissism, and the death drive. They are invoked both in the media vulgate and in many more learned discussions, but always oriented towards desexualization.

Sadism. After all, to speak of sadism is for some no longer to speak of sexuality. Recently, two little girls tortured a third girl

---

5 Robin Fox, *Kinship and Marriage: An Anthropological Perspective* (Harmondsworth: Penguin Books, 1967), p. 54.

almost to death. The media reaction was extraordinary: "But why?" they asked, as if it were necessary to find an exhaustive explanation, a 'why' that would be more acceptable than the sadistic drive itself (even if, of course, the sadistic drive had a particular history in each girl). I am not claiming that the 'sadistic drive' is a final explanation, but rather that we must not skip over sadomasochism in the sexual sense of the term. Generally speaking, whenever it comes to maltreatment, what usually gets left out, without even a mention, is Freud's major reflection on the topic, "A Child is Being Beaten", in which he makes the explicit connection between the fact of beating, even beating with 'educational' motives, and sadism. No less forgotten is Freud's discussion in "Instincts and their Vicissitudes", in which the genesis of sadomasochism is set out step-by-step.

Narcissism is another kind of evasion of the sexual. Here too Freud is passed over. For narcissism would in fact, for many, be the very model of the non-sexual. What is quite simply forgotten is the origin of the concept in Freud himself, and no one takes the trouble to follow its course, not even so as to try to refute it. What is forgotten is that Freud calls 'narcissism' the *libidinal investment* – which is thus something sexual – of the *ego*. He calls narcissism "the libidinal complement of egoism",[6] which clearly shows that narcissism is the sexual complement of something non-sexual, something that he calls, using a completely different term, the 'ego drives',[7] which pertain to the domain of self-preservation.[8] The analysis of megalomaniac delusion, for example, is forgotten. For Freud, and he has yet to be refuted on this point, the megalomaniac delusion is a sexual delu-

---

6 Sigmund Freud, "A Metapsychological Supplement to the Theory of Dreams" (1917d), in *SE* 14, p. 223.
7 [*Trans.*: Freud's German term is *Ichtriebe*, consistently translated as 'ego instincts' by James Strachey. We have used "ego drives" to reflect Laplanche's preference for translating Freud's term *Trieb* as 'drive' (*pulsion*), rather than reproducing Strachey's misleading choice of 'instinct'].
8 See the articles on "Ego instincts [*pulsions du moi*]" and "Ego libido" in *The Language of Psychoanalysis*, trans. Donald Nicholson-Smith (London: Karnac, 1973).

sion. Recently, a killer with megalomaniac delusions was categorized as narcissistic – and was referred to as 'paranoid' in the media and psychiatric vulgate – which supposedly excludes his psychosis from the domain of the sexual. Yet one has only to reread his confession, in which he describes his masturbation as incessant and inadequate and contrasts it with the final grandiose orgasm to which he aspires, and which he was not far off achieving by means of the massacre that still haunts our memories.

Finally, the aggressive drive or *death drive*. Here people do rely on Freud, or think they rely on him, in order, once again, to desexualize the criminal act. This is a complex issue, to be sure, and one which I have attempted to revitalise under the heading of 'the sexual death drive', in an effort to show that in the end what Freud called the 'death drive' is nothing but sexuality in its most destructured and destructuring form.

In either the Oedipus story or the Freudian myth of the primal horde, is the 'murder of the father' purely non-sexual? One might sometimes think so, to read those who set up this mythic act as an absolute, an absolute that is situated at the level of the so-called foundational References. For example, in *Le crime du Caporal Lortie* Pierre Legendre,[9] who doesn't hesitate to capitalize the term Reference, completely scotomises the sexual relation to the father – an instance of Lacanianism pushed to such an extreme that it succeeds in denying the very bases of Freudian thought.

What I am proposing, all too rapidly, is not a dogmatic call to order in the name of Freud, but an attempt at least to ensure that he is not entirely forgotten when trying to seize on something solid in the field of sexual crime. Obviously there is incest and the incest prohibition, and these provide, *a priori*, a good point of departure. In fact, in my seminar I have for several months conducted an examination of this topic, demonstrating that the problem of incest is subject to the

---

9 Pierre Legendre, *Le crime du Caporal Lortie* (Paris: Flammarion, 2000).

greatest variability, in terms of social practice as well as theory, and even as regards the very definition of the term. Among anthropological theories of incest, that of Lévi-Strauss – something of a monument, which Françoise Héritier has described as an 'Impregnable Stronghold' – perhaps owes its solidity to its extreme limitations. It is an appealing theory in that its central proposition is the idea that the incest prohibition is not really negative but in fact has to do with an exchange obligation, a claim that obviously makes the law into a completely positive injunction or invitation to exchange. The limitations of this theory are obvious, as many psychoanalysts have observed. For Lévi-Strauss's theory, working precisely from the point of view of the exchange of possible wives, the basis of marriage, takes sororal incest alone as its paradigm. This leaves aside the very heart of what interests psychoanalysis: intergenerational incest, father-daughter or father-son incest, mother-daughter or mother-son incest. It not only leaves out the intergenerational relation but, what is more, it leaves out *'inter-age'* relations, which are perhaps the essential thing and which I shall have occasion to develop later on. For example, brothers and sisters are of the same generation but they may be in an *adult-child* relationship from the point of view of age and sexual maturation.

On the other hand, Lévi-Strauss's theory (like that of many anthropologists) is one which might almost be described as 'ethnographic', in the sense of being a cultural 'curiosity' itself; for it presumes solidly constituted kinship groups, which are rather difficult to find within, or even to transpose into, societies such as ours, except perhaps in restricted pockets within them. At the same time, it is a theory of matrimonial alliances in which one would be hard pressed to find a single word about *sexual relations* or about sexual incest, including all its so-called perverse gradations, especially its homosexual variant.

On the basis of the conclusion drawn by Levi-Strauss and by many other anthropologists, the incest prohibition – so the argument goes – marks the passage from the state of nature to the state of culture, and brings to an end both promiscuity and confusion between the generations. Even if it does roll off the tongue a little too easily, let us accept this proposition, at least as a kind of provisional clause. Incest would then be correlative to the law; the law instituting social structure would itself be nothing but the prohibition against incest.

Let us turn for a moment to law and criminology. I am by no means an expert in this area, but with a little curiosity even a cursory look reveals the almost total absence of incest in current law. French law does not forbid incest. It prohibits certain matrimonial alliances, but without proposing any penalty other than annulment. After all, the marital situation of Oedipus and Jocasta is not inconceivable, when we have children born 'under the X',[10] and it will perhaps become less and less inconceivable. But if such a marriage came to light, it would not be considered a crime; it would simply be annulled. As for incestuous sexual relations, they are in no way subject to any specific criminalization. It is amusing to see certain authors rising up against those anarchist spirits who supposedly advocate the 'legalization of incest'. No such legalization is needed. Incest between adults is neither an offence nor a crime. I recall (for these are things reported almost every day in the press) the case of a Belgian minister, who for a while was the subject of much discussion. He was prosecuted for paedophilia, and *"furthermore"* lived with his daughter, with whom he even had children. Well, the only offence of which he was charged was, precisely, paedophilia. The one respect in which incest is invoked by the law is as an aggravating factor in relation to the crime of paedophilia, or sexual abuse in general. Incest is included within the acts of those who have power or authority over their victim. A father is scarcely treated any differently than a teacher or a legal guardian in this position.

---

10 [*Trans.*: Laplanche is referring to a provision in French law, known as *accouchement sous x*, which allows new mothers to withhold their identity from the child's birth certificate, and places restrictions on the child's subsequent access to the mother's identity].

Can we get a purchase on incest with reference to the law, when the law itself seems to have allowed incest to escape its grasp (and probably, I suspect, since the Napoleonic Code or the French Revolution)? The definition specified as the juridical one in the *Robert* dictionary attempts to define this sexual aberration with reference to the law. This is not an illogical thing to do, but it continues to refer incest to marriage:

> *Incest.* Noun. Masculine. Law: sexual relations between a man and a woman who are related by blood or marriage to a degree that entails the prohibition of marriage.[11]

Thus it is the prohibition of marriage which is always taken as the starting point and which serves as the benchmark for the offence, the sexual crime itself no longer being regarded as a crime from the point of view of the law. What we have is an attempt to give a broad definition of incest, but one which nevertheless misses out entire areas of it: paedophilic incest, for example – which is perhaps the essential aspect – but also homosexual incest, since there is, after all, no prohibition against homosexual marriage which could serve as a reference point in the above definition, a marriage of this kind not even being envisaged. Homosexual sexual relations, homosexual incest, can in no way be referred to the rules of matrimony.

One gets the continual impression that incest is a poorly conceived category, not only in terms of definition, which would not in itself be of great concern, but more particularly in terms of what it is supposed to regulate. In the case of homosexual incest, we might say that it loses its pertinence as a category; but what, above all, it allows to slip away is sexual crime. And what incest fails to encompass and contain above all is sexual crime. The category of incest is, on the one

---

11 *Le Nouveau Petit Robert*, Paul Robert (Paris: Le Robert, 2010).

hand, too narrow, for it excludes those who are not related by kinship (sexual abuse in the general sense does not come under the heading of incest, even if people sometimes mistakenly use the word 'incest' when referring to sexual abuse committed on minors who are not related to the abuser). But it is also excessively broad, for it includes sexual relations between consenting adults, which are completely ignored by the law. It is as if the incest prohibition had, little by little, been allowed to disappear; what at one time, in rigidly constituted societies, fell within the law, now ends up escaping in every direction.

Can we turn toward psychoanalysis, toward a psychoanalytic framework? I shall not discuss an entire current of thought that claims that incest, as an anthropological or even criminological fact (words which are used with a touch of disdain), has nothing to do with the incest that concerns psychoanalysis. For some: 'In the beginning was the fantasy', even the 'primal fantasy' – a primal fantasy whose origins they don't worry about or trouble themselves to explain. In doing so they completely pass over Freud, who in *Totem and Taboo*, despite the rash character of his speculations, ends his text by asking whether, after all, what he has described is not for primitive humanity pure and simple fantasy already. He then adds: "There is no reason to think so"; and he concludes with Goethe's famous aphorism: "*Im Anfang war die Tat*" ("in the beginning was the Deed"), emphatically placing the real sexual criminal act in the beginning.[12]

"The Deed" means that we are not free to imagine this "In the beginning . . ." in whatever way we wish. Freud, at any rate, gets straight to the point. He speaks of historical or pre-historic stages. There is a beginning, which has to be overcome and regulated. At different moments in his thinking, which are not easily reconciled, Freud makes several different efforts to imagine this first period of prehistory. I can only cover them rapidly.

---

12 Sigmund Freud, *Totem and Taboo* (1912–13), *SE* 13, p. 161.

At one point in his essay on "'Civilized' Sexual Morality and Modern Nervous Illness", he posits a first stage of civilization in which the sexual drive would have been free, functioning "without regard to the aims of reproduction".[13] This is a kind of historical transposition of what he describes in the *Three Essays on Sexuality*, namely the polymorphous perverse sexuality of the child. Thus we have an historical stage modelled upon a stage of a different, ontogenetic kind, and without there being any reason to suppose that the former actually plays an active role in the history of the child.

In Freud, any notion of promiscuity and primary polymorphous perversion becomes blurred with the Oedipus myth. Incest resides in the choice of incestuous objects, which for Freud (as for Sophocles), let us recall, is made at the initiative of the child. There is an endogenous propensity towards it in the little human being, which Freud explicitly connects to the 'primal fantasies'. But in truth, Freud made hardly any effort to explain the origin of these primal fantasies to which so many analysts still refer. He never described any sort of 'Oedipal stage' of humanity.

Finally, there is *Totem and Taboo* and what is referred to as the 'scientific myth' of the 'horde'. I do not think that when Freud describes this as our '*scientific* myth' he is saying that it is 'our myth'; I think he is emphasizing the fact that science has come to occupy the place that others attribute to myth. In any case, the scientific myth of the horde – and I only wish to refer to this indirectly as I'm sure you will have some thoughts on it – is only partially compatible with the Oedipal schema. The parental couple barely appears. The horde is something quite different: everything is centred on the all-powerful father, on the law and on the murder of the father. This father is probably incestuous on all levels, but much more significant than the sexual dimension is the genesis of the law: firstly, a father subject to no

---

13 Sigmund Freud, "'Civilised' Sexual Morality and Modern Nervous Illness" (1908d), *SE* 9, p. 189.

law other than his will, and then, after his murder, the law established by the contract of the brothers.

I am unable to enlarge upon this in detail, but I don't wish to give the impression of wanting to play upon the variability or the difficulty of delimiting incest. There is the variability of incest, and the sheer difficulty of defining it, within the social sciences. There is the variability of ethnological theories of incest among anthropologists. I alluded to Lévi-Strauss. It would be necessary to refer also to Françoise Héritier, whose theory of incest represents, in my opinion, the most extreme form of the desexualizing tendency. Finally, there is the variability within Freud's work, where successive models are not easily reconciled with one another. On the other hand, the historical and cultural variations with respect to incest, the variable delimitations of incest within different civilizations, cannot form the basis of an argument, even if they are a frequent point of reference. How often do we hear about the marriage between siblings in ancient Egypt, etc. As long as there is a stable kinship system, its cement will undoubtedly be the prohibition of incest, however it is defined and however it is prohibited. The principal ingredient of prohibition is naming, the capacity to name and thus to classify and memorize the degrees of kinship. No naming, no incest.[14]

There is a text – some of you may be familiar with it but others may not – which has sometimes been treated with scorn by anthropologists and by psychoanalysts. I am speaking of the text about the Na or Mosuo civilization. Its title is a little provocative itself: *A Society without Fathers or Husbands*.[15] However small in number, this is a society that exhibits an extremely distinctive model of organization.

---

14 "The [incest] prohibition is not always expressed in terms of degrees of real kinship but refers to individuals who use certain terms in addressing one another", Claude Lévi-Strauss, *The Elementary Structures of Kinship*, trans. J.H. Bell, J.R. von Sturmer and Rodney Needham (Great Britain: Eyre and Spottiswoode, 1969), p. 29.
15 Cai Hua, *A Society without Fathers or Husbands: The Na of China*, trans. Asti Hustvedt (New York: Zone Books, 2001).

The demonstrative character of this model has been criticised, even if it is of little importance quantitatively, for its demonstrative aspect is repellent to all our convictions. Here we have a society whose lineage is matrilineal and matrilocal. The designation of degrees of kinship is fully developed within every family line. The incest prohibition is strict and was, in the past at least, if not recently, frequently punished by death. In any case, the prohibition continues to be extremely strict within the entire line, which is solely transmitted by the women. On the other hand, there is *no name of the father*; there is *no father*, no paternal filiation. The very idea that a father could be related to a son is entirely absent from the Mosuo system. The Mosuo are not so naïve that they don't realise coitus is necessary for a child to be born; but a child will be born, as it were, irrespective of whom the coital partner is. As such, the father is not named in their terminology and is in no sense the object of a prohibition. Much has been made of this. Some have said that it was historically linked to social class – I saw this argument in Lévi-Strauss – and others have seen it as a form of organized prostitution, which is slanderous. In any case, here we have a society that knows nothing of the concept of 'father', where there is no *'paternal function'* – I use quotation marks deliberately – and where the role of coitus in impregnation is not unknown but the particularity of any coital act is irrelevant. There is no father-child relation. The father is neither named nor integrated into the child's lineage. There is no marriage and no marriage system.

One often hears, following Freud, the Latin adage according to which *pater semper ignotus*. One never knows who the father is. But in the constellation of the Mosuo, the situation is entirely different. No one wonders *who* the father is, since they know that the answer is always uncertain (at least, it was before the arrival of DNA): the question "who is the father?" has no meaning in itself. There is no father to be identified, to be sought for or even to remain unknown. The dimension of 'paternity' is non-existent. However, watching footage in which the Mosuo people talk, it would never occur to one to wonder whether they are psychotics.

Perhaps, later on, we shall be able speak about this further. It is significant for me, primarily, because of its demonstrative character, which some have found to be entirely contrary to the very idea of the Oedipus complex. A strict kinship system, it bears no relation to the conjugal family. An incest prohibition, it is no less strict even if it is not pronounced 'in the name of the father'. The Mosuo religion, furthermore, is Buddhism, which, it seems to me, is not exactly a religion of the father.

What do we see nowadays, within our modern societies? An erosion of kinship systems and, to that extent, an erosion of the notion of incest and of its prohibition. I am not concerned with celebrating this change or with lamenting it, but primarily with recognising that something is taking place, slowly and unevenly perhaps, but which in a more or less distant future may grow in an exponential fashion. This erosion, which one may try to resist, though with little chance of success, is not a path towards 'sexual freedom'. On the contrary, it lays bare a form of sexual crime which is much more radical, and which the kinship/incest system used to be responsible for controlling.

It is at this point that I would like to emphasize Ferenczi's brilliance. You all know of and have no doubt read his famous article, "The Confusion of Tongues between Adults and the Child".[16] One can of course – as I myself have done – quibble over and criticize some of his terms. It can be pointed out, for instance, that 'confusion' may not be the most appropriate word; that however important it may be, the notion of 'tongues' is not entirely adequate, and that it would be

---

16 Sàndor Ferenczi, "The Confusion of Tongues between Adults and the Child: The Language of Tenderness and of Passion" (1933), in *Selected Writings*, ed. and trans. Julia Borossa (Harmondsworth: Penguin, 1999).

preferable to speak rather of 'messages'. There is also good reason to question the clinical content of the article. For example, it can be pointed out that the language of passion is not exclusive to the adult, and nor is the language of affection exclusive to the child (and here you will immediately remember Freud's text which said exactly the opposite, i.e. that affection was exclusive to the adult and sexual passion was exclusive to the child). Nevertheless, what seems to me to be a stroke of genius on Ferenczi's part is to have dared to use the formulation: "between adults and the child". One can understand why Freud was repelled by this text. He may well have been shocked by the emphasis on real sexual assaults, which, he believed, jeopardised the theory of fantasy. He may well have been equally unsettled, shall we say, by Ferenczi's rather panicked therapeutic reactions to the recognition of the frequency of sexual abuse. But the formulation itself must have been profoundly shocking above all, for it posed a challenge to a very significant aspect of the Freudian edifice. "Between adults and the child" is very different from "between the parents and the child" or "between the two parents and their children". What is called into question here is the Oedipus complex itself.

I shall also cite the title of another article – I like the titles of articles: they are often more interesting than the content – an article which is in the same vein as that of Ferenczi. I ask you to pay close attention to the wording because the title is English. The author is Bennett Simon, who has published several articles with the intention of emphasizing the reality of sexual abuse against children – chiefly incest, but also sexual abuses in general. His title is: "Incest: see under Oedipus complex".[17] This title is an ironic quotation from Fenichel's treatise on the neuroses,[18] where indeed, in the index, under the entry

---

17 Bennet Simon, "Incest: see under Oedipus complex: The History of an Error in Psychoanalysis", in *The Journal of the American Psychoanalytic Association*, vol. 40, 1992, pp. 955–88.
18 Otto Fenichel, *The Psychoanalytic Theory of Neurosis* (London: Routledge, 1946).

for "incest", we find quite simply the following reference: "Incest, see Oedipus Complex". In sum, the article is concerned with a reduction that is common in analytic theory and in analysis itself: the systematic reduction of incest, in all its variations, to the Oedipus complex. What Bennett Simon's title thus emphasises is the way in which Fenichel and psychoanalysis more generally try to reduce the unknown, the unmasterable – incest – to what is known and is masterable; to what is known all too well by psychoanalysis: the Oedipus complex. "See under . . ." "See 'x'". "See at . . ."

For my part, I would take the irony up a notch by proposing something like: "Sexual abuse, see under Incest; Incest, see under Oedipus complex". But this "see under" is not simply the mark of intellectual laziness. It isn't simply a way of escaping the problem by reducing it to the better known paths of the Oedipus complex. It is also a *real* movement of mastery and symbolization. I say 'symbolization' in order to avoid the 'S' or the 'L' of the Lacanians, capitalized as the 'Symbolic' and the 'Law'. For, whatever Freud might think, the law of the Oedipus complex is not universal. It is not the law of God or of the all-powerful father. It is contingent and, unfortunately, it is also porous. And as it disintegrates or rigidifies – which constitute its two types of failure – *it allows sexual crime to slip away.*

To put things in a different way, the regulatory function of the incest prohibition lets something escape from the very beginning. Intended to regulate the order of the generations, it is powerless when it comes to age differences. It reduces age differences to the order of the generations; but age differences do not coincide with generational differences, the latter alone being subject to *named* categorization. It tries to grasp the incongruity of sexual relations between those of different ages (including as well the presence of the child in the adult), it tries to reduce it to a difference that is much easier to grasp: the difference between generations. "Between adults and the child": this expression escapes the purely generational order.

How to define sexual crime? Sexual violence committed within an asymmetrical relation, with rape itself as the model of abuse? Let us add *the essential thing for us as psychoanalysts: committed by someone who is prey to his own infantile sexuality*. Does contemporary sexual crime have an historical or prehistoric correlative? Is it a laying bare within present day societies of a kind of primordial state? No one is immune to the temptation of the prehistoric reconstruction of a savage state of sexuality. Lévi-Strauss with his variations, Freud with his propositions. We might also mention Godelier, about whom we may have a chance to speak in the discussion, with his idea of the 'sacrifice of sexuality' for the good of society. But it is clearly an illusion to posit a state of primal savagery at the origin of the individual or of society, and especially to do so with reference to what Freud calls 'polymorphous perversity'. In fact, we must get to the point of admitting that 'the animal in man' is not that real, adapted animal that we know, but the savage, sexual brute. And this sexual brute is not there in the beginning; it is not the 'true' animal. We don't have a prehistoric animal lurking within us from the start. We ourselves have brought this animal into being. It is said that "man is a wolf to man". As I have had occasion to explain in a different lecture, man has become a wolf to man – or rather a bestial 'lupus', for the real wolf is not a wolf to man. By the same token, the unconscious and the id are not there from the beginning, and perverse fantasies are the very consequence of repression. But a point of view of this kind is no doubt difficult to assimilate.

I do not want to end this rather meandering discussion without pinpointing some clear points of view:

1 — The fundamental sexual crime is sexual abuse. The model for this is the abusive adult-child relation, but also rape and other variants.

2 — Sexual crime is characterized not only by asymmetry, which is present in many other kinds of relation, but also by the position of dominance.

3 — Beyond this (and this point is crucial from the point of view of metapsychology) we must not neglect the fact that the infantile aspect also has an essential function on the side of the abuser. It is infantile sexuality, sadistic infantile sexuality in particular, which is at work in the abuser.

4 — The disorder generated by sexual crime strikes much farther and deeper than the social damage it causes. Internal disorder is also at stake, the internal unbinding which is characteristic of unbound infantile sexuality: this is what I theorize under the heading of the sexual death drive.[19]

5 — Even if it is intellectually illusory to displace 'polymorphous perverse' sexuality into a mythic 'beginning' of individual or collective history, it is nevertheless this sexuality which the so-called 'symbolic' systems of kinship, incest prohibition, Oedipus, etc. labour to bind. I say 'etc' in order to emphasise the diversity of such systems and the fact that they are not God-given.

In modern civilization the more or less gradual dehiscence of these systems permits the re-emergence of the very essence of sexual crime, in all its brutality. It will perhaps be for future generations to invent new modes of binding. But we are not there yet.

To conclude, I should like to make two further points:

1) I have not discussed anything touching on the 'psychology' of sexual crime, in terms of the criminal or the victim. This is an immense problem but, once again, we cannot begin to approach it if we forget Freud, infantile sexuality, and the Unconscious... I have also omitted any discussion of the clinical approach, which must at the same time be connected to a *practice*. I shall only indicate what seem to me to be two major imperatives:

to look for the *infantile* in analytic investigations;

---

19 Cf. Jean Laplanche, "The So-Called 'Death Drive': A Sexual Drive", in *The British Journal of Psychotherapy*, vol. 20, no. 4, 2004, pp. 455–71.

to look for the *message*, the residue of message and communication, which are always present, even in what are apparently the crudest of acts. It is this which leads me to reject as insufficient such notions as the 'predator', and the idea that the victim is treated purely as an 'object'. Even when enslaved, the victim is never treated purely and simply as a 'thing'. And the fact of sadism (need we recall, *with Freud*?) presupposes at least a minimum level of masochistic identification with the victim. The only guiding thread within practice is the patient, desperate search for a thread of message. Need we recall – in a scarcely different register – those victims who have saved themselves by establishing a minimal dialogue with their aggressor?

2) My title could be read differently, it could be read to mean 'crime is sexual'. In other words, it poses the question of the role of the sexual in *all crime*, even the most ordinary, the most banal, the most 'realistic'. No analyst can elude this question, even if it is not every day that he has a 'criminal' on his couch.

9

GENDER, SEX AND THE *SEXUAL*[1]

<u>Gender</u> *is plural. It is ordinarily double, as in masculine-feminine, but it is not so by nature. It is often plural, as in the history of languages, and in social evolution.*

<u>Sex</u> *is dual. It is so by virtue of sexual reproduction and also by virtue of its human symbolization, which sets and freezes the duality as presence/absence, phallic/castrated.*

The <u>sexual</u> *is multiple, polymorphous. The fundamental discovery of Freud, it is based on repression, the unconscious, and fantasy. It is the object of psychoanalysis.*[2]

<u>Proposition:</u> *The* sexual *is the unconscious residue of the symbolization-repression of gender by sex.*

What I present here is a sort of synthesis – one which is too abbreviated and which merits further development – of a work that we have pursued for about three years in my teaching and research

---

1 First published in Libres cahiers pour la psychanalyse. Études sur la Théorie de la séduction (Paris: In Press, 2003) pp. 69–103.
2 [*Editor*: On Laplanche's French neologism 'sexual' (as distinct from the normal 'sexuel'), see the Editor's note to the Forward of this volume. The term is usually printed in italics to mark it off from the standard English term with the same spelling].

seminar; the basic question being, to put things in a very classical manner, the question of sexual identity – as it is called in psychoanalysis.

The current tendency is to speak of gender identity, and the question immediately arises whether this is simply a change in vocabulary or something more profound. Is it a positive development or the mark of a repression, and if there is repression, where is it? As you may know, I tend to think that 'repression in theory' and 'repression in the thing itself'– that is to say in the concrete evolution of the individual – often go hand in hand.

My plan will be very simple. First, I shall spend a little time on conceptual distinctions and on the question, "why introduce gender?" and then, for the second part, I shall sketch the functioning, in the early history of the human being, of the triad gender–sex–*sexual*.

*

* *

Conceptual distinctions are not worthwhile in themselves but only for the conflictual potentialities they harbour; if they are binary they are often the mark of negation and therefore of repression. Some displacements may hide repressions. So it is with the displacement of the question of sexual identity onto the question of gender identity. What this displacement perhaps conceals is that the fundamental Freudian discovery does not lie in gender identity but – besides gender, besides sex or the sexed – in the question of the *sexual*.

Following Freud, I would like to distinguish between the sexual (*le sexuel*) and the sexed (*le sexué*) or that which concerns 'sex'. It has been claimed, perhaps correctly, that the etymology of 'sex' is from '… cut', because the 'sexed' clearly entails the *difference* of the sexes or the *difference* of sex, which in German is called an *'Unterschied'*.[3] There is

---

[3] In a quite general way, although not systematically, Freud uses the term *Unterschied* (difference) to indicate a binary opposition and *Verschiedenheit* (diversity) when there is a plurality of terms: difference between black and white, diversity of colours. [*Editor*: cf. "18th December, 1973", *Problématiques II: Castrations-Symbolisations*, (Paris: Presses Universitaires de France, 1980), pp. 44-58].

the '*sexual*', for example, in "The Three Essays on *Sexualtheorie*", that is to say on the theory of the sexual (*le sexuel*) or rather what I would call 'the *sexual* (*le sexual*)'. It is perhaps an eccentricity on my part to speak of *le sexual* and not *le sexuel*, but I do so in order to indicate clearly this opposition and the originality of the Freudian concept.[4] In German, there are two terms. There is '*Geschlecht*', of course, which means 'sexed sex', but there is also '*Sexual*', the sexual (*le sexuel*), which I am calling the '*le sexual*'. When Freud speaks of enlarged sexuality, the sexuality of the *Three Essays*, it is always the *sexual*. It would have been unthinkable for Freud to have entitled his inaugural work, "Three Essays on the Theory of the Sexed – or of Sexuation". '*Sexualtheorie*' is not a '*Geschlechtstheorie*'.[5] It is a sexuality that has been called 'non-procreative' and even primarily non-sexed, as distinct from what is called precisely 'sexed reproduction'. The *sexual*, then, is not the sexed; it is essentially perverse infantile sexuality.

'Enlarged' sexuality is the great psychoanalytic discovery, maintained from beginning to end and difficult to conceptualize – as Freud himself shows when he tries to reflect on the question in, for example, his *Introductory Lectures*. It is infantile, certainly, more closely connected to fantasy than to the object, and is thus auto-erotic, governed by fantasy, governed by the unconscious. (Isn't the unconscious ultimately the *sexual*? One can legitimately ask this question). So for Freud, the '*sexual*' is exterior to, even prior to, the difference of the sexes, even the difference of the genders: it is oral, anal or para-genital.

Nevertheless, whenever Freud tries to define it he is brought back to the need to put it into relation with what it is not, that is to

---

4 In German the derivation of the terms *sexuell* and *sexual* is very close. The provenance of both is the Latin *sexualis*. 'Sexual' is more erudite and more Germanic; 'sexuell' has more a flavour of the Romance languages and has more common currency.

5 Conversely, Freud employs the term *Geschlechtlichkeit* in a quite specific sense, different from that of 'sexuality'. This is the case in *The Interpretation of Dreams* (1900a) where there is "a conversation in which 'it was just as though we had become aware of our *sex*, it was as though I were to say: 'I'm a man and you're a woman'", *SE* 4, p. 333.

say, with sexed activity or with sex; and he does this according to the three classic paths of the association of ideas. First, the path of *resemblance*: Freud seeks resemblances between the pleasures of the *sexual*, the pleasures of infantile sexuality or perverse pleasures, and what is characteristic of genital sexuality, namely the experience of orgasm. Some of the resemblances are more or less valid; some are more or less artificial, such as that claimed between the "blissful smile" of the sated nursling and "the expression of sexual satisfaction in later life".[6] Second and above all, there are the arguments of *contiguity*: contiguity since the *sexual* is found in foreplay and in the perversions contiguous to genital orgasm; and even the argument of 'anatomical' contiguity, which Freud already calls a sort of 'destiny', in which the contiguity is between the vagina and the rectum.[7]

But what I would like to stress instead is association 'by *opposition*', which among the associationists is typically referred to as the 'third type of association'. Does *sexual* pleasure exist in *opposition* to sexed pleasure? Doubtless this is often true in reality, in the pursuit of erotic activities, even in terms of economic characteristics, since one may imagine – I shall perhaps return to this – that the economic functioning of the *'sexual'* is aimed at the pursuit of tension, whereas the 'sexed' aims rather at the classic pleasure of relaxation. But this is not the true opposition. We encounter a sort of subversion of the very notion of logical opposition, which itself suddenly becomes an opposition in the real, i.e. a prohibition. In other words, the *sexual* is defined as 'that which is condemned by the adult'. There is not a single text by Freud in which he speaks of infantile sexuality without putting this opposition forward, not as a sort of contingent reaction to infantile sexuality, but as something that truly *defines* it. I believe that even these days infantile sexuality, strictly speaking, is what is most repugnant in the eyes of the adult. Even today 'bad habits' remain the most difficult

---

[6] "Infantile Sexuality", *Three Essays on the Theory of Sexuality* (1905d), SE 7, p. 182.
[7] "On the Universal Tendency to Debasement in the Sphere of Love (Contributions to the Psychology of Love II)" (1912d), SE 11, p. 189; ibid., p. 187, note 1.

thing for adults to accept. So it is a curious definition, by opposition. By a sort of circular reasoning the sexual is condemned because it is sexual, but it is sexual, or *'sexual'*, because it is condemned. The *sexual* is the repressed; it is repressed because it is the *sexual*.

Here, then, we confront the great difficulty of having to define an enlarged sexuality that we appear to be able to grasp only in terms of its relation to what is sexed, to sexuality in the classic sense. Will introducing a third term save us, or will it rather add to the confusion, add to the repression?

The third term is 'gender', which was first introduced in English, but which came to be translated or transposed into different languages and in particular into French. The notion of gender is currently enjoying such success among sociologists, feminists, and especially among feminist sociologists, that it is supposed to have been introduced by them. In fact, it is now established that the term was introduced by the sexologist John Money in 1955, and later reintroduced, with well-known success, by Robert Stoller, who in 1968 created the term 'core gender identity'. He thus integrated the term into specifically psychoanalytic thought.[8]

Here it would be necessary to enter into the infinite and powerfully seductive variations of Stoller's thought – a non-conventional thinker who is very interesting even if he often contradicts himself. I particularly like to cite what he says about contemporary psychoanalytic thought when he compares it to the Pantheon of imperial Rome, where temples to the most diverse divinities coexisted in a kind of joyous jumble.[9]

However, my main argument is that with Stoller, and after him, the notion of gender becomes a synonym for a set of convictions:

---

8 Robert Stoller, *Sex and Gender* (London: The Hogarth Press, 1968), which was published in a French translation under the title *Recherches sur l'identité sexuelle* (Paris: Gallimard, 1978). The transposition of the title alone shows the difficulty classical French psychoanalytic thought has in integrating the term and the idea of gender.
9 *Presentations of Gender* (New Haven and London: Yale University Press, 1985), p. 82.

the conviction of belonging to one of two social groups defined as masculine or feminine, or else the conviction that the assignment to one of these two groups is correct. I shall come back to this term 'assignment'.

I shall not follow Stoller's thinking here.[10] What interests me is the appearance of this new anglophone binary, the sex-gender couple. 'Sex' being understood principally as biological, and 'gender' as socio-cultural but also as subjective. The problem thus arises of the politics of translation into languages with no common usage of the word 'gender'. French more or less had this, but mainly in connection with 'grammatical gender', a very rich and tricky question on which I shall offer a few notes in an appendix at the end of this essay.[11] Notably, German does not have a term that corresponds exactly. Without going into detail, German has *'Geschlecht'* which means 'gender' and 'sex' at the same time. Thus Freudian German only has the opposition *'Geschlecht/sexual'*. In fact, when they translate English texts, Germans are led – and this is important because it amounts to a veritable interpretation – to translate the English 'sex' by 'biological sex', and 'gender' by 'sociological sex', which is already, and obviously, an entire theoretical option itself – one which remains undiscussed.

Terms and concepts are weapons, weapons of war: gender against sex and, one could say, gender and sex allied against the *sexual*. Gender against sex in Stoller because under the single banner of gender he removes all conflictuality from a large part of the problematic of gender. The German author Reimut Reiche devoted an article titled "Gender ohne Sex"[12] to the way in which, in his view, the introduction of gender – "gender without sex" – leads to a biased conceptualization that completely erases the problem of sex and sexuality. Notably, Reiche criticizes the notion of 'imprinting' and especially of a non-conflictual imprint, which belongs to Stoller's attempt to define

---

10 Cf. "Appendix I: Stoller and Gender".
11 Cf. "Appendix II: Linguistic gender".
12 In *Psyche*, 1997, 9/10. This title is a mixture of the English words 'gender' and 'sex' and a German word (*ohne*): "Gender without Sex".

gender. But it seems to me that what Reiche does not see is that the gender/sex pair serves as an even more formidable machine against the Freudian discovery.

It is here that the feminist movements as a whole enter the battle. Whether or not they are 'differentialists', as it is said, in the end the sex/gender binary is always more or less preserved. In de Beauvoir, the distinction between the terms is not posed; I mean that at the time of her book the difference between the category of sex and the category of gender was not yet explicit but was, as can be shown, already functioning implicitly. One could say that her general position is that biological sex must be postulated as a foundation, even if this foundation must be completely subverted. I cite a passage from *The Second Sex*:

> Certainly these facts [of biology, of the physical differences between men and women] cannot be denied – but in themselves they have no significance … It is not merely as a body, but rather as a body subject to taboos, to laws, that the subject is conscious of himself and attains fulfilment.[13]

This is evidently a passage characteristic of the atmosphere – let us call it voluntarist and existentialist – in which this book was written (a book which in other respects continues to be very interesting because of its numerous descriptions). Yet it is clear that there is a double movement in the work of most feminists – the most theoretical and the most radical. There is a first movement, which subverts the notion of sex to the point of annihilating it, in a purely retroactive fashion, by gender; and then there is a moment when it is realized that, in spite of everything, it is necessary to postulate something

---

13 Simone de Beauvoir, *The Second Sex*, trans. H.M. Parshley (London: Picador, 1988) pp. 66–8.

foundational, a sort of pure nature, or, as de Beauvoir says, "facts" that "in themselves ... have no significance", even if it is precisely to subvert and annihilate it.

This is the case with Judith Butler, whose second book, *Bodies that Matter*, constitutes a thorough revision of her first, *Gender Trouble*, in that it immediately reintroduces the 'biological' aspect of 'sex' and its 'constraints', explaining that their omission in the preceding work had the 'good tactical reason' of acting as a counterbalance: "doesn't everybody else talk about that?"[14]

This is the case with Nicole-Claude Matthieu, one of whose articles, which is extremely difficult, is titled "Three modes of conceptualization of the relation between sex and gender".[15] You can see from the title alone that in the end she still needs the notion of sex. Gender, she says, can "translate" sex, or can "symbolize" sex or can "construct" sex, which is to say, construct it by reconstructing it, even "by destroying it". But this positions sex as a kind of biological precondition, since gender "translates", "symbolizes" or "constructs" a sex that is already there before it. Thus, implicitly or even surreptitiously, a sort of biological definition of sex is ultimately restored.

Here is a more recent passage by Nicole-Claude Matthieu: "As with the replacement of the term 'race' by the term 'ethnic group', to leave sex out of gender risks preserving its status as an inescapable reality by forgetting that biology, and *chiefly* the physiology of fertility, is *largely* dependent on social environment".[16] I have emphasized the words "chiefly" and "largely" in this excerpt. You see that in a body of thought that aims at great rigor, she nonetheless introduces large tracts of indeterminacy by saying that biology is "chiefly" the physiology of fertility. If it is "chiefly" so, then it could nonetheless also be

---

14 Interview in *A Critical Sense*, ed. Peter Osborne (London and New York, Routledge, 1996), p. 112.
15 "Trois modes de conceptualisation du rapport entre sexe et genre", in *L'anatomie politique*, (Paris: Côté femmes, 1991).
16 In *Dictionnaire critique du féminisme* (Paris: Presses Universitaires de France, 2000), pp. 197–98, emphasis added.

something else. That it is "largely" dependent on social environment means that it may not be totally dependent on it, etc. "Chiefly": sex is accepted in the domain of procreation. "Largely": one escapes by a partial dependence.[17]

In short, the feminists in general, including the 'radicals' – or, one could say, the less radical of the radicals – need sex in order to subvert and 'denaturalize' it in gender. But is it necessary to return to the good old sex/gender sequence and in the following order: sex before gender, nature before culture, even if one agrees to 'denature' nature?[18] Of course, in all of this, the Freudian *sexual* risks becoming a major absence. Psychoanalysis is mentioned but as something listed under the class of ideologies that subordinate gender to sex, the first being the 'translation' of the second (Matthieu).

Does introducing gender into psychoanalysis entail allying oneself with those who would banalize the Freudian discovery? Or paradoxically would it be a way to reaffirm the *sexual* as the intimate enemy of gender?

I have at least one excuse for introducing gender into psychoanalytic thought: it has a presence, more or less sketchy, throughout Freud. To be sure, he never used the term; the German language scarcely permits him to because '*Geschlecht*' means both 'sex' and 'gender'; the word *Geschlecht* is used even in connection with humankind [*le genre humain*]. Thus Freud lacks the word, even though it could probably be reinvented in German using the scholarly term

---

17 Unless one goes as far as the radicalism of certain feminists who, in order to suppress the notion of sex completely find themselves led to combat the very notion of difference at the level of logic (e.g. Monique Wittig). But I can only gesture towards this point here.

18 It is precisely here that I am opposed to hastily positioning (and translating into French) *gender* as 'psychosocial sex' and *sex* as 'biological sex'. Such a categorization reduces the gender-sex opposition to the old sociology/biology refrain, whereas the opposition is much more fruitful and complex. Further on I shall show in particular that the sex that enters into a symbolic relation with gender is not the sex of biology but in large part the sex of a fantasy anatomy, profoundly marked by the condition of the *human* animal.

'*Genus*'.¹⁹ But although the word 'gender' is lacking, the thing is not completely absent. Freud insists – I recall this briefly – on the existence within the human being of three pairs of opposites: 'active-passive' and 'phallic-castrated' but also, which is what interests us here, the third, 'masculine-feminine'. He tells us that the third pair is the most difficult to think; it may even be essentially resistant to thought. At the two ends of the evolution that leads to adulthood, one finds the masculinity-femininity enigma. In the adult, it is the enigma of something that is neither purely biological, nor purely psychological, nor purely sociological, but a curious mixture of the three. As Freud says: "When you meet a human being, the first distinction that you make is 'male or female?' and you are accustomed to make the distinction with unhesitating certainty".²⁰ The 'first sight' of a human being, of a fellow creature, differentiates in an 'unthought' way between masculine and feminine. At the other end, and this interests us even more, at the other end we have a famous text, "On the Sexual Theories of Children", where Freud creates the amusing and curious hypothesis of a traveller who comes from another planet (from Sirius let's say) and whose curiosity is aroused by the presence of these two 'sexes'. If one wished to modify Freud's text slightly one would have to say 'genders', for it is actually the 'habitus' of these two categories of human being that counts and not the genital organs as such, which are usually concealed.[21]

Further on I shall come back to this problem of the *enigma* because in this case the human being is not envisaged in terms of a succession, whereby the child becomes adult or whereby the adult recalls the child that he was, but rather in terms of a simultaneity: it is the child *in the presence of* the adult who asks himself the question

---

[19] A term used in relation to linguistic 'gender' but whose usage could have been enlarged.
[20] "Lecture 33: Femininity", *New Introductory Lectures on Psychoanalysis* (1933a), SE 22, p. 113.
[21] (1908c), SE 9, pp. 207–226.

about this difference present in adults. But Freud very often forgets this questioning. What I mean is that the category of gender is often absent or unthought. One could mention, for example, the whole problematic that Freud constructs concerning homosexuality and paranoia in the Schreber case. Freud writes the basic statement, which he will play with by modifying each of its terms, in the following way: "*I* (a man) *love him* (a man)".[22] Furthermore, we know how Freud's entire dialectic concerning the different modes of delusion consists of modifying the "I" of "I love", the "him" of "him (a man)" and also, of course, the verb 'to love' which can be transformed into 'to hate'. Thus, the whole dialectic of "I (a man) / I love him (a man)" is centred on the *second part of the sentence* without ever calling into question what is meant by "I, a man". To do so would constitute a problematic, however, that is precisely that of Schreber himself, and which with good reason many analysts have aligned with that of transsexualism.

In psychoanalysis, and generally in clinical practice, the vast majority of 'observations' – if not all of them – begin unthinkingly with: "This is a 30 year old man…" or 'A woman of 25…" Is gender truly non-conflictual to the point of being unquestioningly assumed from the beginning? Has gender, so to speak, expelled the conflictual outside of itself in the form of the *sexual*?

*
* *

I now come to my second part, which is the history of the gender-sex-*sexual* triad. By 'history' I mean purely and simply the infantile genesis of this triad in the human being, the little human being; a genesis that psychoanalysts must not hesitate to approach.

There generally exists a kind of foundational 'adulto-centrism'. I have spoken of the feminists but they are certainly not the

---

22 "Psychoanalytic Notes on an Autobiographical Account of a Case of Paranoia (Dementia Paranoides)" (1911c), *SE* p. 63.

only ones – one could say the same thing of the ethnologists. I say this about ethnologists because, if you take Lévi-Strauss, for example, the theory of the incest prohibition is a theory situated entirely on the level of the adult. Besides, the major incest prohibition in Lévi-Strauss is the prohibition against sororal incest, which clearly shows that it is a question of adults of the same age, a world of only adults. There certainly is a post-Cartesian prejudice there, a kind of adulto-centrism that is not even close to being abolished.

In a few lines that were circulated before this presentation, I have contrasted two sentences: de Beauvoir's, "One is not born a woman, but becomes one"[23] and Freud's, "In conformity with its peculiar nature, psycho-analysis does not try to describe what a woman is – that would be a task it could scarcely perform – but sets about enquiring how she comes into being".[24]

One could say many things about the similarities between these two sentences. First of all and strikingly, de Beauvoir in 1949 does not feel the need to cite Freud's statement, which is so close to her own. Although quite close, it is certainly different; and yet, in spite of everything, it is the precursor to her work.

In what respect are they close and in what respect remote? They are remote insofar as, in a certain way, one could say that de Beauvoir shows herself more 'naturalist' than Freud. She accepts 'woman' as a being, as a given, as a sort of nature, a raw given that evidently one is led to take up subjectively, whether to become it or to refuse it. 'She becomes *it*.' In Freud, on the other hand, we have something quite extraordinary in that his statement is completely contradictory. Freud tells us: "She becomes what we are incapable of *defining*". In a certain sense, Freud is here more existentialist than Simone de Beauvoir. One could also situate them in *the dispute over 'afterwardsness'*. On one side, that of de Beauvoir, we have retroactive interpretation, the

---

23 *The Second Sex*, op.cit. p. 295.
24 " Lecture 33: Femininity", op. cit., p. 116.

omnipotence of changing afterwards the meaning of the past, 'resignification': this was already the Jungian thesis of *Zurückphantasieren*, 'retrospective fantasizing'. In this line of thought there is the 'performative', gender as performative, as certain feminists say. On the other side, that of Freud, there is determinism, which is also confirmed at the end of the lecture on femininity in *New Introductory Lectures*, where Freud accentuates this determinism in a caricatured and rather unpleasant way, in order to assert that a woman, once she has become an adult, has a "psychic rigidity" and "unchangeability" that he has never encountered in young men of the same age.[25] The responsibility for this assertion I leave entirely to him.

Thus one could identify a point of view that splits de Beauvoir-Freud on the question of afterwardsness between 'retroactive modification' – the action of the future and of the present upon the past – and 'deferred action' – a determinism, however delayed it may be, of the present by the past. I have tried to go beyond this split by introducing two essential elements into afterwardsness: one element is the *primacy of the other* which, because they remain in the frame *of a single* individual, is precisely what these conceptions of afterwardsness do not mention. They do not bring the presence of the other into play in the process of afterwardsness. The second element, equally lacking from these conceptions, is child-adult *simultaneity*. What I mean is that the child-adult couple should not be conceived essentially in terms of one succeeding the other, but rather of one actually finding itself in the presence of the other – concretely so, in the first years of life, from the first months. I think that *the key to the notion of afterwardsness* is to take it beyond the consideration of just the single individual, where one remains enclosed in an opposition with no exit: asking whether the child is the cause of the adult, or whether the adult freely reinterprets the child; asking whether determinism follows the arrow of time or whether, on the

---

25 "Lecture 33: Femininity", op. cit., pp. 134–5.

contrary, it moves in the opposite direction. It is an opposition that can only be overcome if one positions the individual in the presence of the other, if one positions the child *in the presence* of the adult and as *receiving messages* from the adult, messages that are not a *raw given*, but are 'to be translated'.[26]

So, for this talk I have proposed, *in this order*, 'gender, sex, the sexual'. To speak of the little human being in this order is to put gender in first place. *It is therefore to call into question the primacy of sexual difference as a foundation.*

Subjectively speaking – and here the discussions and the observations are quite numerous – nothing permits the claim that biological sex is intimately perceived, apprehended and lived by the subject in any way at all in the first months of life. Here I have in mind texts such as that of Person and Ovesey,[27] which Kernberg summarizes in his book on "love relations,"[28] and in particular Roiphe and Galenson's book on *The Infantile Origins of Sexual Identity*,[29] which was published in French some years ago.

Gender, according to all these authors and according to all the observations they report – I cannot cite them here but they are completely convincing – gender would be first in time and in becoming conscious, and it would start to become stable toward the end of the first year. But – and we must immediately add a *but* – gender is *neither* a hypothetical cerebral impregnation, which would be a sort of hormonal impregnation (although we know that there is a certain perinatal hormonal impregnation; it ends rapidly and has *no* influence on the choice of gender), *nor* an imprint in Stoller's sense, *nor*

---

26 Cf. "Notes on Afterwardsness" in *Essays on Otherness*, ed. John Fletcher (London & New York: Routledge, 1999), pp. 260–65.
27 Ethel Person and Lionel Ovesey, "Psychoanalytic Theories of Gender Identity", in *The Journal of the American Academy of Psychoanalysis*, vol. 11, 1983, pp. 203–226.
28 Otto Kernberg, *Love Relations* (New Haven and London: Yale University Press, 1995).
29 (New York: International Universities Press, 1981).

a habit. All these notions are, in the end, what I call 'ipso-centrist', which is to say centred on the individual alone.

To define gender in my sense, and I am not alone in saying this, the crucial term is '*assignment*'. Assignment underlines the primacy of the other in the process – whether the first assignment is the declaration at the town hall, at the church or in some other official place, a declaration involving the assignment of a first name, the assignment to a place in a kinship network, etc., or very often the assignment to membership in a religion. But I want to emphasize this important point: it is a process that is not discrete, not done once and for all, not limited to a single act. In this I distinguish myself clearly from all that could be said, for example, of 'determination by the name'. This is a field already opened up by Stekel, but which only received further development (partly unwarranted) with the Lacanian inflation of the notion of the signifier. That the assignment of the first name can carry unconscious messages is one thing. But the 'signifier' is not a determining factor in itself. Assignment is a complex ensemble of acts that go on within language and within the meaningful behaviour of the family circle. One could speak of an ongoing assignment, of a veritable *prescription*. Prescription in the sense in which one speaks of messages called 'prescriptives'; it is therefore of the order of the message, even a bombardment of messages.

A word of warning! It is said that 'gender is social', 'sex is biological'. Caution must be taken with the term 'social', because here it covers up at least two realities that intersect. On the one hand there is the social, or the socio-cultural, in general. Of course it is in 'the social' that the assignment is inscribed, if only in that famous declaration at the beginning of life that is made at the level of the institutional structures of a given society. But the inscriber is not the social in general; it is the little group of close *socii*, of friends and blood relations. This is, effectively, the father, the mother, a friend, a brother, a cousin, etc. Thus it is the little group of *socii* who inscribe *in* the social, but it is not Society that does the assigning.[30]

This idea of assignment or of 'identification by' *completely changes the vector of identification*. Here there is a way to get out of the aporia of Freud's 'O so beautiful' formula which has caused so much thought and commentary: "an individual's first and most important identification, his identification with the father in his own personal prehistory".[31] As you know, this beautiful formula is immediately contradicted by a note in which Freud says: "Perhaps it would be safer to say 'with the parents'; for before a child has arrived at definite knowledge of the difference between the sexes, the lack of a penis, it does not distinguish in value between its father and its mother" (op. cit. p. 31, n.1).[32] This primitive identification with the father of personal prehistory, which has been revived as 'symbolic' identification by certain Lacanians (I am thinking of Florence, for example, in his work on identification),[33] is considered more or less the matrix of the ego ideal. I simply ask the following question, or rather I propose this: instead of being an 'identification with', wouldn't this be an '*identification by*'? In other words, I would say: 'primitive identification *by* the socius of personal prehistory'.

Because I am not the first to go in this direction, I shall pause for breath a moment to cite Person and Ovesey in their very impor-

---

30 At the beginning of *Group Psychology and the Analysis of the Ego* (1921c) Freud affirms that "... from the very first, individual psychology ... is at the same time social psychology as well", (*SE* 18 p. 69). But one quickly sees that the "social psychology" of which he speaks is that of close interactions within the narrow circle of the *socius*: "his parents and ... his brothers and sisters, ... the object of his love, and ... his physician" (ibid. p. 70).
31 *The Ego and the Id* (1923b), *SE* 19, p. 31.
32 For a critique of these passages of Freud's, which are absolutely enigmatic and symptomatic, cf. Jean Laplanche *Problématiques I L'angoisse*, (Paris: Presses Universitaires de France, 1980), p. 335–37.
33 Jean Florence, *L'identification dans la théorie freudienne* (Universités Saint-Louis: Brussels, 1978).

tant article on the question of gender identity. Person and Ovesey completely invert the commonly accepted sequence – that is, of the biological coming before the social – by saying the following (you will see which aspects can be accepted and which can be criticized or modified): "In this sense, one can say that gender precedes sexuality in development and organizes sexuality, not the reverse."[34] A formula that I accept, though only partially. As to the idea of precedence, you can see that I subscribe to this absolutely – that is to say, to the precedence of gender in relation to anything else. As to the term 'sexuality', I think it is too vague to be accepted (except as a sort of general term, a kind of bridging term). For my part, I would say, "gender precedes sex"; and furthermore, differing from Person and Ovesey, who say, "gender precedes sex and organizes it", I would say, "Yes, gender precedes sex. But, far from organizing it, it is organized by it".

I am tempted here to call upon the schema of what I have called the 'general theory of seduction'. The general theory of seduction starts from the idea of messages from the other. In these messages, there is a code or a carrier wave, that is to say a basic language, which is a conscious/preconscious language. In other words, I have never said – I do not think I have ever said – that there are unconscious messages from the parents. On the contrary, I think that there are conscious/preconscious messages and that the parental unconscious is like the 'noise' – in the sense of communication theory – that comes to perturb and *to compromise* the conscious/preconscious message.

But the code, or the language that corresponds to a code – the carrier language – is not necessarily always the same. Until now, in the general theory of seduction, which aims to explain the genesis of the drive, I have mainly focused on the code of *attachment* in so far as it is carried by bodily care given to the child. Thus, in this case, communication takes place within the attachment relation. Here, today, I

---

[34] Ethel Spector Person, *The Sexual Century*, (New Haven and London: Yale University Press, 1999), p.70.

try to advance a second, more hypothetical step that demands to be articulated with the former. Communication does not only occur with the language of bodily care; there is also the social code, the social language; there are also the messages of the *socius*: these messages are chiefly *messages of gender assignment*. But they are also the carriers of a good deal of 'noise', all that is brought by the adults who are close to the child: parents, grand-parents, brothers and sisters, their fantasies, their unconscious or preconscious expectations. A father may consciously assign the masculine gender to his offspring but have expected a daughter, even have unconsciously desired to penetrate a daughter. Actually, this field of the unconscious relation of parents to their children has been very poorly explored; the first messages are generally maternal (but not necessarily solely maternal), and I don't think that the parental unconscious is limited to infiltrating the care given to the infant's body. These unconscious wishes also infiltrate the assignment of gender. Therefore it's what is 'sexed' and also and above all the '*sexual*' of the parents that *makes a noise* in the assignment. I say the *sexual* above all because I want to hold onto the idea that adults in the presence of a child will, most importantly, reactivate their own *infantile sexuality*.

The theory of seduction, as I have attempted to formulate it, postulates a translation, and so a translation code. Here it is evidently on the side of sex that one must search. Gender is acquired, assigned, but enigmatic, until about fifteen months. Sex comes to stabilize and to translate gender in the course of the second year, in what Roiphe and Galenson call 'the early genital phase'.

The *castration complex* is at the centre of it. Of course it offers some certainties, but these very certainties are too clear-cut and must be questioned. The certainty of the castration complex is based upon ideology and illusion. Freud said: "Destiny is anatomy".[35] This des-

---

[35] As a translation, this is preferable to "Anatomy is destiny". German permits the phrase to be translated in this way, and I believe it is more striking to say "Destiny is anatomy".

tiny is that there are two sexes, separated, he says, by "The Anatomical Distinction Between the Sexes".[36] But here Freud's argument cannot dispense with a certain slight of hand, which consists in introducing a confusion between *anatomy* and *biology*. Indeed, at other moments, he speaks of the 'bedrock' of biology, in effect making this destiny a biological fate. Many people see an affirmation of Freud's 'biologism' in the phrase "Anatomy is destiny". But *anatomy* is not biology, nor is it physiology, and still less is it hormonal determinism. There are several levels (not to mention other registers) within anatomy itself: there is scientific anatomy, which may be purely descriptive or may be structural – for example, the anatomy of specific apparatuses, which describes the function of the genital apparatus on the basis of its anatomical structure – and then there is 'popular' anatomy. But the anatomy that is a 'destiny' is a 'popular' anatomy, and moreover it is perceptual, even purely illusory. 'Perceptual' in what respect? In animals that do not have an upright posture there are *two* groups of external genitals *perceived* as such, that is to say visualized as such, the female genital organs being perfectly perceptible – visible and also, above all, perceived by smell. So, for the animal there are *two sexes*. For man, owing to his erect posture, there is a double perceptual loss: the loss or regression of olfactory perception, and the loss of the sight of the external female genital organs. Perception is then reduced to what Freud sometimes calls 'inspection' (*Inspektion*), that is to say pure visualization in the medical sense of the term. For the human being, the perception of genital organs is no longer the perception of *two* genital organs but of only one. The difference between the sexes becomes a 'difference of sex'.

    In Spinoza there is a passage of which I'm especially fond, which does not seem to do anything but in reality works perfectly. He says: "For the intellect and will that would constitute the essence of

---

36 Freud, "Psychical Consequences of the Anatomical Distinction Between the Sexes" (1925j), *SE* 19, p. 243.

God would have to be vastly different from human intellect and will, and would have no point of agreement except the name. They could be no more alike than the celestial constellation of the dog and the dog that barks."[37] Well, this is a disparity between two things that actually have nothing in common except the name: "the celestial constellation of the dog" and "the dog that barks". I would say that this can be transposed onto the question of the difference of the sexes: the perceptible difference of sex as sign or as signifier has practically nothing to do with biological and physiological male/female difference.

Isn't *this contingency an extraordinary destiny?* The erect posture makes the female organs perceptually inaccessible; but this contingency has been raised by many civilizations, and no doubt our own, to the rank of a major, universal, signifier of presence/absence.

Is perceptual anatomical difference a language, a code? It is certainly not a complete code, but it is at the least something that structures a code – a most rigid code at that, structured precisely by the law of the excluded third, by presence/absence. It is rather a skeleton of a code, but of a logical code that for a long time I have referred to as 'phallic logic'.[38] This is the logic of presence/absence, of zero and one, which has received an impressive expansion in the modern universe of computer science.

Thus it is difficult to disengage the question of the difference of sex from the castration complex.

Once disentangled from certain ideological presuppositions, studies such as those by Roiphe and Galenson, long-term observations of an entire population of closely observed children, appear emphatically to reinforce the idea of a very widespread, even universal castration complex. But in contrast to Freud, the castration

---

37 Spinoza, *Ethics,* Part 1, "Prop. 17, Schol", in *The Essential Spinoza: Ethics and Related Writings,* trans. Samuel Shirley, ed. Michael L. Morgan (Indianapolis: Hackett Publishing Company, 2006), p. 15.
38 Cf. *Problématiques II, Castration, symbolisation* (Paris: Presses Universitaires de France, 1980).

complex according to Roiphe and Galenson is not initially bound up with the Oedipus. They speak of an 'early genital phase', a 'castration reaction', which is actually a reaction *by* means of the castration complex.

Many questions may be opened up here – those that I evoked quite a while back in one of my *Problématiques* called *Castration, Symbolisation* where I asked whether the universality of the castration complex in its rigid form, with its logical opposition of 'phallic/castrated', is inevitable, or whether there are more flexible, more varied, more ambivalent models of symbolization.

Does the inevitability of the logic of the excluded third in the equipment of our western civilization necessarily go hand in hand with the reign of the castration complex at the level of the individual or of the little group, which is to say as *ideology*? After all, in analyses, memories bound to the castration complex are often encountered in attenuated form: attenuated in that they are compromised by what they seek to repress.

Yet what they seek to repress is precisely 'the *sexual*'. What sex and, as one might say, its secular arm, the castration complex, tend to repress is infantile sexuality. Repress it or, more precisely, create it by repressing it.

Here I can only mention what recently emerged from a dialogue with Daniel Widlöcher concerning 'attachment and infantile sexuality'.[39] Infantile sexuality, the *'sexual'*, is the very object of psychoanalysis. It is drive-based, and not instinctual. It functions according to a particular economic regime that seeks tension rather than the reduction of tension, and it has the fantasy object at its source and not at its end-point, thus reversing the 'object relation'. Consequently the *sexual* will occupy the entire domain and attempt to organize itself but in a way that is always precarious, until the upheaval of puberty when the genital instincts will have to come to terms with it.

---

39 See "Sexuality and Attachment in Metapsychology" in this volume.

I shall shortly close this presentation in order to give way to discussion, which is to say to uncertainties.

*
* *

I wanted to provide a precise framework in order to open up some hypotheses and some uncertainties. As to the *hypotheses*, some of these profoundly unsettle commonly accepted views:

— Precedence of gender: gender comes before sex, a point that upends habits of thought, the ruts of routine thought that put the 'biological' before the 'social'.
— Precedence of assignment: assignment comes before symbolization.
— Primary identification: far from being a primary identification 'with' (the adult), this is, I propose, a primary identification 'by' (the adult).
— The contingent, perceptual and illusory character of anatomical sexual difference, the veritable destiny of modern civilization.

As to the *uncertainties*: these are numerous, and I'm sure you will raise them. I shall point to the question of knowing how the two lines of enigmatic messages which I am currently trying to define come to be combined: that is to say, we must make room for the second line, that of social assignment, next to the line of attachment. How are the problems of femininity and bisexuality to be positioned with respect to this double line? What is the relation between what I have suggested concerning 'identification by' and the notion of the ego ideal? I have certainly not addressed all of the uncertainties, the questions and the objections that you will want to raise.

APPENDIX I

STOLLER AND GENDER

I would like to start off by *noting a few impressions* that arise from reading Stoller – Stoller as researcher and thinker.[1]

Stoller shows a strikingly impressive freedom of style, in fact he flaunts it. He doesn't hesitate to criticize and reconsider his own observations (e.g., in Chapter 5 of *Presentations of Gender*, "How Biology Can Contribute to Gender Identity"). Sometimes he makes fun of himself, or of explanations that are too complete. Among many other examples, there is the moment in *Perversion* (pp. 81–82) where he throws into a single rag-bag non-analytic psychological or physiological theories as well as analytic theories, and concludes that "psychoanalytic theory is the most syncretic system since the Pantheon of the Romans" (*Perversion*, p. 82 n).

Or again in *Presentations of Gender* (pp. 3–4) he criticizes psychoanalytic jargon, while also showing a mistrust of "case reports" (pp. 2 and 9) – a mistrust concerning theory that can, however, end up in a curious scepticism: "A last hopeless mutter: of what practical importance is it whether perversions are classified as neuroses or as something different?" (*Perversion*, p. 101 n).

Excessively simplistic biological explanations are shown no mercy, especially those drawn from animal experimentation concerning the erection centre in monkeys (*Perversion*, pp. 21–22); Stoller returns here to explanations that take account of fantasy, while underlining the fact that fantasy is no less neurophysiological than the rest. Similarly, in Chapter 5 of *Presentations of Gender* cited above, he finally gives pre-eminence to the individual acquisition of gender over the

---

[1] Works referred to: *Sex and Gender* (London: Karnac, 1984 [orig. 1968]); *Perversion: the Erotic form of Hatred* (London: Karnac, 1986 [orig. 1975]); *Presentations of Gender* (New Haven: Yale Univeristy Press, 1985).

hypothesis of hormonal determinism.

Nevertheless, Stoller's positions in relation to biology remain ambiguous. One has the impression that he sprinkles his writings with allusions to sexual physiology so as to avoid dealing with the question in real depth. One of the most explicit passages is in *Perversion* (p. 15 ff), but in the end the confusion is only multiplied. Here Stoller starts out from a passage in which Freud speaks of the biological "bedrock"[2] without noticing that Freud himself performs a sleight of hand by equating the anatomical difference of the *observable external genital organs* with a biological difference.

Stoller goes on to refer to the Freudian notion of complementary series, which positions the 'constitutional' (innate, endogenous, atavistic) in opposition to the 'accidental' (acquired, exogenous).

However, by an unjustified slippage this opposition is superimposed onto the opposition between the biological and the psychosocial.

| innate | acquired |
| biological | psychological-social |

This assimilation is unwarranted and misleading: it encourages a return to the old soul-body problematic and it neglects:

1) the fact that the biological can have a mental expression (hunger) and that the mental necessarily has a neurophysiological counterpart;

2) the fact that there may be biological characteristics that are acquired, even at the level of the individual, and that there is a given, pre-existing 'psychosocial' domain (social categories, symbolic systems, etc.).

The criticism of simplistic thinking or of the useless complication of current explanations falls flat when confronted with the extremely simplistic aspects of certain Stollerian developments. For

---

2 "Analysis Terminable and Interminable" (1937c), *SE* 23, p. 252.

example, the summaries that Stoller gives of Freudian theory are so cursory and superficial that one wonders where or even whether he has really read Freud at all.

For example, in chapter 8 of *Perversion*, we read among other things that "[Freud] saw homosexuality in males especially as a pathology of the resolution of a boy's oedipal conflict with his father" (p. 144). A purported summary that is completely silent about the maternal aetiology (cf. the Leonardo text), which, in addition, Stoller attributes to other authors: "others emphasized that male homosexuality, which seemed to Freud to spring primarily from a son's disturbed relationship with his father, could be traced back to preoedipal disturbances in mother-son relationships" (ibid.). Furthermore Stoller attributes this to some of the 'moderns', without mentioning the 'Leonardo theory' that can be found regularly in Freud.

Stoller's capacity for mockery and his freedom of style can be seductive, but they all too often mark an absence of serious thinking. This applies not only to his reading of Freud, but to his own thought. Take his explanation of 'perversion'. The suggestive title *Perversion: the Erotic Form of Hatred* does not live up to its promise. For the "hatred" in question has nothing to do with the death drive or with unbinding; in the end it is related, in an unambiguous fashion and apropos of all perversions, to a desire for vengeance experienced by the boy, following a humiliation ('trauma') undergone in childhood.

Another type of explanation, reduced to a strict minimum, is that which relates transsexualism to "too much mother, too little father" (*Presentations of Gender*, pp. 28, 63), a formula so general and so abstract that one can find it in innumerable attempts to identify a psychogenesis of neuroses, psychoses and perversions, all the way up to and including Lacanian foreclosure (although Lacan had criticized this type of "lame reply" in advance).[3]

---

3 Jacques Lacan, "On a Question Prior to any Possible Treatment of Psychosis", in *Écrits*, trans. Bruce Fink (New York: WW Norton), p. 480.

On the same level of theoretical prestidigitation, one will note the answer to the question: how is femininity transmitted? Stoller says: "I do not know ... I doubt if there is a more intense way available to humans for merging with each other than to look deeply into each other's eyes; lovers have always known this, as have mothers ... Perhaps in this way, especially, the boys drink in, merge with, sense they are a part of their mothers' femaleness" (*Presentations of Gender*, p. 33).

Another subterfuge, mostly used when criticisms of his theory accumulate, consists in acknowledging that what he is describing (the "primary transsexual", the "very feminine" boy) is an extremely rare condition that may never have existed (ibid., pp. 40–42) or is only an identikit picture.

*
* *

Let us enter into the *question of gender*, without losing sight of what serves as a point of reference for Stoller: the discourse of adult transsexuals, and, to a certain degree, the discourse and/or behaviour of "very feminine" boys.

The central affirmation of this discourse is: "I have the soul of a woman in the body of a man". Taken at face value, it is a discourse that confirms *gender* as something psychological, as a matter of belief, and which affirms *sex* as a purely somatic reality. Gender would be the subjective aspect, the consciousness of sex. Although Stoller sometimes maintains the soul-body dichotomy, he only partially adheres to it.

A more tautological but perhaps more interesting definition is found in *Presentations of Gender* (pp. 10–11). Here, gender is defined as the belief or feeling that one belongs to one of the two genders. Thus, the transsexual does not believe that he is of the female sex, but of the female *gender*. One sees that we are pulled toward several convergent ideas: "a dense mass of beliefs" and "convictions"; the feeling of belonging to a group (one of the two large human groups); and, finally, an element that is situated on the side of the subject or the ego, and not on the side of the object or "object choice".

My commentary on this – not Stoller's – would be as follows: gender choice, even if it is correlated with object choice, is fundamentally different from it. Recall Freud's basic formula in the Schreber case: "I (a man) love him (a man)".[4] In this formula the 'I' may be (or may consider himself to be) a man or a woman: this is the question of gender. So again in the formula for homosexuality in the Leonardo case study, Freud establishes the following connection:

Mother – loves – Leonardo
Leonardo – loves – a boy in the image of the child Leonardo.

For all that, Leonardo is not identified with the gender of the mother whose place he takes.

The genesis of *gender* is thus clearly independent of the genesis of object choice.

Let us now turn to the aetiology that Stoller postulates as the origin of gender identity. In *Presentations of Gender* (pp. 11–12), Stoller sums up this aetiology according to five factors:

1. A biologic force
2. Sex assignment at birth
3. The attitudes of the parents (the way in which the child is perceived and raised)
4. 'Biopsychic phenomena'
5. The developing body ego

Some of these factors are eliminated or regrouped:

---

[4] "Psycho-Analytic Notes on an Autobiographical Account of a Case of Paranoia (Dementia Paranoides)" (1911c), *SE* 12, p. 63.

No. 5, the developing body ego, corresponds to different self-perceptions by the child of its own sexed body (ibid., p. 14). But Stoller eliminates this last factor as being secondary in the little child: "Even when anatomy is defective ... the individual develops an unequivocal sense of maleness or femaleness if the sex assignment and rearing are unequivocal" (ibid.). Stoller often combines factors 2 and 3 (assignment + parental attitudes). This leaves three factors to be discussed.

A. The biologic force

The influence of genetic and hormonal factors on gender choice is fiercely debated; indeed there are two ways to conceptualise this influence. The idea of hormonal determination in the 'brain' (a somewhat debatable idea, from an experimental point of view) may, theoretically speaking, be manifested:

— directly by a male or female 'psyche', though there is nothing to bear this out (cf. two the notes on pp. 22 and 23);

— or indirectly through the determination by the 'brain' of anatomical appearance. This then returns the matter to our factor of 'assignment + parental attitudes'. This second option is clearly preferred by Stoller. I can only make reference to the long case report and the related follow-up data presented in chapter 5: "How Biology can Contribute to Gender Identity".

Thus the only factors left in play are 'biopsychic phenomena' and 'assignment + parental attitudes'. Since Stoller's own theory remains essentially that of 'biopsychic phenomena', I shall begin with that factor.

B. Under the term 'biopsychic phenomena'

The notion of biopsychic phenomena comprises an entire theory founded on the idea of *symbiosis*, which turns up repeatedly.

It can be found on p. 16 ff and p. 25 ff (in chapter 3, "An Emphasis on Mothers"); and also, for example, in *Perversion* chapter 8 ("Symbiosis Anxiety and the Development of Masculinity").

The essential reference point is the theory of Margaret Mahler, and it is difficult for us in France to imagine the hold this notion has had on Anglo-Saxon thought from 1952 almost until the present day.

In a word, Margaret Mahler inferred from the observation of *autistic* and *symbiotic* children the postulate that in the course of its development every child necessarily passed through these two phases, to which the subject could subsequently regress. On the other hand, a normal development is presumed to entail a 'separation-individuation' phase in terms of the child's relation to the mother, an evolution that Mahler was led to divide into four sub-phases.

To be sure, this theory had some influence in France. But very quickly it was sharply criticized, both in its own right and by virtue of its affinity with the Freudian theory of a primary narcissism understood in the literal sense, that is, as something that exists from the first days of life. Here I can only mention in outline a few stages of this critique:[5]

For a critique that is much more recent and is based on child observation, one should refer to Martin Dornes and to the cluster of arguments he assembles.[6]

Dornes's article demolishes the idea of a primitive symbiotic phase in the child, acknowledging that at most there are symbiotic *moments* in *some* children.

---

[5] See Jean Laplanche and Jean-Bertrand Pontalis, "Primary Narcissism" in *The Language of Psychoanalysis*, trans. Donald Nicholson-Smith (London: Karnac, 1973) and Jean Laplanche, *Problématiques*, vols. I to V: refer to the index to the *Problématiques* at the end of *Nouveaux fondements pour la pyschanalyse* (Paris: Presses Universitaires de France, 2008 [orig. 1987]) p. 187). See also the arguments against Winnicott's idea of a 'first not-me possession', which presupposes an original lack of differentiation between mother and child (*Nouveaux fondements* index, ibid., p. 172). See Jean Gortais' survey article, "Le concept de symbiose en psychanalyse", in *Psychanalyse à l'Université*, vol. 12, no. 46, April 1987, pp. 201–38.

[6] Martin Dornes, "La théorie de Margaret Mahler reconsidérée", in *Psychanalyse et psychologie du 1er âge* (Paris: Presses Universitaires de France, 2002).

The way in which Stoller adheres to Mahlerism is, however, quite peculiar:

1) He doesn't care at all about the 'autistic phase'.

2) He postulates that in the process of going from symbiosis to separation-individuation there is a particular symbiosis, one that is gendered and is *different from symbiosis in general*. In other words, in the case of "primary transsexuals" the boy could *separate himself from the mother* and become completely independent of her in all other respects, but *without managing to separate himself from the femininity of his mother* (*Presentations of Gender*, pp. 16–18).

As to the aetiology, we have seen that it always comes back to 'too much mother, not enough father', a generalization in which Stoller, good 'scientist' that he is, would like to find elements of predictability (if a mother is like that, the son will be like this; if a son is like this, the mother must have been like that (pp. 33–34)). However, this desired predictability is at odds with the fact that one practically never finds the exemplary case of a son who is 'like this', that is to say a pure 'primary transsexual'. Stoller affirms that:

1. cases of 'very feminine boys' are a small minority and should not be confused with homosexuals (p. 41);

2. he has never followed one of these 'very feminine boys' so far into adulthood as to be able to see them transform into 'primary transsexuals';

3. not one of the cases followed by Richard Green became a 'primary transsexual' (p. 41 n. 12).

When Stoller tries, in one case, to demonstrate "predictability" (p. 38ff), it concerns a boy who did not begin to dress as a girl until 3¾ years old and whose description is profoundly at odds with the "type" (or identikit picture) described previously (p. 19ff).

Conclusion

The Stollerian explanation of gender identity collapses on all sides:

1) Its Mahlerian foundation is contested. Already in the debate with Stern in *Presentations of Gender* (p. 39 n. 9, and pp. 39–40) one can see all the 'complementary hypotheses' that Stoller is forced to demand his reader accept in order to try to 'save' a theory that is contradicted by the facts. At that point, when the Mahlerian foundation collapses (a debate that I shall not take up again here), the whole Stollerian aetiology collapses.

2) In addition, the latent idea according to which symbiosis = identification is thoroughly questionable. The biological model of symbiosis implies complementarity and not assimilation. Why would it be otherwise in a 'psychic' 'symbiosis'?

3) Even supposing that there is a primary identification with the *mother* (whether or not by means of symbiosis), why would this be a primary identification with the mother as a *woman*? And why in particular with *femininity*, which is a very elaborated trait?

4) Why would 'disidentification' (Greenson's term) or 'separation-individuation' (Mahler's terms), succeed on all levels *except* on the level of gender? How could such a split be conceived? (cf. pp. 40–41).

5) The appearance of masculine and feminine traits happens when the child begins to be socialised (at the end of the first year and the beginning of the second). Who would say of a nursling that it is a masculine rather than a feminine creature (even if *we* project: "It's a boy!")?

Nevertheless, Stoller's work has the following immense merits:

1) To have underlined the early appearance of gender identity.

2) To have, in his moments of greatest lucidity (*Presentations*, p. 73ff), attributed gender identity to the complex unity created by "assignment" and the "endless messages reflecting parents' attitudes delivered to the child's body and psyche" (ibid. p. 74–75) (one can see

a door opening up to the general theory of seduction). Finally, of the three factors singled out above the only one remaining is 'assignment + parental attitudes' (factors 2 and 3 of his aetiological series).

In the very important ending of Chapter 5 (ibid. pp. 73–76), Stoller vigorously refutes the notion of the *direct hormonal determination of gender*: hormones, even when administered in massive doses, generally only lead to small or modest changes in gender behaviour. Even though, with the sceptical style he often adopts, Stoller ends on a *non liquet*, his preference is for the psychological and relational hypothesis (ibid. pp. 75–76).

APPENDIX II

LINGUISTIC GENDER

In what follows, we shall designate as gender (S) the gender that is at stake for analysts, psychologists and social science specialists more generally. Here (S) stands for 'sexological'. We introduce this clarification so that in all cases in which confusion would be possible we are able to distinguish between 'gender (S)' and linguistic gender, or 'gender (L)'. We are well aware that by introducing this (S) we are to some extent raising questions about the distinctions between gender, sex and the *sexual*.[1] But we have never claimed to be creating a categorization that would be clear-cut, as if by a knife, so to speak. Far from it! To repeat our point about assignment, gender is intrinsically freighted with contents that are conceptually 'impure'; that is to say, to a great extent unconscious and bearing on sex and sexuality.

1. – We are led, then, to an important excursus on linguistics. Why venture into what might appear to be a digression?

a. In part, the feminist (and antifeminist) battle crystallizes around gender (L). Beyond those aspects of this which are anecdotal and somewhat ridiculous – in particular, the desire to modify mental attitudes by artificially modifying language[2] – it is worth taking seriously the notion of 'symbolic systems' that impose their supremacy – Bourdieu's notion of 'masculine domination' being a case in point.

---

1 [*Editor*: On Laplanche's French neologism 'sexual' (as distinct from the normal 'sexuel'), see the Editor's note to the Forward of this volume. The term is printed here in italics to mark it off from the standard English term with the same spelling].
2 In a separate domain, Roy Schafer's attempt to create a 'new language for psychoanalysis' moved in the same direction: from the moment analyst and analysand agree to replace the substantive or the adjective 'unconscious' with the adverb 'unconsciously', we are already a long way on the road towards disalienation. See Agnès Oppenheimer, "Le meilleur des mondes possible. À propos du projet de R. Schafer", in *Psychanalyse à la Université*, vol. 9, no. 35, p. 467

b. Gender (L) eminently relates to language or, more precisely, to *language as a system* [*la langue*]. Since we have a tendency to see in the assignment of gender (S) an act of *utterance* [*parole*] (a message), and to see the assumption of gender as a process that could be understood as the translation of a message, it is even more urgent to pose the *distinction* between these two types of gender (S and L), whose resemblance risks leading us down the wrong path.

2. – Throughout the course of its innumerable variations and complex historical evolutions (which we couldn't possibly claim to cover exhaustively), gender (L) seems to us to have entailed a tendency towards a logic of the excluded third, which irresistibly evokes the binary and exclusive logic of the castration complex (phallic–castrated; or: phallic–all the rest). To this extent, what we see emerging is that the problematic of gender (L), far from being situated at the same level as gender (S), in fact corresponds to, or at least has a tendency towards correspondence with what I call 'sex', that which translates and organises gender (S).

3. – The two authors from whom we shall take our bearings (even though it means expanding our documentation) are Greville Corbett, in his book *Gender*,[3] and Raoul de la Grasserie in his "La catégorie psychologique de la classification, révélée par le langage"[4]

No doubt the difference of nearly one hundred years which separates these two authors gives Corbett superiority in terms of information, linguistic 'scientificity', etc. Yet one cannot help but be struck by the narrowly technical and restricted character of Corbett's approach, despite the extent of his documentation.

This approach is characterized from the start by a restriction of the problematic of genders, which (following Charles F. Hockett) are narrowly defined as "classes of nouns reflected in the behaviour of associated words" (quoted in Corbett, p. 1). Gender is a *property of*

---

3 (Cambridge: Cambridge University Press, 1991). Corbett's text was analysed at length in my seminar by Christophe Dejours.
4 In *Revue philosophique*, vol. 45, 1898, pp. 594–624.

the substantive that has *consequences* for agreement (the agreement of articles, adjectives, pronouns, even of verbs, and so on).

This deliberate, technical restriction of gender mutilates the anthropological dimension of Corbett's book:

a – Unlike La Grasserie, Corbett prohibits himself from connecting 'gender' in this narrow sense with the presence of noun classes in *languages that do not require agreement* (non-inflected languages). In such languages, gender – understood in the broad sense given by La Grasserie: "families of things" (La Grasserie, p. 624) – manifests itself in, for example, the presence of classificatory words and affixes.

Thus, in Chinese, all the names of trees are followed by the generic name: tree (*chou*) (ibid. p. 598).[5]

A pine would be a pine-tree (*song chou*); a pear, a pear-tree (*ly chou*). Sometimes the affix retains its meaning even when it is separate (*chou* by itself means 'tree'); sometimes it has no more than a classificatory value, which is dependent on its affixed position (e.g. in Algonquin where "every second word becomes an empty word which serves to form the substantive" (ibid. p. 600)). This is a little similar to the *e* ending in French, which is used to mark the feminine: the *e* by itself has no meaning.

This entire domain is excluded from Corbett's investigation.

b – Corbett asks artificially complex questions concerning what he calls "the assignment of gender", which is to say "the way in which native speakers allocate nouns to genders … How native speakers know that the word for 'house' is masculine in Russian, feminine in French and neuter in Tamil" (Corbett, p. 3).[6]

All of which is fine so long as the subject has semantic criteria at his disposal. Thus "'house' in Tamil is neuter because it does not

---

[5] It will be immediately noticed that the notion of class or of gender in linguistics in no way implies distinction by sex. As Christophe Dejours has pointed out, the number of genders (L) can vary from 2 to 20 or more, among which sexual distinction is possible but not always present. In our example, 'tree' is a gender, in the same way that 'insect' could be a gender, or 'non-meat food', etc.

[6] Here I am summarizing, on the basis of Dejours' work.

denote a human" (ibid.).

But the problem becomes more complicated when there are no semantic criteria: why is 'house' masculine in Russian?

Corbett has, then, to make do with 'phonological and morphological' criteria.

His reasoning is as follows. It would be too complicated for each speaking subject to *learn* the gender of each noun when gender is not determined by meaning. There must therefore exist formal rules (phonological or morphological) which are more or less hidden and which have not been formulated by linguists. In this regard Corbett relies on certain regularities (e.g. in French the words ending in 'son' are feminine) and on experimental studies in which one presents to native speakers words borrowed from a foreign language, or words created artificially, in order to see how they make gender assignments.

Here one can see that the term 'assignment' has taken on two meanings: from spontaneous assignment by a speaker, it becomes assignment by a linguist or by a subject in an experiment. Of course certain regularities are uncovered but they are not sufficient to explain how a native speaker almost never makes a mistake (see ibid. p. 7). Hence Corbett's quasi-mystical appeal to 'hidden rules'.

It seems to me that that Corbett makes a simple error with respect to both the speaking subject and the subject learning a language. It consists in making gender an intrinsic property of the noun, which is "reflected in the behaviour of associated words". This is clearly true in the context of an *experiment*, where one presents a subject with an isolated substantive: *verre* (glass). But when one learns a language (whether as a child or as an adult) one is never presented with '*verre*', but always with '*le verre*'. The associated word, the article, is a part of one and the same syntagm, which the subject learns at a single stroke (it's as easy to learn '*le verre*' as to learn '*verre*'). One could even say that in French the article plays precisely the role of 'gender classifier' as it is defined above on the basis of La Grasserie:

> '*Le-verre*' relates '*verre*' to the masculine gender
> just as
> 'pine-tree' relates 'pine' to the gender[7] tree

3 – One more word on the term *assignment* as it is used both by linguists in relation to gender (L) and by psychologists in relation to gender (S).

Gender (L) defines noun classes.

Gender (S) applies to *classes of living or human beings*, classes which have a certain relation (yet to be determined) to sexual reproduction.

The assignment of gender (L) is a *phenomenon of language* which includes a noun (itself already something collective, generally speaking) within a class of nouns that share certain properties.[8]

The assignment of gender (S) is an *act of communication* (a message, in fact), which declares that an individual belongs to a particular class of being.

There are thus two reasons not to let oneself be misled by words: gender (S) is not the same as gender (L); assignment (S) is not the same as assignment (L).

4 – Having cleared the field, let us try to draw some positive conclusions about the notion of gender (L), taking it, as does La Grasserie, in the enlarged sense of linguistic classes.

These conclusions are provisional and open to further enrichment in the light of more extensive information. In particular we would have to take account of a second article by La Grasserie: "De l'expression de l'idée de sexualité dans la langage".[9] What a surprise it is to bring this author back to light and to see how between his two

---

7 [*Trans.*: see note 5.]
8 It is to be noted that in certain countries the registration of a birth may involve other categories than that of gender (S): racial assignment ('white'), religious assignment (Catholic, Muslim, no religion, etc.) racial-religious assignment, etc.
9 *Revue philosophique*, vol. 57, September 1904.

articles he moves from the general problem of classification to a piece specifically on sexuality (Freud's *Three Essays* was published in 1905!)[10]

For my part, I shall use the term 'gender (L)' in the general sense of 'a category of classification revealed by language', including all the classes of substantives of which La Grasserie speaks, whether or not the language in question requires 'agreement'.

A. La Grasserie and Corbett agree in saying that genders (L):
— are not limited to the sexual domain. The sexed classification may even be absent;
— can be multiple;
— often include a 'residual' category: 'All the rest'.

B. La Grasserie links gender to an "instinct for classification". He analyzes this instinct in terms of a transposition of "kinship in man" into a "kinship among objects" ("La catégorie", p. 596).

Language would then be a revealer of, or a "litmus test" for, this instinct: "Psychic need becomes grammatical need"; "Grammar translates the idea, just as the idea translates the object" (ibid.).

(With this idea of *kinship* between things – of a passage from families of people to families of things – we find a prefiguring of Lévi-Strauss's *The Savage Mind*).[11]

C. La Grasserie tries to bring order to this often dense multiplicity of classifications by distinguishing between

---

10 Raoul de la Grasserie (b. 1839 d. 1914) was a Doctor of Law and a judge at many tribunals in Brittany. He was a member of the Société de linguistique de Paris and of many other learned societies. The author of numerous books and articles (more than 200 titles) on law, sociology, linguistics, psychology and philosophy, he was held in unanimous regard in his own era: "He is to be classed among those who tried to found a new philosophy – not a general philosophy, but a philosophy within each specific science – and to bring out the laws which govern the observation of facts, and create from them a precise synthesis" (H. Carroy, *Dictionnaire biographique international des écrivains*; vol. 4, 1903–1909).
11 Claude Lévi-Strauss, *The Savage Mind*, trans. John and Doreen Weightman (Chicago and London: Chicago UP, 1968).

— concrete classifications, and

— abstract classifications.

His definition of *"concrete" classifications*, if taken literally, could seem absurd. How could certain peoples "limit themselves strictly to what is individual"? How could one have "languages devoid of all classification"? Isn't the substantive itself a classification? If Chinese has no word for 'brother' but only 'older' and 'younger', there are, at least, those two classes! (ibid. p. 598).

What La Grasserie seems to want to say by means of this distinction is:

a. that certain languages – those said to be without classification – do not go beyond the substantive, that is to say do not go so far as to have a class of classes;

b. that at a level which is already superior to the absence of classification, *concrete classification* proceeds, so to speak, little by little, by means of analogy between the members of the class (and perhaps also by contiguity), but without logical opposition, without thinking of the exclusion between classes.

Concrete classification would be "down to earth"(ibid. p. 610). According to our own terminology, this would be a classification in terms of *diversity* and not a classification by *difference*. In my view, this would be a new reason for a *rapprochement* with Lévi-Strauss, as much with the notion of the 'savage mind' as with his revitalised conception of 'totemism'.[12]

According to La Grasserie, the concrete classifications could be:

"objective": aimed at identifying "kinship" among objects or actions (might we say 'metaphoric'?);

"subjective": that is, those which "are connected to a part of the human body, either as an object, as an instrument, or as a movement of the body" (ibid. p. 608) (might we say 'metonymic'?)

---

12 Claude Lévi-Strauss, *Totemism*, trans. Rodney Needham (Boston: Beacon Press, 1963).

D — Part II (ibid., p. 610ff) deals with *abstract classification*. The term *"difference"* appears immediately, which is a good confirmation of our hypothesis: *abstract classification* is that which is formulated more or less in terms of differences, or which at least aims towards difference.

La Grasserie proposes a typology of abstract classifications:

1st) The *vitalist* classification into animate and inanimate.
2nd) The *rationalist* one, into beings with and without reason.
3rd) The *hominist* one, between human and non-human beings.
4th) The *virilist* one, between male humans and other beings.
5th) The *intensivist* one, between strong beings and weak beings.
6th) The *gradualist* one, between diminutive and augmentative beings.
7th) The *masculinist* one, between male beings and all the other beings.
8th) The *sexualist* one, between masculine, feminine and asexual.

Corbett refers to La Grasserie and raises only relatively minor objections to this classification.

E — One of the advantages of La Grasserie's work is to show that there is a kind of *evolution* and a trend in the history of classifications. The *'vitalist'* classification (animate – inanimate) would be one of the most primitive.

The 'sexualist' classification, on the other hand, would be the one toward which the movement of civilization tends:

> This *vitalist* distinction is the most solidly grounded; we find it, combined with others, in most of the Caucasian languages; indeed,

it is founded on movement, one of the most general and most important of the physical factors. Because of its clarity it seems preferable even to the sexualist classification; for the vitalist classification encompasses all beings, which it divides up more equally and according to a positive classification, whereas in order to include all beings the sexualist classification must institute a negative category, the neuter or asexual. So the vitalist classification could have been adopted by more civilised peoples and to better advantage. However, the opposite occurred, the *vitalist* classification remained restricted to peoples with an inferior civilization, while those with a superior civilization adopted the *sexualist* classification.[13]

F — The *sexualist* classification often includes three genders: masculine, feminine, neuter. Neuter being the asexual and not the inanimate (ibid. p. 618).

G — So according to La Grasserie again, there would be:
a) A general evolution of 'vitalism' toward 'sexualism'.
b) Some superimpositions of one system over another, and some survivals – in particular, the survival of the inanimate classification within sexualism.
c) "*Some usurpations, or rather, some expansions*" or "*invasions*" (ibid. p. 614).
In particular: "within the sexualist classification, one endeavours to give a grammatical gender to many objects which do not naturally possess one" (ibid. p. 618).
This happens according to two mechanisms:
a 'psychological' mechanism: semantic analogies (a certain object resembles the masculine or the feminine)
a 'morphological' mechanism: words ending in *a*, in Latin, are feminine.

---

13 La Grasserie, *Revue philosophique de la France et de l'étranger*, vol. 45, p. 616.

H — For my part, I would propose the following idea:

— that because it uses the *difference* of the sexes, the *sexualist system* is the one which lends itself best to a rigorous classification; this is probably by virtue of the binary logic (phallic–castrated) to which this difference lends itself;

— that, paradoxically, it is also the one which lends itself most to *usurpations* of territory between genders: whether it be the usurpation by masculine/feminine difference, which, in French for example, has almost entirely overrun the territory of the neuter; or whether it be the encroachment of one gender upon another. This latter usurpation is most often, but not always, the usurpation of the feminine gender by the masculine gender, on the grounds that the masculine gender is 'unmarked' (*Madame le ministre*, etc.).[14]

On the other hand, in French the word *'personne'*, which is feminine, is said to be 'unmarked', while in German *Mädchen* is neuter (L) but feminine (S).

To return to assignment (S), the parent at the town hall who is registering the birth of *ein Mädchen*, does not suppose himself to be registering a neuter or asexual being!

So it is only with immense caution that one might suppose the existence of a relationship between this 'war of the genders (L)' and a 'war of the sexes (S)'! At most one might propose that in the 'war of the genders (L)' a certain 'masculinism' (whose classification is: the masculine *versus* 'the rest') is the 'objective ally' of a certain 'sexualism' (the only logical difference, since it is clearly symbolizable in terms of the phallus, is sexed difference) and the 'objective ally' of the 'digital' binarism or system (1 – 0), whose success in the contem-

---

14 [*Trans.*: Laplanche's parenthesis gives an example of standard French linguistic practice whereby a grammatically masculine professional title (*le ministre*) retains its grammatical gender even when collocated with *madame* to indicate that the holder of the post is female].

porary world is well known.

It is no less remarkable that, just at the point of being 'acquired', masculine-feminine difference is immediately doomed to a troubling or contamination. Is this the sign of an instability within binary logic? The victory of a certain 'gender trouble' (Judith Butler)?

10

THREE MEANINGS OF THE TERM 'UNCONSCIOUS' IN THE FRAMEWORK OF THE GENERAL THEORY OF SEDUCTION[1]

I.1   The General Theory of Seduction has its origin in a generalisation of Freud's theory of seduction. Formulated in the years 1896–97, Freud's theory gave an account of repression but within the limits of a situation that was contingent and restricted: it was confined to the domain of psychopathology. To coin a phrase: 'for every neurotic daughter, a perverse father'. A variety of elements was lacking for any reconstruction of the theory by Freud through a generalisation of it, as an alternative to the repudiation of it that took place in the famous letter to Fliess of 21st September, 1897. What was lacking was the concept of the polymorphous perverse and a conception of sexuality in general, such as he was to describe in the *Three Essays* of 1905. What was lacking was the concept of primordial communication and of a message. What was also lacking was an in-depth theorisation of the notion of *translation* as the mechanism of repression. The notion of translation is congruent with the conception of the human being as a being of language and communication; it can be aptly substituted for the mechanical schemas drawn on in the classical theory of repression.

---

1 Paris, 2003.

I.2   The general theory of seduction seeks to give an account of the genesis of the psychosexual apparatus of the human being, starting from interhuman relationships and not from biological origins. The human psychical apparatus is above all wedded to the *drive*, to the sexual drive (under the form of both the life and death drives). The somatic *instincts* are not denied, but they are neither the origin of *infantile* sexuality nor involved in the genesis of the repressed unconscious.

I.3   Seduction is not a contingent, pathological or episodic relation – even though it can sometimes appear in that form. It is based on a situation that no human being can escape, which I call the 'fundamental anthropological situation'. This situation is the adult-infant relation, the relation between the adult and the *infans* (lit. without speech). The adult has an unconscious such as psychoanalysis has described, a sexual unconscious, made essentially of infantile residues, an unconscious that is perverse in the sense of the *Three Essays*; the infant is without genetic sexual instincts, without hormonal activators of sexuality and at the beginning without sexual fantasies. The idea of an endogenous infantile sexuality has been thoroughly criticized, and not only by me, but this criticism has on occasion led to the denial of infantile sexuality in general, or to its being assimilated into an ill-formulated theory.

I.4   How can we locate here the contributions of contemporary psychology of the early infant years? There is much to add from the work of recent observation studies. There has been, notably, considerable development of what Freud had previously called 'self-preservation'. Freudian self-preservation returns under the rubric of 'attachment', with all the developments and observations organised around this theme. On an evident genetic instinctual basis a dialogue, an adult-*infans* communication, develops very quickly, even immediately. The old theory of 'symbiosis' (a state from which it is impossible to say how one would exit), has disappeared thanks to the observation of early relations that are organised, differentiated, reciprocal from the beginning, and where from the beginning the 'not-me' is marked by a relation of personal belonging.

However, what the theory and observations of attachment fail to take into account is the *asymmetry* on the sexual plane. What is missing is an insistence on the fact that the adult-*infans* dialogue, reciprocal as it may be, is nevertheless *parasited by something else* from the beginning. The adult message is scrambled. On the side of the adult there is a unilateral intervention by the unconscious. Let us even say, an intervention by the *infantile* unconscious of the adult, to the extent that the adult-*infans* situation is a situation that reactivates these unconscious infantile drives.

I.5   In order to underline these points, let us ask the question: why speak of *the adult* and the fundamental anthropological situation? Why not speak of a fundamental familial, even oedipal, situation? We do so because the adult-*infans* relation, in its generality, even its universality, goes beyond the parent-infant relation. The fundamental anthropological situation would exist between an infant without a family and an absolutely non-familial educational environment. In this fundamental anthropological situation the important terms are 'communication' and 'message'. Here I would insist that, in speaking of adult messages, we don't mean unconscious messages. All messages are produced on the conscious-preconscious level; when I speak of an enigmatic message, I speak of a message 'compromised' by the unconscious. I insist on the compromised character of the message and this only on the side of the adult at the beginning, even if a reciprocity is established very quickly afterwards, even on the sexual level. What counts, finally, in this situation is in fact what the recipient does with the message, that is to say, precisely the attempt at translation and the necessary failure of that attempt.

I.6   Let me add here a remark on the question of *the biological dimension*. The general theory of seduction and its postulate of a fundamental anthropological situation absolutely does not involve taking a position against biology. In my view, all human processes are indissociably biological and psychic. Even the most abstract mathematical reasoning cannot be conceived without a biological and corporeal correlate. When Freud abandons the theory of seduction in his famous 'letter of the equinox' in 1897, he doesn't say, "I am turning back to the biological" but "I am turning back to the innate, the hereditary". He doesn't at all say that the *biological factor* regains its place, for there isn't anything to be regained. The biological always remains present as the other side of the psychological. On the other hand, this reconquest by the hereditary announced by Freud, the return of the innate factor, runs throughout the history of Freudian metapsychology of which I shall only mention three moments: the 'primal fantasies', *Totem and Taboo* (1913), *Moses and Monotheism* (1939).

As regards the biological, this can be acquired as well as being innate. It is therefore the primacy of the hereditary that I challenge as regards infantile sexuality. I say precisely *sexuality* and *infantile*, in order to indicate that there is certainly an innate and hereditary programme *in what is not sexual* ('self-preservation'), and equally *in non-infantile sexuality* (adolescent gonadal sexuality). There exists, I would argue, a fundamental difference between the sexual drive of infancy and what kicks in at the moment of *adolescence*, which is the effective appearance of the sexual instinct. The sexual *instinct* then has to catch up with the *drive* of intersubjective origin that has developed autonomously over a long period, and there emerges a serious problem of integration and cohesion between the two.

What I would equally challenge is the notion of a *primordial id* at the origin of psychic life, an idea that contradicts the novelty implied by the notion of the drive as a sexual process not adapted (in human beings) to a pre-established aim. If the notion of an id retains a meaning, it is in order to characterise the repressed unconscious, which, in its otherness, *becomes* a veritable 'thing in us' or 'internal foreign body', an 'it'.

*Primal Repression, Translation,
the Constitution of the Unconscious
and the Psychical Apparatus in its Normal and Neurotic Form*[2]

II. 1 The fundamental anthropological situation confronts an adult, who has an unconscious that is sexual but essentially pregenital, with an infant, who has not yet constituted an unconscious nor the opposition unconscious-preconscious, in a dialogue that is both symmetrical at one level and asymmetrical at another. The sexual unconscious of the adult is reactivated in the relation with the small infant. The messages of the adult are conscious-preconscious and are necessarily *compromised* (in the sense of a return of the repressed), by the presence of unconscious scrambling or interference. These messages are therefore *enigmatic*, both for the adult sender and for the infant recipient.

While in a normal dialogue (verbal or non-verbal) there exists a common code and there is no need of translation (or it is instantaneous), in the primordial communication the adult message cannot be grasped in its contradictory totality. For example, in the typical model of breast-feeding, there is a mixture of love and hate, appeasement and excitation, milk and breast, the 'containing' breast and the sexually exciting breast, etc.

The 'codes', innate or acquired, that the infant makes use of are therefore insufficient to cope with this enigmatic message. The infant must resort to a new code, at once improvised by him and invoking the schemas furnished by his cultural environment.

---

2 See my "Short Treatise on the Unconscious" in *Essays on Otherness*, ed. John Fletcher (London: Routledge, 1999), pp. 84–116.

II.2 The translation of the enigmatic adult message doesn't happen all at once but *in two moments*. This schema of two moments or times is the same as that of the model of the trauma: in the first moment, the message is simply inscribed or implanted, without being understood. It is as if maintained or held in position under a thin layer of consciousness, or 'under the skin'. In a second moment the message is reactivated from within. It acts like an internal foreign body that must at all costs be mastered and integrated.

It is a question, Freud tells us, of "experiences which occurred in very early childhood and were not understood at the time but which were *subsequently* [*nachträglich*] understood and interpreted".[3]

II.3 The translation or attempt at translation establishes in the psychical apparatus a *preconscious* level. The preconscious – essentially the ego – corresponds to the way in which the subject is constituted and represents its own history. The translation of messages is in essence the production of a history, more or less coherent.

But because the message is compromised and incoherent, located on two incompatible planes, the translation is always imperfect, with certain *residues* left aside. These are the remainders that constitute *the unconscious in the proper Freudian sense* of the term, in opposition to the preconscious ego. It is clear that the unconscious is marked by the sexual, since it owes its origin to the compromising of the adult message by the sexual. But it is not in any way a copy of the adult unconscious, because of the double 'metabolism' that the sexual has undergone in its trajectory: a distortion in the compromised message on the part of the adult, and a work of translation that revises completely the implanted message on the part of the infant recipient.

II.4 The typical characteristics attributed to the unconscious by Freud himself are the direct consequence of its origin in repression:

---

3 "Remembering, Repeating and Working Through" (1914g), *SE* 12, p. 149.

— the *absence of time* in the unconscious, since it is what escapes, in the process of repression, from the constitution of the domain of the temporal that is the flowering and enrichment of the preconscious personality;

— the *absence of coordination and of negation,* since it is precisely what escapes from coordination that is indispensable to the process of translation;

— the *realism of the unconscious,* corresponding to Freud's 'psychical reality', is repudiated as scandalous by a large number of modern interpretations. This realism opposes the idea that the unconscious is *a second meaning* subjacent to the 'official' and preconscious meaning proposed by the subject. On the contrary, the unconscious is what has escaped from that construction of meaning that I call translation. It isn't part of the domain of meaning, but is constituted by signifiers deprived of their original context, therefore largely deprived of meaning, and scarcely coordinated among themselves.

In a word, the repressed unconscious is at the origin of the *drives,* sexual life drives and sexual death drives, drives that one can consider – by inverting Freud's famous formulation[4] – as 'the demand for work' imposed on the body by its relation to the repressed unconscious signifiers.

The Psychotic and the Borderline: the Radical Failure of Translation and the Untranslated Enclave

III.1   The partial failure of translation accounts for the 'classical' normal-neurotic unconscious. Alongside this, we should make room for the possibility of a radical failure of translation. Nothing is translated, the original message remains as such in the psychical apparatus,

---

4 [*Editor*: cf. "an 'instinct' appears to us ... as a measure of the demand made upon the mind for work in consequence of its connection with the body", "Instincts and their Vicissitudes" (1915c), *SE* 14, pp. 121–2].

whether implanted or intromitted.[5] It thus constitutes what one might call an 'inserted' / 'enclosed' unconscious [*l'inconscient enclavé*].[6]

What are the characteristics and the causes of such an 'unconscious'?[7]

III. 2   This unconscious enclave is not correlated with the preconscious system. With the psychotic there is little or no narration of a history. The unconscious enclave remains, so to speak, just below consciousness. It is maintained by a thin layer of conscious defence, functioning according to an apparently logical, 'operational' mode whose principle modality of defence would be disavowal (Freud's *Verleugnung*) rather than that of repression-translation. It is often said that defence (conscious reasoning) is like the inverted reflection of what is disavowed. Only the "symbol of negation" separates them.[8]

III. 3   Among the untranslated messages constituting this unconscious, one notes in particular the messages of the superego. I have

---

5 [*Editor*: cf. "While implantation allows the individual to take things up actively, at once translating and repressing, one must try to conceive of a process which blocks this, short-circuits the differentiation of the agencies in the process of their formation, and puts into the interior an element resistant to all metabolisation", "Implantation, Imtromission", Jean Laplanche, in *Essays on Otherness*, op.cit., p.136].

6 [*Editor*: Laplanche has previously formulated in an earlier text the idea of the intromitted, unmetabolisable messages from the other as "*psychotic enclaves* within the human personality as such", *New Foundations for Psychoanalysis*, trans. David Macey (Oxford: Basil Blackwell, 1989) p. 139. He here extends this notion of an 'enclave', from untranslatable messages to include messages awaiting translation. Lacking verbal forms for the English noun enclave (the French have *enclaver, enclavé*), I have specified the double and linked meanings of 'insertion / enclosure.']

7 I find Christophe Dejours' proposal of the term 'amential unconscious' difficult to accept, for it presupposes that repression-translation is a process of mentalisation which the psychotic unconscious does not undergo. It therefore presupposes that the messages of the other are not 'mental' but must become so. I have trouble accepting any such opposition as soul/body, *mens/soma*.

8 {*Editor*: cf. "A negative judgment is the intellectual substitute for repression; its 'no' is the hallmark of repression, a certificate of origin – like, let us say, 'Made in Germany'. With the help of the symbol of negation, thinking frees itself from the restrictions of repression ... ", Sigmund Freud, "Negation" (1925h), *SE* 19, p. 236].

often argued that the Kantian categorical imperative is untranslatable into anything other than itself, being impossible to metabolise: 'you must because you must'. It is impossible to give an account of it by reference to any other justification.

III. 4   What are the conditions and causes of such a radical failure of translation?

The conditions are probably multiple. I have opened up here a line of investigation, which I am not the only one to explore and I leave to others the task of continuing it, if it turns out to be viable.

The failure of translation can result notably from an intergenerational transmission, without any metabolisation. The question of 'the intergenerational' must be developed by asking what are its conditions of existence from the point of view of the very structure of the message and from the point of view of the recipient of the message. Many are already working on this: the line of investigation and the theoretical framework have been formulated especially for psychiatrists confronted more and more, as it seems to me, with these problems. Is there even a message that is not so much compromised as inhabited by the unconscious, without any distance from it? Is this even possible? Is there a message that carries and imposes its own code, and so imposes a translation that is nothing other than the message itself? Or when the message is paradoxical? What are the possible applications of the notion of the paradox, if it is used in a rigorous way?

A book such as Tarelho's *Paranoïa et la théorie de la séduction généralisée* opens up interesting paths of investigation in this area.[9] Can someone be 'possessed' by the messages that he fails to translate? It is here, in my view, that a major set of problems is posed for psychoanalytic psychopathology.

---

9 Luiz Carlos Tarelho, *Paranoïa et la théorie de la séduction généralisée* (Paris: Presses Universitaires de France, 1999).

Three Meanings of the Term 'Unconscious'

Towards a Unified Theory of the Apparatus of the Soul

IV.1 The Freudian model of the 'apparatus of the soul' is a normal-neurotic model. Confronted more and more in their practice with cases deviating from this model (limit cases, psychoses, mental illnesses, perversions) a large number of theoreticians have *put to one side* the Freudian conception, founded on repression and the unconscious, as being relevant only to a small number of cases. They have then constructed other models *alongside* the Freudian edifice, without seeking to keep a consistency with Freudian thought. Furthermore, these models are, most of the time, desexualised, and they scarcely make use of the notion of the unconscious. It is as if, in another theoretical register, faced with different aspects of the world, one were to propose two perfectly distinct cosmologies, each without communication with the other.

IV. 2 On what basis does the general theory of seduction propose a unitary view, subsuming the so called separate models of normal-neurotic and borderline-psychotic functioning?

a) by referring them to a common basis in the fundamental anthropological situation and the translational hypothesis;

b) by recalling that the untranslated, the unconscious enclave, is not the exclusive result of a single radical failure of translation. Indeed we should remember that in the model of neurosis the translation process always happens *in two moments*, the first being that of the latent dimension of the other's message in an untranslated state, in waiting, an actual state of 'sub-conscious' inscription, without having yet been "understood and interpreted."[10] There would exist, therefore, not only in the infant but in all human beings, a *stock of untranslated messages*: some practically impossible to translate, others temporarily in waiting for translation. Translation can only be got under way by a reactivation, a reactualisation. This unconscious enclave can therefore be a place of stagnation, but

---

10 "Remembering, Repeating and Working Through", op.cit., p. 149.

also a place of waiting, a kind of 'purgatory' of messages in waiting.

IV. 3   It is pertinent to recall here Freud's description, in his article on the splitting of the ego, of the existence side by side in the same individual of two mechanisms: the neurotic mechanism of repression (*Verdrangung*) and the perverse or psychotic mechanism of disavowal (*Verleugnung*). I would propose, following Christophe Dejours, to generalise to all human beings what Freud describes as being present only in certain individuals.[11]

IV. 4   The psychic life of all human beings can be understood to consist of two parts, each ignorant of the other but with pathways between them. Between these parts the border fluctuates from one individual to another and, at different epochs of life, within the same individual. The frontier of this splitting, a vertical frontier in relation to the 'horizontal' barrier of repression, isn't a site of conflict but, as with Freud's account, a separation between two 'processes of defence'. Furthermore, this frontier can be crossed, for example when a new process of translation is triggered off. [see figure 2.1]

In the case of the normal-neurotic, part A is very much larger than B. It is the reverse with the non-neurotic. But, as Dejours underlines, in certain circumstances the right-hand side (B) can take the upper hand: "no subject is totally sheltered from somatisation or from delirium, even if certain structures are better protected than others" (ibid. p. 95).

IV. 5   In repression, and specifically in primal repression, the messages of the other come from the sole reality for the human being, *the reality of the other*. They come in a first moment and are inscribed in the unconscious or 'sub-conscious' enclave, and are then taken up again, translated and henceforth divided between a preconscious translation and its repressed unconscious remainders. [see figure 2.2]

---

11 Christophe Dejours, *Le corps, d'abord* (Paris: Payot, 2001 [orig. 1986]), pp. 39–117.

Three Meanings of the Term 'Unconscious'

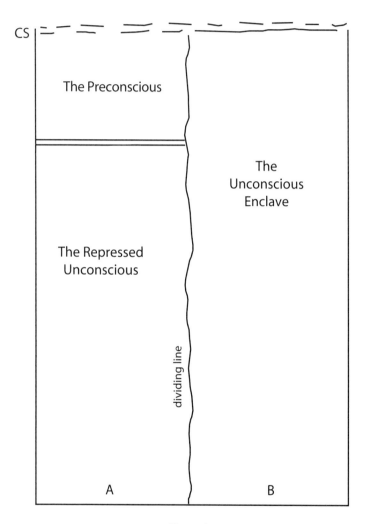

Figure 1

Three Meanings of the Term 'Unconscious'

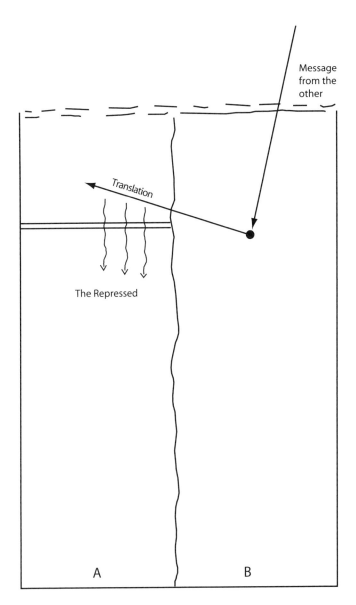

Figure 2

IV. 6   Once these two parts A and B have been postulated, how can one reconcile the idea, on the one hand, of a "mutual ignorance" (Dejours, p. 98) between two parts that are separated by the borderline of a split, and, on the other, the possibility of a phenomenon of communication, of communicating vessels on either side? We refer here to the productive developments of Christophe Dejours, who appeals to what he calls a "zone of sensitivity of the unconscious" (p. 97), and above all to the mechanisms of working through in dreams.[12]

To return to the topographical model common to both neurosis and psychosis, this has the major advantage of proposing a frame of reference to situate a double problem: the possibility of a new translation of the 'inserted' messages [*messages enclavés*], notably in the psychotherapy of borderline or psychotic cases, and, conversely, the possibility in all human beings (even if it is a weak one) of a delirious instability.

Let us note, furthermore, in another domain, that the classic treatment of neuroses, by its main action of *detranslation*, has the effect of temporarily enriching the stock of messages to be retranslated, resymbolised. What is interpreted must therefore pass again through part B of the schema, before being reintegrated into a richer preconscious.

Translation and Neo-code: the Mytho-Symbolic Order

V. 1   Confronted with adult messages that are compromised by the unconscious and are therefore enigmatic, untranslatable by the only means at his disposal (the relational codes which belong to the order

---

[12] For my part, both with and after others, I have tried to describe a creative function of the dream, by conceiving of the dream not just as an expression but as a 'crucible' of the unconscious, a crucible of working though and neo-creation by the sexual unconscious; see Jean Laplanche, *Problématiques* V: *Le Baquet* (Paris: Presses Universitaires de France, 1987), p. 197–210. The same aim can be found in my essay, "Dream and Communication", in this volume.

of attachment, self-preservation), the *infans* must seek for new codes. But he doesn't invent these from nothing. Very soon he has codes, preformed narrative schemas, within reach in his general cultural (and not only familial) environment. One could speak here of a veritable 'aid to translation' offered by the surrounding culture.[13]

V. 2   What is called the universe of the 'mytho-symbolic' intervenes here, including, as well as those classic codes of the Oedipus complex, the 'murder of the father' and the 'castration complex', the more modern narrative schemas, partly related to the previous ones but partly innovatory.

The mistake of psychoanalysis in relation to the mytho-symbolic is double.

First, there is the attempt to include among the truths that it has effectively discovered (concerning the 'apparatus of the soul' and the intersubjective situation of the adult-infant couple) and which are 'metapsychological' truths, the more or less contingent schemas of narration which enable human beings in a cultural situation to put their destiny into an order, a history. This is very much the case with the Oedipus complex, which, however general it may be (with numerous variations), isn't a universal characteristic of the human, as it is not necessarily present in the fundamental anthropological situation.

Second, there is the attempt, more or less explicitly, to index the myths according to the psychosexual evolution of the individual. One generally lists together as formations of the unconscious: symptoms, bungled actions, jokes, etc ... and myths. But myths are not a production or even a sketch of individual evolution. They are part of the cultural universe, where they can be observed, described and possibly explained.

On the other hand, psychoanalysis must not abandon the attempt to give an account of the *intervention* of the mytho-symbolic

---

13 The idea of an 'aid to translation' has been proposed and developed by Francis Martens (verbal communication, *Journées Jean Laplanche*, Lanzarote, August, 2003).

in the constitution of the human psychical apparatus and particularly in the model of translation, which is one of its essential mechanisms.

V. 3   Among ethnologists, the description and theorisation of myths that have been elaborated for some decades now begin principally with the thought of Lévi-Strauss. The notion of a code has become more and more productive. Myth works by offering a code, or perhaps a plurality of codes. They are mutually convertible, beginning with simple logical schemes.[14] Each of them is readable from the point of view of the others, but in itself, without any interpretation, it remains opaque. The meaning is latent so that one cannot say finally that any one myth reveals a final, ultimate meaning.

One can make two major objections in particular to the ethnologists, especially the students of mythology:

a) they proclaim their wish not to be called 'anthropologists', while very often they confine themselves to very particular sectors of the human condition , namely the so-called 'primitive societies', thus leaving to one side contemporary societies and their own very specific myths;[15]
b) another limitation is that they confine themselves to the adult universe, without ever investigating the manner in which mytho-symbolic thought is offered and communicated to the child, even the *infans*.

V. 4   The ethnologists closest to psychoanalysis most often only retain those aspects of it that fit in with their framework. They privilege those aspects closest to symbolism, those conceived as universal

---

14 Claude Lévi-Strauss, *The Savage Mind*, trans. John and Doreen Weightman (London: Wiedenfield and Nicholson, 1966), and *The Jealous Potter*, trans. Bénédicte Chorier (Chicago and London: Chicago University Press, 1988).
15 Modern myths such as that of the 'proletariat', or more recently that of the 'star', leave nothing to be desired for complexity and efficacy in comparison with 'the epic of Asdruval'.

in nature, rather than the associative-dissociative method, which has the individual psychoanalytic treatment as its field of application. It is in this restricted sense that they are ready to speak of the 'unconscious', when they discover a readability proper to myths, using perhaps some psychoanalytic 'keys', but without having to overcome any censorship or repression, and without having recourse to any other than intellectual means. In this they approximate to the manner in which Freud described the domain of symbolism and myth, a domain in which it is legitimate to read myth 'as an open book', for there is no need of the *analytic* method to access it.

Such a conception of psychoanalysis isn't so far removed from the current Vulgate concerning the unconscious: it is a question of a *hidden meaning*, whether universal or trans-individual, which one can access without too much effort, other than being a little informed. The Oedipus and castration flourish in these writings whether they be in the media or more so-called specialist works. The 'realism of the unconscious', such as I have sought to recover in Freud, has given place to a universal readability of certain grand mythic schemas of understanding.

For Freud, however, the 'symbolic method' never substitutes for the individual associative method: it complements it. However, as this 'complementarity' is not adequate in my view, I intend to offer an alternative mode of articulating the two methods.

V. 5   I am far from refusing the idea of the implicit (which others would perhaps call the 'unconscious') in the domain of the mytho-symbolic. Myths are interpreted in terms of each other, as are symbols.[16] It is a question of a universal reversibility, which sometimes seems to be what Lévi-Strauss is saying, in which case there would be no question of a final interpretation. Only the totality of myths would permit

---

16 Lacan remarked that nothing would prevent a penis in the manifest content of a dream from referring to an umbrella in the latent content, as well as the reverse. See Jacques Lacan, *Écrits* , trans. Bruce Fink (New York and London: W.W. Norton), p. 594.

the uncovering of general structures, organising structures, referring for example to the container-contained opposition (*The Jealous Potter*), or to the notion of 'thirdness'.

Thus the conception of the individual repressed unconscious, such as I would maintain, does not exclude taking into consideration alongside it the notion of the *implicit,* which many other thinkers unwarrantably substitute for the Freudian unconscious. Whatever conception one may hold of the superimposition of codes in a mythic scenario, whether one admits a hierarchy of levels or not, it remains appropriate, nonetheless, to give a place, not to *another* unconscious, but to another kind of latency, which is common most noticeably in collective cultural productions. This latency is of the order of the implicit; the movement of its interpretation is that of an explication (*Auslegung*): a work that does not require the overcoming of resistances.

V. 6 What is in every case decisive for us is the way in which collective narrative structures – whatever their level of generality or, inversely, their concrete, anecdotal aspects – *are inscribed in the schema of the psychical apparatus.*

Contrary to general opinion, and especially to that of Freud who saw the oedipal relation as the 'kernel' of the unconscious, it is necessary to situate such structures *not on the side of the repressed but of the repressing*; not on the side of the sexual but of that which organises it, and finally desexualises it in the name of the laws of alliance, of procreation, etc. . . . There is nothing in the least sexual (in the original sense of the *Three Essays*) in the myth of Oedipus and the tragedy of Sophocles; nothing that speaks to us less of sexual jouissance or of the pursuit of sexual excitation.

The great narrative schemas, transmitted then modified by culture, come to help the human subject to process, that is to bind and to symbolise, or to translate, the messages, both enigmatic and traumatising, which come to him from the adult other. Very obviously this relation is indispensable for the human being's entry into his humanity.

Conclusion

To invoke the fundamental anthropological situation is to consider primarily the enigmatic message from the other and its translation.

From this point of departure, the word 'unconscious' can acquire three meanings, each corresponding to three elements referring to the schema of the apparatus of the soul.

The unconscious in the proper Freudian sense can only be *the repressed*, that is to say, in our terms, the remainder of the always imperfect translation of the other's message. It is in opposition to a preconscious ego, the domain in which, through the narration of its own history, a personality is constituted, a personality that contains the unconscious under pressure, while at the same time being infiltrated by it.

The *unconscious enclave* can be called 'sub-conscious', in that it is only kept latent by a thin layer of conscious defence. Composed of untranslated messages, it would be wrong to consider it as co-extensive with a psychotic part of the human being. A fuller examination allows us to distinguish – alongside what has truly undergone a radical failure of translation, and which would be unassimilable, pre-psychotic – some components of the message that are not yet translated, awaiting translation, and perhaps also detranslated messages awaiting a new translation. As well as a zone of stagnation, such an enclave would also be a zone of passage, of transit.

Finally, there is the pseudo-unconscious of the mythosymbolic that does not find its place in the *interior of the psychical apparatus*. It can be described as implicit: as to its origin, the structural and sociological dimensions are undecidable from a solely psychoanalytic viewpoint. Its *psychic function* must be distinguished from its nature and its historico-social genesis. This function, crucial for the little human being, is to furnish him early on with an 'aid to translation', so as not to leave him helpless, faced with the task of containing, symbolising, of 'processing' the adult messages that never cease to assail him, a task of narrating his history, both thanks to them and against them.

11

FOR PSYCHOANALYSIS AT THE UNIVERSITY[1]

In October 1994, after nineteen years, the journal *Psychanalyse à l'Université* ceased publication, not owing to an internal decision, but solely to the decision of the publisher. At the time, I wrote: "This experiment, which we are proud of having sustained for nineteen years, has been supported by a limited but faithful readership, and organized by an Editorial Committee whose choices were always marked by rigour when it came to judging what was serious, innovative and – not the least of virtues – readable in terms of style and thought. All of which are qualities that derive primarily – but by no means exclusively – from what is called, quite simply, the university spirit. Laying claim to the Freudian example, we have always understood that 'academic' and 'university' are terms that remain fundamentally opposed, and which only a pen dipped in venom and envy would care to confuse".

In one short page I announced even at that 'end' a 'sequel', and, it's worth noting, under the anticipated title of *La Recherche psychanalytique*.

It would be ten years before this project was reborn, and in the same place: the University of Paris VII. The very title of the

---

[1] First published in *La Recherche psychanalytique*, the journal of the psychoanalysis laboratory at the University of Paris VII, no. 1, 2004.

old journal rang out as a challenge, or at least as an affirmation that Psychoanalysis, at the University, must win back and maintain its merited position as an entirely distinct discipline. The history of the journal was marked by the parallel presence and the good fortune of Psychoanalysis at Paris VII.

The good fortune, that is, of the *Unité d'enseignement et de recherche (UER) des sciences humaines clinique*,[2] created amidst the fervour of 1968 and the emancipation of a clinical psychology inspired by Psychoanalysis (which must be constantly reclaimed) from what was then known as 'experimental' psychology (only the epithet has changed). Also the good fortune of a 'Psychoanalysis laboratory', which was immediately established, and which did not profess to unify but to enrich, and to do so by means of the passionate yet objective confrontation of different points of view. Finally, the good fortune of a doctoral programme in Psychoanalysis, which was attacked violently, and sometimes in bad faith, by those who thought they saw in it an 'institution' threatening their own, but which survived against all the odds. Beyond these specific institutional transformations, some major problematics came into play and remain present today. I shall cite just a few, which were the object of much debate.

1) Is psychoanalysis a scientific discipline? A branch of knowledge? Or, to put things a little less abruptly, is it open to discussion, to refutation, in the same way as are other university disciplines? It is true that nowadays the question may seem old-fashioned to some, inasmuch as the 'postmodernist' fashion goes so far as to deny the term 'knowledge' even to disciplines which have a much more rigorous appearance. Given that the notion of the 'rationally correct' is subject to mockery, how would the frequent reduction of psychoanalysis to one narrative schema among others, avoid ending up a vague hermeneutics, itself not so different from the 'anything goes' position so dear to someone like Feyerabend?

---

2 [*Trans.*: The Centre for Teaching and Research in the Clinical Human Sciences].

Personally, I have always maintained that the presence of psychoanalysis within the University is one guarantee among others of a rigorous confrontation of positions, of argumentation, of a taking up of clear positions, and even of refutation.

None of which is without difficulties, one of the most significant being the relationship between psychoanalysis and psychology. It may be a theoretical problem – the problem of the "unity of psychology", as Lagache put it[3] – but it is one that has very often been resolved on a simply pragmatic basis by including Psychoanalysis within university departments entitled 'Psychology'.

To explain in detail why psychoanalysis, even under the name of a 'Psychology of the unconscious', cannot be considered a branch of Psychology is beyond the scope of this short introduction. I shall give only the thrust of the argument. By a kind of reversal that 'turns the glove inside out', it is psychoanalysis – or more exactly that which is at the heart of psychoanalysis, enlarged sexuality – which reinvests the totality of psychic or psychological processes. What is referred to as Freud's 'pansexualism' (the fact that sexuality can be *found everywhere* even if it *is not everything*) corresponds to a legitimate 'panpsychoanalyticism': the primary processes, which are unconscious and sexual, work covertly within psychology, with the result that, at the level of the human being, psychology – the purported agent of 'inclusion' – is in fact invaded by what it purports to include. It is precisely this that drives and legitimates the undertaking of the psychoanalytic treatment.

Another way of 'relativising' psychoanalysis is to be found in the titles that collocate it with 'psychopathology'. In doing this, one blithely combines what is a specific mode of approach (even a 'doctrine', according to Freud) with one field of exploration among others. It is a discreet trick to effect a dilution. Even in Freud's day the first

---

3 Daniel Lagache, *L'unité de la psychologie: Psychologie expérimentale et psychologie clinique* (Paris: Presses Universitaires de France, 2004 [orig. 1949]).

publication (the *Jahrbuch*, an annual journal) was, in a concession to Jung, called the "*Jahrbuch* of research in psychoanalysis and psychopathology". As soon as Freud took back control of the journal after the break with Jung, it went back to being a "*Jahrbuch* of psychoanalysis".

2) More insidious still is the question of whether research at the University – doctoral dissertations, but also teaching seminars, etc. – can address clinical themes. The very simplistic objection is that since the University is not a site of clinical practice, it should limit itself to research that is 'theoretical', 'applied', and so on. But by the same token, where in the world are reflection and research on practice carried out in the same place as practice itself? Are societies and groups of analysts *as such* places of practice? Yet it is in such places, and rightly so, that clinical material is generally presented, commented on and discussed. One could also ask whether the very idea of a place in which research and practice are tightly connected (there are rare examples, such as the Tavistock Clinic in London) does not involve a practice that is reoriented toward some form of experimentation, which is quite contrary to the spirit of the psychoanalytic method. Psychoanalytic research is and will always remain at a distance from the clinical experience to which it relates, and so much the better. In this respect as in others, University research is in no way restricted or inferior. In any event, the place(s) where treatments take place will never be those in which we reflect on the treatments or on clinical phenomena in general.

All valid psychoanalytic reflection makes reference, in variable combinations, to four essential coordinates: the theoretical, the clinical, the extra-mural and the historical. There is no need to install couches or consulting rooms at the University for psychoanalytic observation and psychoanalytic experience to have a rightful place there.

3) Objections of this kind are sometimes augmented by another, which, in a certain way, goes back to the earliest period of psychoanalysis, not to say to Freud himself. Can one teach – and above all discuss and work collectively with – others who are not 'in

analysis'? This is an objection that I have tried to put into perspective, and even to refute, from the time of my earliest seminars, notably during the seminar of December 14, 1971.[4] There, I developed the following argument: "We postulate, of necessity, that communication between us is potentially possible because, potentially, it is possible for one to communicate with oneself, that is, with one's own unconscious" (ibid. p.154).

This argument does not take its principal support from the social aspect of analysis, but from "certain temporal structures regarding one's relation to oneself, the temporal categories which are justly brought to light by Freudian thought. To enumerate a few: 'repetition', the 'already-there', and 'afterwardness' – this last category, 'afterwardsness', above all, because it forms the basis for the very possibility of treatment, for it means that something can be reworked, acquire meaning belatedly, come back to life, and acquire truth in a different way. But if an afterwardsness is possible at the level of the treatment, it is based on the fact that there are other kinds of afterwardness, which are already there within the existence of each of us. In this limited but very precise sense, and without demagogy, all of you are in a situation of 'having been' and 'having to be' in analysis" (ibid. p. 155).

A little mischievously, I added: "The one category I would perhaps exclude is that of currently *being in it* ... As to the fact of being in analysis, going a certain number of times a week to lie down on a couch, I would say that if taken as a concrete stipulation, the Freudian requirement that one be in analysis if one is to understand any discourse about analysis, immediately turns against itself and against analysis. The requirement that one be in analysis emerges from every direction – in order that one may occupy a post within a clinic, in order that one may conduct psychotherapies, in order that one may attend closed seminars; so why not in order that one may attend this course?

---

4 *Problématiques I. L'angoisse* (Paris: Presses Universitaires de France, 1980) p. 153 ff.

Are you in analysis? Are you on a 'waiting list' (which is almost as good as being in analysis)? With whom? Is it a 'training' analysis or not?" (ibid. p. 154–5)

Here we can see another problem emerging: behind the enigma of 'being in analysis' in order to understand and discuss it, there emerges in a different light the requirement of having had a 'training' analysis on an accredited couch. In short, there is a constant slippage between teaching, research, personal analysis and … indoctrination. The proliferation of Societies, Associations and Institutes has changed nothing: it only reflects the proliferation of allegiances. Although it is not infallible, *the universality and the freedom of thinking* in the University constitute a certain antidote to this.

4) The next episode – in which the same protagonists played for the same stakes – was the creation of a 'Doctorate in Psychoanalysis'. This quickly gave rise to offense, with some claiming that the University intended it as a diploma in psychoanalytic practice. Yet these criticisms emanated from precisely the side (and from all directions: IPA as well as Lacanian) where what is considered the most important part of one's training – the personal analysis – must be framed institutionally, from its initiation through its trajectory and to its recognition by institutions which, while not being official, are all the more insidiously constraining. These are old questions, but ones that have been renewed in the recent debates where they have been re-engaged.

To finish, briefly: far from constituting a sort of institutional and official enclave, psychoanalytic research at the university is able to offer a double guarantee: the rigor and boldness of debate, and the recognition of an *epistemological field* that is rightfully independent. All of which, by a sort of paradox, constitutes a pledge of the *extraterritoriality of analytic practice* vis-à-vis *all* institutions.

Intervention in a Debate

12

**INTERVENTION IN A DEBATE
between
Daniel Widlöcher and Jacques-Alain Miller:
"The Future of Psychoanalysis"**[1]

This debate was published by Le Cavalier Bleu in 2004,[2] and was subsequently reviewed in a very detailed and precise way by Bernard Golse in *Le Carnet psy*.[3] I take the liberty of intervening because the debate touches on themes to which no one who is concerned with psychoanalysis today can remain indifferent.

The Psychotherapies

As Golse rightly emphasises, this aspect of the debate has not been tackled in depth. Daniel Widlöcher touches on the matter apropos of the social demand for psychoanalysis and psychotherapy. Jacques-Alain Miller, if I understand him correctly, touches on it apro-

---
1 First published in *Le Carnet psy*, no. 96, February 2005.
2 *L'avenir de la psychanalyse: débat entre Daniel Widlöcher and Jacques-Alain Miller* (Paris: Le Cavalier Bleu, 2004).
3 no 94, November 2004, pp. 13–16.

pos of the cultural danger of that demand. However, neither one risks distinguishing firmly between psychotherapy and psychoanalysis. Yet the distinction is simple, if one merely refers to what is specific to the Freudian invention: *analysis*. Psychoanalysis furnishes itself with the means of dissociating, of *unbinding* [*délier*] the ties that uphold conscious discourse, our personality (our ego), our symptoms, the ideologies that orient how we tell ourselves our own histories. This allows something to manifest itself, something we repress and which to a large extent governs our lives: the repressed sexual unconscious.

Conversely, psychotherapy – *the psychotherapies that have existed for as long as man has been man* – seeks to *rebind*, to reassemble, to synthesise whatever, arising from our unconscious fantasies, makes dominant within us the unbinding whose most extreme form is the death drive.

So we have:

— what has always existed and still exists today: psycho*therapies* of the most diverse kinds; shamanistic, supportive, containing and persuasive psychotherapies, counselling, cognitive therapy, etc.; all diverse paths towards cohesion that only confirm the ego's natural tendency towards synthesis;

— since Freud, psycho*analysis*, whose axis is the reverse principle: namely, the *unbinding* that aims to bring out something of the buried unconscious. But psychoanalytic practice does not consist of analysis alone. The movement of unbinding and the ineluctable tendency towards rebinding coexist within it side by side (Freud uses the image of a chemical entity that always tends to reunify itself after its elements have been separated).[4] The tendency towards binding is the work of the analysand, and ordinarily the analyst has no need to bring into play his own choices (his own ideologies) in this work. This psychotherapeutic aspect exists, in the most varied proportions, within every psychoanalysis. But the situation is in fact more complex

---

4 "Lines of Advance in Psycho-Analytic Therapy" (1919a), *SE* 17, p. 161, n 1.

still, for there are cases in which the analyst has no choice but to make binding interventions: for instance, if the patient is, as they say, 'completely unhinged'.[5]

Thus, simply put, our distinction is directed not at two techniques that are susceptible to being categorised separately, but at two dimensions that may coexist within a single practice. A little further on we shall come to how this allows us to characterise Lacanian practice.

The Instrumentalisation of the Countertransference

There is a mystification around this which can be very exactly dated to 1950 and the initial article written by a misguided psychoanalyst, Paula Heimann.[6]

This illusion is related to the increasing neglect to which the Freudian *unconscious* is subject. For one can hardly advocate the analyst's 'use' of his countertransference in the treatment if one holds firmly to the notion that the countertransference pertains to the register of the unconscious, a register to which the analyst can only gain access with great difficulty. But from the moment one assimilates to the unconscious (which is perhaps the least 'subjective' thing within us) all the analyst's reactions in the course of the treatment (affects, thoughts, acts) the field is open to what is banally referred to as the 'transference-countertransference' dynamic. To break up this *false reciprocity* it is sufficient to point out that a patient has *one* transference (an unconscious transference towards his analyst) whereas we maintain without raising an eyebrow that the psychoanalyst has 5, 10 or 15 countertransferences towards his patients, countertransferences that he would change – as the surgeon does his scrubs – for each new ses-

---

5 [*Trans*: There is a play on the word binding {*liante*} here. The colloquial idiom *fou à lier* literally means 'mad enough to need binding or tying up'].
6 Paula Heimann, "On Counter-Transference", *International Journal of Psycho-Analysis*, 1950, vol. 31, pp. 81–4.

sion of the day. Fifteen 'transference-countertransference' dynamics, which is rather a lot for just one man or one woman!

This transference-countertransference mess has affinities with the so-called intersubjective practices that we hear about endlessly (reciprocity, self-disclosure, etc.).[7] Ferenczi confronted the question – not without getting himself burnt, but at least he approached it seriously – with the notion of 'mutual analysis', which he ultimately maintained could only take place between *two* people, and not between a single analyst and several patients.

It should also be noted that among more than one committee or inner circle tasked with evaluating a future colleague a little countertransferential 'touch' will always get a warm welcome. One colleague will allude to the death of his mother during the analysis of his patient, another to a traffic accident that he witnessed just before the session. The committees always fall for this; and yet it is nothing but a matter of insubstantial allusions to conscious or preconscious events or affects experienced by the analyst during the treatment. Where is the unconscious in all this? The candidate will, moreover, be careful not to communicate anything further about his associations to or investigations of such affects and events.

One can only deplore the fact that the 'handling of the countertransference' has almost become a 'shibboleth' within the most widespread circles, the very ones in which the word 'unconscious' is articulated least.

The Debate on the Countertransference

Let us exclude from this debate about the countertransference what Golse calls *"the nature of psychoanalytic listening"*[8] and what

---

7 [*Trans*: 'self-disclosure' in English in the original].
8 Golse, op. cit., p. 14.

Widlöcher calls "co-thinking". Widlöcher tells us that "co-thinking", "shared associative work", *"implies the countertransference"*,⁹ and one is inclined to believe him. I have no wish to depreciate this exploration of a parallel or complementary movement of associations between the analysand and the analyst. But the rule of 'evenly suspended attention' – whose very wording refers us to the 'well-tempered' (*gleichschwebende*), i.e., 'balanced' musical scale – does not always seem to be in accord with this kind of preconscious accompaniment. On the contrary, it often underlines and accentuates what the patient is inclined to leave in the shadows. In short, it too operates in the service of unbinding and does not always correspond with the picture of two thought processes that are perfectly in tune.

The Short, Foreshortened or Scanned Session

Here my position is clear, even though my grounds would not be the same as those of Widlöcher. In a word: the short session is a psychotherapeutic practice.

a) The short session, whose duration is subject solely to the good will of the 'analyst', does not permit the free development of associations, and thus does not permit *analysis*. It submits the patient to a constraint that must put pressure upon the course taken by his thoughts: what will I say of any importance, and how will it be judged by my 'analyst'? We have few accounts of short sessions. In contrast we have numerous reports from sessions with a normal and contractual duration. In the latter, one can follow the movements, the different libidinal movements, the defences, the inflection provoked by an intervention from the analyst – in short, a whole dynamic in which the unconscious sometimes surfaces.

b) To characterise the analyst, Lacan introduced the 'subject

---

9 Miller and Widlöcher, op. cit., p. 47; emphasis added.

supposed to know' – such a beautiful formula! Alas! Things have changed greatly since then, for the 'analyst' is 'the one who knows' – period! Whether or not he knows by means of the 'matheme' is of little importance. In any case, one only needs to prick up one's ears to realise that in certain psychiatric services the diagnosis of 'foreclosure of the name of the father' is used in everyday practice, and means that the patient should be directed down the path of medication without any concern for listening, for dialogue or psychotherapy.

As Jacques-Alain Miller emphasises, 'knowledge' is no less implicated within individual Lacanian practice, and here too it is not subject to appeal: the decision to interrupt the session and the word on which to interrupt it.

c) The 'short-session analyst' not only *knows* the 'Structure' and the Unconscious, he *knows* the Law and the Symbolic. The repeated blows of interruption to the session ("cut!" as the film director says) can only be understood as the enforcement of Castration, based on the imposition of the arbitrary and tyrannical Law of the Father. Could there be a more violent – not to say effective – instrument of binding than the Law and its privileged declaration, "thou shalt be castrated"? It is in this sense that the practice of short, scanned, arbitrary sessions seems to me to bring us back to the *normative*, and, as such, to a mode of psychotherapy: it aims to impose upon the patient a certain ideology.

In two words:

— in opposition to *a certain* conception that is pervasive in the IPA we must be wary of the 'transference-countertransference' theme, which negates the asymmetry essential to the treatment.

— in opposition to (*certain*?) Lacanians it must be understood that the short session is an instrument for the enforcement of the 'Law', towards normative and psychotherapeutic ends.

Levels of Proof

13

LEVELS OF PROOF[1]

I suggested the slightly austere "Levels of Proof" as a title simply because Bertrand Hanin asked me for one. But permit me to give this presentation the form of a wider ranging talk, rather than holding me to that restricted theme, though it will come up at a certain point. I speak first and foremost in honour of Daniel Widlöcher who has for years deepened the theme of 'debate in psychoanalysis', which is essential. Before listening to the introductory talks I was asking myself once again whether those of us who still speak about debate are not dinosaurs. Every day the mail floods us with programmes for congresses, meetings and conferences on the most tempting themes – classic as well as new – yet one can see that for the most part there is no real question of debate. Even when what is proposed are 'roundtables', they are not really roundtables; the talks are parallel and never come into contact with each other; and, finally, the time given for discussion is minimal. But it doesn't matter. Speakers do not try to convince each other; they come, they do their thing and then leave.

Is this what's called postmodernism? I agree with the idea

---

1 Delivered at *Débat en Psychanalyse*, the sixth colloquium organized by the APEP (Association psychanalyse et psychothérapies), the CHU Pitié-Salpêtrière and the Association de santé mentale, Thursday, March 10, 2005. Discussion opened by Professor Daniel Widlöcher.

235

that the truth remains always out of sight, but on the other hand this doesn't mean that 'anything goes', as Feyerabend put it in a depressing phrase.²

Shall I say a word or two about truth? I have no need of a capital 'T' in order to speak about it, but truth is nevertheless at the heart of debate. Let's say truth or simply reason, a certain discursive coherence. This requirement of coherence is applicable not only to the so-called hard sciences but also, if one wants to engage effectively in debate, to the human sciences. The 'hard' sciences are frequently invoked in connection with the 'uncertainty principle'. But one would be quite wrong to use this as a weapon in the service of irrationalism or relativism; for the uncertainty principle is itself mathematized; it is itself something argued through and refutable precisely by virtue of being a principle. Even if it asserts an uncertainty in the object (or in the observation of the object – the debate remains open) the *affirmation of the uncertainty principle* is a rational affirmation, which does not present itself as being uncertain.

Psychoanalysis can often get bogged down in an excessive transposition of relativism into our own domain. "Your transference as against mine", says one; "your mother as against mine", says another. This is the tendency that for my part I call 'postmodern', and that has become breathless in its horror of 'the theoretically correct'.

Not that there is no debate these days; but, it must be said clearly, debate is dominated by the media. Of course we have our groups, our seminars, our private meetings, but ultimately the real debate takes place in the media. Here, two points return consistently: one concerns therapy as a 'technology', the other concerns the question of normativity. As to therapy as a technology, it seems to me that our predecessors bear the greatest responsibility, and did so from the moment when the official organizations – I am thinking particularly

---

2 Paul Feyerabend, *Against Method* (London: Verso, 2010 [orig. 1975]).

of the International Psychoanalytic Association – agreed to modify Freud's own position, which defined psychoanalysis above all as method and as science, before defining it as a therapy. From that moment the therapeutic aim has been made the primary goal. We are *de jure* an association of practitioners. This moves us away from the scientific goal of truth, which was Freud's constant goal. With my experience as a translator, since I am immersed in Freud's original terminology, I simply point to the German term *Erfolg*, which can mean 'success' or 'result'. Thus an *Erfolg* may be an adverse result. One could say, as one did in old French, *cette aventure a eu un succès déplorable* ["this venture has had an unfortunate outcome/'success'"]. Which means – and Freud himself testifies to this – that any kind of 'tendentiousness', even the tendentiousness which claims that this or that is the correct procedure for therapy, is alien to Freud. At least, it is not his major concern. If psychoanalysis wishes to be *a part of the scientific community*, where I believe it certainly belongs,[3] it must accept that there are some propositions without any practical consequences. There are results of our work which are failures from the point of view of a certain norm of healing, of happiness, even of life. The theory of gravitation, to refer to Newton, is verified by a bridge that collapses just as much as by one which stays up; and yet none of us escapes this fascination with the technology of therapy. This includes those who, in France, have succeeded in inscribing psychoanalysis in the corpus of psychotherapies and, in doing so, have only extended the general aim of the International Psychoanalytic Association; and it includes, on the other hand, those who claim to represent 'absolute knowledge' by the ways of the matheme. In this manner they have succeeded – I am referring to the current situation, which everyone can confirm – they have succeeded by means of an outcry in having a Government Minister censor the text of a report, which was published on the inter-

---

3 Cf. Jean Laplanche, "La psychanalyse dans la communauté scientifique", in *Entre séduction et inspiration: l'homme* (Paris: Quadridge/Presses Universitaires de France, 1999), pp. 173–188.

net, on the evaluation of psychotherapies.[4] I haven't read this report, I cannot judge its worth; but it is astonishing that the problem of truth should be resolved by an outcry, by an assembly, so we're told, of a thousand psychoanalysts. Censorship, pure and simple, takes the place of argument and debate.

The other offshoot of this current debate – a media 'debate', to be sure, but a debate all the same – is the issue of *normativity*. I shall simply offer one thought about this: psychoanalysts are now invited to give their judgment on all the current social issues. Which psychoanalysts? one might ask. They are *ex-officio* members on all the committees on ethics, violence, civil marriages, cloning, homophobia, etc. In each instance they intervene in the name of a norm, and it must be said that the norm to which they return is a Lacanian norm, which passes as the psychoanalytic point of view. The Symbolic, the Name of the Father, the Law. Psychoanalysis is reduced not to the ten commandments but to two or three. Psychoanalysis becomes a sort of Law of the social.

Freud says repeatedly that bias is quite alien to him. All "tendentiousness [*Tendenz*]" – this is his word – is alien to him.[5]

After these excursions into therapy as a 'technology' and normativity, I return to what is the central concern for me today, a problem at a tangent to that of *debate* – the problem of *scientificity*, of verification or proof: 'psychoanalysis in the scientific community'. Although I don't have time to go into detail, I allude here to what we might call the parallel trajectories of Freud and Popper. These two men of genius, even if one doesn't measure the genius of one against the other, are at cross-purposes to an incredible extent. There is a lack of awareness on the side of Freud, who I don't think ever cited Popper; and on Pop-

---

4 [*Trans.*: The report to which Laplanche is referring was published in February 2004 by the Institut nationale de la santé et de la recherche médicale (INSERM), and was deeply critical of psychoanalysis. The report was initially published on a Government website but subsequently withdrawn from it, allegedly under pressure from certain figures in the French psychoanalytic community].
5 "On Narcissism: An Introduction" (1914c), *SE* 14, p. 89.

per's side there is misunderstanding. One of Popper's most important works is *Conjectures and Refutations*.[6] A *conjecture* is a model that is devised to account for observed facts, which are themselves already partially constructed on the basis of other, pre-existing models. As such, for Popper science is never drawn from facts, is *never inductive.* Here, Popper takes up Hume's old argument about habit. I leave my office, I open the door. I go into the adjacent room. I can open the door a hundred times, a thousand times, ten to the power of ten or however many times, and I will always come out on a floor. What would happen if one day the door opened onto the void? Nothing permits the assertion that the door will not, one day, open onto the void. This is the proposition that Hume and Popper defend with vigour. *Induction cannot lead* to a certainty. One can speak of statistics, but no law is 'statistically true'. One cannot say, "This is 95% true." One must say: it is 100% true that this phenomenon will happen 95% of the time. Which is very different. There is no such thing as statistical truth and the attempt to rebuild induction on the basis of statistics is a logical fallacy.

However, Popper does not embrace the notion of an absolute truth in the Platonic or any other sense. On the contrary, for him the only truth is a provisional, even imaginary truth. He starts from the idea of 'conjecture' – subsequently taken up under the names of 'model' or 'paradigm' – as something that remains provisional until it is refuted, falsified. Is this so far away from Freud? There are certain fragments of epistemology in Freud. There is the familiar passage in "Instincts and their Vicissitudes" in which Freud focuses more perhaps on concepts than on the relations between them, and in which the concepts are considered provisional. When they are no longer adequate, he says, we change them. In contrast to Popper, he formulates things in terms of inadequacy rather than refutation. The idea that one day the theory will be contradicted by what is observed:

---

6 Karl Popper, *Conjectures and Refutations: The Growth of Scientific Knowledge* (London: Routledge: 1963).

this aspect is sometimes present in Freud. It is interesting to detect the rudiments of Popperian thought in Freud. Think, for example, of the title of a text that is single-handedly Popperian in its implicit programme, "A Case of Paranoia Running Counter to the Psycho-Analytic Theory of the Disease". Whatever the fate and the truth of this text, its purpose is to test a falsification of a theory, in Popper's sense, within a case of paranoia – a case of female paranoia in which the underlying homosexuality had not been apparent.

Here, though, the following question might be posed: if the case really did contradict the theory, would everything collapse? Would the whole of metapsychology come crashing down? Here is where the question of the levels of statements and the coherence of theories arises. It is true that in Popper as well as Freud one sometimes encounters an absolutism that may lead one to believe that 'the throne and the altar' ultimately depend on a certain number of shibboleths, such that the refutation of one small point of the metapsychology might imperil the entire system. This is clear in Popper because he takes the Einsteinian revolution as his model. Yet this revolution is actually a very unusual case, where ultimately a single experiment, that of Michelson and Morley, was the origin of the falsification of Newtonian theory. But is it the case that things always happen this way? I think not; and along with many epistemologists who have followed up Popper's thought, developing and nuancing it, I accept that there are intermediate levels between what one might call 'psychoanalytic doctrine', to use Freud's term, or general metapsychology, and something I shall shortly call the 'mytho-symbolic'. Between these two levels there are the intermediate levels of theories of conflict, of psychopathology, of symptoms, of *Witz*, etc., even the theory of dreams. Would a modification of the theory of dreams necessarily entail a falsification of the whole of metapsychology? I don't think so.

You see that the idea of a theory that is ultimately supple and open to reworking, a theory containing on the one hand a relatively dense kernel and on the other hand statements that are not deduced from the general theory, is valid not only for psychoanalysis but for every science. So, a hard kernel, a suppler periphery. What would be the hard kernel of psychoanalysis for which we could claim to devise (is this possible?) Popperian procedures? No mistake, what causes scandal today, the hard kernel, what's constantly being left to one side, is infantile sexuality, the unconscious and the paths of access to it, and repression. These may well be objects, but above all they are constructed models and their centre is the infantile sexuality that Freud first formulated in the *Three Essays* (1905). I cite a short passage from the *Three Essays*, which involves some simple epistemology:

> The direct observation of children has the disadvantage of working upon data which are easily misunderstandable; psycho-analysis is made difficult by the fact that it can only reach its data, as well as its conclusions, after long détours. But by co-operation the two methods can attain a satisfactory degree of certainty in their findings.[7]

You can see the image of a tunnel being dug from both ends and by way of rigorous understanding. I emphasize this because it is not simply a question of 'observation'; it is observation itself that must be *understood* – on the one hand the observation of infants, and on the other hand psychoanalytic experience.

All of which seems simple, and yet what a concatenation of discord is thus created. Prominent among the voices are the categorical positions for or against *the psychoanalytic observation of children*, that is, for or against one end of the tunnel. In his 1979 article "L'enfant modèle" (I don't think he has changed his opinion on the subject), André Green immediately contrasts two types of science: 'sciences of

---

7 *Three Essays on the Theory of Sexuality* (1905d), *SE* 7, p. 201.

observation' and 'sciences of interpretation'.[8] Things start out from an epistemological dilemma of the most radical kind. The Popperian epistemological sequence, which would be *observation, conjecture, refutation*, is displaced into an opposition between 'observation' and 'interpretation'. An opposition which itself corresponds to two forms and domains of knowledge: on the one hand, psychological knowledge of the child, observations devoted to what is purely 'perceptible'; and on the other hand, psychoanalytic knowledge of the adult, which would be the domain of representation and interpretation.

I am revisiting this question because it is important to reject this opposition between the science of observation and the science of interpretation, which is posed as a general opposition pertinent to all knowledge, and not specifically to psychoanalysis. First of all, apropos of *observation*, there is *no such thing as* a science of observation, not even observation of the stars. Observation functions only if guided by conjecture. The idea of direct observation is a poor one in respect of nurslings just as much as galaxies. There is no observation that is not oriented by hypotheses: there is no domain of pure observation. Even the observation of the stars by the ancients presupposed reference points, charts, suppositions, conjectures.

Thus Green places into one bag psychology, child psychology and an empiricism that operates without reference to any principle. Yet modern psychology, such as that of Stern or Dornes, can only function when supported by conjectures that often are quite elaborate. What he places in opposition to this are the sciences of *interpretation*. But here the ambiguity becomes total, since 'interpretation' is a word with which psychoanalysis is well acquainted. Is it really psychoanalytic interpretation that is at stake here? Psychoanalysts interpret in their practice; but they have never wanted to make that interpretation – psychoanalytic interpretation – the path of science. For example,

---

[8] André Green, "L'enfant modèle", in *Nouvelle revue de psychanalyse,* 1979, vol. 19.

one cannot say that the Freud's metapsychology – the first or the second topography for example – is the result of an 'interpretation' in the psychoanalytic sense of the term. It is a *conjecture* in Popper's sense. Yet, by a slippage of meaning, Green gets very near to maintaining that that psychoanalysts who treat adults would constitute a model for science because they think by interpretation: conjecture, construction, scientific hypothesis.

This debate is important. It has been somewhat distorted by Freud and by all those who, a little imprudently at certain moments, have spoken of the *direct* observation of the child as a scientific finding.

In my opinion, the central problems of psychoanalysis remain the unconscious and the paths of access to it (for Freud this is the very definition of psychoanalysis), and the position and genesis of infantile sexuality or, if one prefers, of the sexual drive. I speak of infantile sexuality in the sense of the *Three Essays*, that is to say in the sense of what I call the '*sexual*'[9] beyond the 'sexed', beyond the difference between the sexes and beyond even the diversity of genders.

It is interesting to read the *Three Essays* of 1905. Once separated from the later additions, the original essays emerge as a composite being, an enigmatic sphinx, which is often ambiguous and sometimes contradictory. Nevertheless, these essays are consistent in their affirmation of the notion of an *enlarged sexuality* – the major problem that is also the most denied and the most repressed, even though we sometimes dedicate study days to it. Freud begins his "Second Essay" with two subchapters, entitling the first "Neglect of the Infantile Factor" and the second "Infantile Amnesia". This immediately underlines the repression that affects not only the child with respect to his own sexuality, but also the adult parent and the adult observer. If we take account of this neglect of the infantile factor and take account

---

9 [*Editor*: On Laplanche's French neologism 'sexual' (as distinct from the normal 'sexuel'), see the Editor's note to the Forward of this volume. The term is printed here in italics to mark it off from the standard English term with the same spelling].

of infantile amnesia, what we discover is not the root of attachment theory, but the root of its hypertrophy and its tendency to occupy the entire domain of the infantile. My concern is not that attachment theory should have no place in this domain, but that it takes up all the space. Infantile sexuality is, for its part, watered down and barely mentioned. If paediatric and perinatal specialists overrun the whole field – albeit with certain concepts that have a psychoanalytic flavour, such as 'drive' or 'attachment drive' – some psychoanalysts would, for their part, be ready to abandon the whole field to these theoreticians of attachment, since, according to a certain conception, infantile sexuality is only a retrospective projection into the past by the adult (a re-signification, as it's sometimes called).

I do not have the time to dwell upon this distorted conception of afterwardsness as a matter of pure back-projection. The notion of afterwardsness is completely transformed when one assumes a particular point of view that seems to have been neglected by everyone, including Freud.[10] In Freud himself and among all those who have studied the child and the adult-child relationship, child and adult are always envisaged from the beginning and primarily in terms of a *succession*: the child is the antecedent of the adult, the prehistory of the adult; the adult regressively finds the child and the traces of the child within himself. The point I have tried to hammer home is that the child and the adult – before the first is the antecedent of the second, and before the second finds within himself the traces of the first – must be conceived by psychoanalysis as being from the beginning *simultaneous*, in *dialogue*, engaged in an *exchange of messages*. The adult *in the presence of* the child is an adult who sees re-burgeoning within himself all the pre-genital, partial sexuality that is aimed at partial excitations and pleasures. Here is how Freud in 1908 summarizes infantile sexuality as it emerges in the *Three Essays*: "in man the

---

10 Cf. Jean Laplanche, *Problématiques VI, l'après-coup* (Paris: Presses Universitaires de France, 2006).

sexual instinct does not originally serve the purposes of reproduction at all, but has as its aim the gaining of particular kinds of pleasure".[11]

I shall not unpack here my own 'conjecture' – the theory of messages that are compromised by the sexuality of the adult and then translated by the child. It is a theory of the genesis of the unconscious and of the genesis of the 'apparatus of the soul', which for me is at the heart of metapsychology.

What truth is there in what here must be named the 'general theory of seduction', what falsification is possible? Surely we are a long way from having found the means of falsifying Freud's first or even second topography, and no less so the theory of seduction as I propose it. But this is so *precisely to the extent that one is not in the position to consider the adult and the child as a simultaneous and asymmetrical couple*. Not an interaction but an asymmetry of communication. That is, to consider in particular the analysis of the parental adult (or caregiver) as being no less pertinent to the situation than conjectures about the genesis of the psyche of the child. This taking into consideration of the unconscious of the adult in the adult/child situation is what is lacking, and what will always be lacking, in the infinite developments of 'the experience of satisfaction' (nursing), which is habitually reduced to a single person: namely, the child.

How is it possible to set forth and perhaps refute or falsify a process that bears on messages (primarily nonverbal messages), their reception, their translation, and even the failure of this translation?

In a sense, observations, which are at once individual and collective, such as those of Roiphe and Galenson in *The Infantile Origins of Sexual Identity*,[12] show us one possible path. In any case they demonstrate that, in a given adult/child situation, it is a matter of putting conjectures to the test, and not of lining up meaningless 'observations'. Furthermore, where they fail somewhat is where it comes to conjecturing about

---

11 "'Civilised' Sexual Morality and Modern Nervous Illness" (1908d), *SE* 9, p. 188.
12 Herman Roiphe and Eleanor Galenson, *The Infantile Origins of Sexual Identity* (New York: International Universities Press, 1981).

the impact and the evolution of parental messages. Where they fail is precisely in the observation – by which I mean the psychoanalytic observation – of adults, the caregivers or the parents of these children.

I shall now return to the question of levels before coming back to the possibility of some kind of observation and conjecture about the processes leading to the formation of the 'apparatus of the soul'.

Popper showed us the way forward by opposing, somewhat schematically, the scientific and the metaphysical. The *scientific* is that which is susceptible to being falsified and indicates the paths of its possible falsification. The *metaphysical* is that for which no falsification is possible. Don't suppose that Popper devalues the metaphysical, however. He considers Darwinism, for example, to be a fruitful metaphysical system, some of whose consequences can themselves be falsified, but which as a system cannot. Since Popper's own writings, 'Popperism' has been significantly modified and improved. The all-or-nothing of great changes of system, such as Newton being eliminated by Einstein, is now considered to be exceptional. In fact, as I indicated above, in each theory there is most frequently a hard kernel – the most difficult to endanger – as well as an entire series of hypotheses subject to testing and falsification but whose refutation does not directly endanger the centre.

In psychoanalysis, this can be found in what I call levels of truth or of proof. I spoke of the intermediate level. I have already cited the example of the case of paranoia but I could give another example of the same level. Interestingly Freud employs the term "negative case" here. The discovery of a single "negative case" would permit bringing down a hypothesis. It comes up in respect of neurasthenia. In his early texts, Freud says: "neurasthenia is always caused by a genital dysfunction" (he is thinking essentially of masturbation), and "so far as the theory of the sexual aetiology of neurasthenia is concerned, there are no negative cases".[13] Here we are at what I would call an intermediate

---

13 "Sexuality in the Aetiology of the Neuroses" (1898a), *SE* 3, p. 269.

level: a psychoanalytic theory that does not, of course, call into question the hypothesis of the unconscious. In this we encounter something quite close to Popper, and above all to his successors.

We have thus discerned the existence of one or several intermediate levels, but the major opposition is the one between the two extreme levels, the opposition founded by the theory itself. There is *on the one hand* the Sexual Theory or the Metapsychology, the theory of the unconscious and its genesis, centred on infantile sexuality; and *on the other hand* there are the 'sexual theories' of children or adults. Yet Freud left a certain ambiguity – which some have rejoiced in – between the sexual theory of the *Three Essays*, which is the theory of the scientist, and the sexual theories of every individual, the theories that the individual creates for himself about his own existence and his own sexuality. We thus have psychoanalytic theory at one extreme, and at the other extreme the way in which the human being 'theorises himself', on the basis of messages from the other which he has to translate and which he must integrate by assimilating. The most conspicuous example in the article on "The Sexual Theories of Children"[14] is the castration complex, which is a way for the child to represent for itself in a 'story' or a narration the difference between the genders as communicated by the parental messages that assign gender to the child.[15]

The castration complex and the Oedipus complex are mythic theories that do not require proof. In Popper's terms, they belong to the level of metaphysics; what I call the 'mytho-symbolic' is presented to the human being largely by his cultural surroundings. Unfortunately, however, Freud ended up regarding the sexual theories of children – the apparatus best suited to repressing the unconscious – as the very kernel of the unconscious.

The strength of the theory of seduction consists in its ability to account for the non-scientific function of psychoanalytic myths. It is

---

14 (1908c), *SE* 9, pp. 209–26.
15 Cf. "Gender, Sex and the *Sexual*" in this volume.

thus necessary to situate the two Popperian levels carefully. Metapsychology is *scientific* in Popper's sense of the term. The mytho-symbolic is *narrative* and its principal function is both sublimatory and repressive, helping to give form to a personal history that is clearly of crucial importance for the human being.

There is no denying the difficulties for observation that could arise here – for the observation of what I call the fundamental anthropological situation. The latter requires conjoint rather than successive observation, psychoanalytic observation, psychoanalytic investigation of the adult-child dialogue in its entirety, and of the resurgence of infantile sexuality in the adult protagonist. It is important to underline that the adult in the situation of relating to an infant experiences a resurgence of his own infantile sexuality. Freud underlines this several times and everybody realises it.

We should, then, pay close attention to the two warnings Freud puts at the beginning of his "Second Essay" on sexual theory: "Neglect of the Infantile Factor" and "Infantile Amnesia". These are one and the same: the repression of the sexual.

Finding a joint methodology for the observation and interpretation of adult-child communication and its results would reopen the question of the "neglect of the infantile factor": is it the result of repression or an absence? I believe that a large part of so-called psychoanalytic child psychology – which has existed for decades and has taken on a new *élan* with 'attachment theory' – however scientific the psychology may be, must begin by questioning (and trying to eliminate) the repression of infantile sexuality in the adult and of course, above all, in the 'observer'.

14

THE *THREE ESSAYS* AND THE THEORY OF SEDUCTION[1]

The titles that I initially proposed for the present talk were eventually abandoned for the more traditional "The *Three Essays* and the Theory of Seduction". The titles that came spontaneously to mind were, "The *Three Essays* as Enigmatic Message" or "The *Three Essays* as Traumatism". You can see, then, that I count this work of Freud's, this episode in Freudian thought, as an event at the very heart of the 'theory of seduction' and of Freud's struggles with and against that theory.

In order to experience fully this 'enigmatic' or 'traumatising' aspect it is important to refer to the event of 1905 – that's to say, to the *first edition* of the *Three Essays*. In the French edition,[2] of which I am the scientific director, we have decided to mark with a continuous line in the margins all the passages dating from the subsequent editions: 1910, 1915, 1920, 1924. I advise you to do something similar with your own copy of the *GW* or the *SE*, then read it following just the 1905 version. The effect is startling, deeply disruptive. Everything

---

[1] Delivered at the congress of the Deutschen Psychoanalytischen Gesellschaft, Saarbrucken, 05/06/2005.

[2] *Sigmund Freud: Oeuvres complètes: Pscyhoanalysis*, Vol. VI, "Trois Essais de la théorie de la sexualité, dir. J. Laplanche, André Bourguignon, PIerre Cotet (Paris: Presses Universitaires de France, 2006).

that seems to be well known – the 'stages' of libidinal development, narcissism, the progressive evolution towards genital primacy – all of it has disappeared. We are left with a strange, even baroque text, but one that is nevertheless supported by solid fundamental ideas. First and foremost there is the incessant affirmation of infantile sexuality, with its particular characteristics – partial drives, erotogenic zones, leaning-on, etc. – and with its mysterious, if not insoluble economic problem: the difference between the pleasure of excitation and the pleasure caused by the reduction of tension. There is also the affirmation of original 'polymorphous perversity' and of its eventual integration into genital pleasure in the form of fore-pleasure. I pause here to emphasise that in the course of the text these fundamental themes are frequently resumed in a somewhat contradictory way. I shall return to this point: we are in the presence of an entity that is somewhat composite, an enigmatic and seducing sphinx. Don't suppose that the portions added in later editions will clarify things. They will only enable a historico-genetic schema to make a forcible entry into the text, linking the sexuality of the infant to that of the adolescent by a series of stages or 'organisations'. Freud does not, however, give himself the insurmountable task of remodelling the whole text as a consequence – as one can see, for example, at the beginning of the third chapter where an emphatic opposition is delineated between puberty and the whole anterior sexual life in which

> [t]he sexual drive has hitherto been predominantly auto-erotic … a number of separate drives and erotogenic zones … independently of one another have pursued a certain sort of pleasure as their sole sexual aim.[3]

---

[3] *Three Essays on the Theory of Sexuality* (1905d), *SE* 7, p. 207. Page numbers will henceforth be cited in parenthesis in the text. [*Trans*: the Standard Edition translation has been altered here and throughout to reflect Laplanche's preference for rendering Freud's German term *Trieb* as 'drive' (Fr. *pulsion*) rather than the more familiar but misleading 'instinct'].

The Three Essays *and the Theory of Seduction*

We could discourse at length on this view formulated in 1905 – so distant from simple observation of the child – which persistently sets up a clear barrier between an auto-erotic childhood and the pubertal period, and sketches a sort of model of a child who for a long time exists without fantasies, the latter not being explicitly mentioned except in relation to puberty and in connection with masturbation. One could give no better outline of the *Three Essays* of 1905 than the following few lines with which Freud himself summarises them in 1908:

> [t]he sexual drive does not originally serve the purposes of reproduction at all, but has as its aim the gaining of particular kinds of pleasure. It manifests itself in this way in human infancy, during which it attains its aim of gaining pleasure not only from the genitals but from other parts of the body (the erotogenic zones), and can therefore disregard any objects other than those convenient ones. We call this stage the stage of auto-erotism, and the child's upbringing has, in our view, the task of restricting it.[4]

With this overview having sketched things out in broad strokes, it is time to indicate the two lines of thought that link the *Three Essays* to the theory of seduction:

1. In what ways does this text, coming eight years afterwards, contribute some starting-points for a reconsideration of 'the abandonment of the seduction theory'?

2. What to make of the role played by seduction in the text itself?

1. – *On the first point*, it should be recalled that the Freudian theory of seduction (1895–1897) was essentially intended to explain

---
4 "'Civilized' Sexual Morality and Modern Nervous Illness" (1908d), *SE* 9, p. 188.

pathological phenomena: the aetiology of hysteria and the constitution of the unconscious in that illness. The seduction theory can be summed up in the following formula: 'hysterical daughter, perverse parents'. As such, Freud's abandonment of the seduction theory amounts to a veritable 'falsification', in Popper's sense of the term. Without entering into detail about the calling into question of the 'neurotica', let us emphasise a single argument, statistical in appearance and almost irrefutable: to produce one hysterical patient, says Freud, at least one perverse parent (the seducer) is required. And if it is the case that parental perversion must be allied with other pathogenic factors in order to give rise to a hysteria, one would need a still greater proportion of perverse parents in the previous generation:

> Then the surprise that in all cases the *father*, not excluding my own, had to be accused of being perverse – the realisation of the unexpected frequency of hysteria, with precisely the same conditions prevailing in each, whereas surely such widespread perversions against children are not very probable.[5]

However, the *Three Essays* of 1905 will belatedly supply a decisive argument against this objection: namely, that all 'the children of men' carry within them from childhood a polymorphously perverse potentiality. What is more, this polymorphous perversity does not pass away with childhood: whether repressed or sublimated, it persists as a potentiality in every adult:

> No healthy person, it appears, can fail to make some addition that might be called perverse to the normal sexual aim… (p. 160)

---

5 *The Complete Letters of Sigmund Freud to Wilhelm Fliess: 1887–1904*, trans. Jeffrey M. Masson (Cambridge Mass. and London: Harvard University Press, 1985), letter dated 21 September 1897.

Or again:

> ... it becomes impossible not to recognize that this same disposition to perversions of every kind is a general and fundamental human characteristic (p. 191).

Moreover, this infantile sexual potentiality is awakened within the adult carer in the course of his relation with the child:

> [T]he person in charge of [the child], who, after all, is as a rule his mother, herself regards him with feelings that are derived from her own sexual life: she strokes him, kisses him, rocks him and quite clearly treats him as a substitute for a complete sexual object (p. 223).

The 'statistical' argument against the seduction theory thus collapses: *all* parents, *all* Pflegepersonen [caregivers], *all* adults are potentially perverse seducers.

This is something that of course obliges us to reconsider the terms of the letter of 21 September 1897: seduction has in fact every chance of being produced within *every* relation of care (*Pflege*).

This is not to claim that the *Three Essays* of 1905 constitute the unique missing link for a restoration of the seduction theory. Many other steps would still have to be taken in order to acknowledge that repression and the unconscious are not exceptional, pathological phenomena, but are the lot of humanity as such. In this progression towards the general theory of seduction, further theoretical elements are absent: the generality of the 'fundamental anthropological situation' between the adult and the child, which extends beyond even the familial or oedipal situation; the notion of the message, and of the enigmatic message originating from the adult; the attempt to apply to repression a model much more removed from a pure mechanical play of forces and much closer to a communication theory: message – translation – failure of translation.

2. – The sexual theory thus comes too late to save the theory of seduction in all its amplitude. But *what is there, within the text, of seduction itself?* This second point will require a lengthier development.

Let us emphasise first of all that seduction is omnipresent in Essays two and three. The major text of his own to which Freud makes reference in the *Three Essays* is, as it happens, "The Aetiology of Hysteria" (the text that develops the theory of seduction most explicitly), not only as regards the importance of infantile sexuality –

> As long ago as in the year 1896 I insisted on the significance of the years of childhood in the origin of certain important phenomena connected with sexual life, and since then I have never ceased to emphasise the part played in sexuality by the infantile factor (p. 176)

– but also seduction:

> I cannot admit that in my paper on "The Aetiology of Hysteria" (1896) I exaggerated the frequency or importance of [seduction], though I did not then know that persons who remain normal may have had the same experiences in their childhood … (p. 190).

The argument is worth pausing over for a moment: according to the *Three Essays*, seduction is not more exceptional but *more frequent* than Freud believed in 1896. It is just as likely to show up among normal people… From which Freud might have drawn the conclusion that it explains the normal unconscious as well as pathological facts. But he does not do so, for he has not established, so it would seem, the idea of a 'normal' unconscious.

From this very complicated text where arguments intersect and do not always agree, let us try to bring out *some lines of discussion*.

A) *The biological line*. The origin of the drive is beyond dispute related to innate biological factors:

> There seems no doubt that germs of sexual impulses are already present in the new-born child and that these continue to develop for a time, but are then overtaken by a progressive process of suppression (p. 176).

The general theme is well known: infantile sexuality is bound to erotogenic zones and subdivided into component drives, each seeking pleasure on its own terms. But these erotogenic zones are in turn part of a potential erotogeneity of the whole body. The entire body surface, the whole skin, is equipped with a potential erotogeneity:

> We have already discovered in examining the erotogenic zones that these regions of the skin merely show a special intensification of a kind of susceptibility to stimulus which is possessed in a certain degree by the whole cutaneous surface (p. 201).

The same would apply (this is a later addition) to the internal organs. All are capable of sexual excitation. This raises multiple problems. Firstly, the problem of excitation in its relation to pleasure. Freud leaves open – mysterious and unelucidated – the fact that excitation (that's to say, the increase of tension) might in itself be a pleasure, something that contradicts the general idea of pleasure. He returns several times to this paradox of excitation-pleasure:

> This strikes us as somewhat strange only because, in order to remove one stimulus, it seems necessary to adduce a second one at the same spot (p. 185).

Furthermore, however fertile is the notion of a somatic 'source' of the drive, the enlargement of its application also entails many difficulties. It may appear obvious for certain zones – oral, anal, genital – but there are many deficiencies that ought to be underlined. The *erotogenic zone of the woman's breast* is never mentioned; and once we move away from the simplest cases, the original schema fits poorly. Freud persists, for example, in considering the *eye* as the source, the erotogenic zone of *Schaulust* (voyeurism/exhibitionism). Yet the conception of an organic tumescence of the organ of vision is utterly improbable. Moreover, Freud quite creatively emphasises that certain events or general processes can be at the origin, at the 'source of infantile sexuality' (and adult sexuality): train journeys, affective processes, intellectual work . . . Yet, in many of these cases the mediating function of cutaneous erotogeneity seems uncertain.

B) Moving beyond these difficulties, which will later bring us back to the general question of fantasy, let us now recall the *function or the major role attributed to seduction in the birth of sexuality*. Freud is clear, even categorical: seduction occurs with great frequency, and its significance cannot be overestimated. But conversely:

> Obviously seduction is not required in order to arouse a child's sexual life; that can also come about spontaneously from internal causes (pp. 190–1).

Having thus set down the limit to a psychogenesis or an intersubjective genesis of the drive (which is our own thesis), Freud is then free to give a broad description of the modalities of the influence of seductive gestures on the part of the adult. It is interesting to note the linking of seduction with the notion of polymorphous perversity: the child brings with him at birth only an innate disposition:

> It is an instructive fact that under the influence of seduction children can become polymorphously perverse (p. 191).

Freud even goes so far as to propose that the same process can be produced in many women who are "uncultivated":

> In this respect children behave in the same kind of way as an average uncultivated woman in whom the same polymorphously perverse disposition persists (p. 191).

We shall return below to this theme of seduction and polymorphous perversity, on the basis of the question of the object.

Let us conclude this initial revisiting of the texts with some reflections of our own.

First of all, it is important to establish the difference between *the facts* of seduction and the '*theory* of seduction'. The latter has the aim of explaining the specifically sexual character of the excitation. The old theory, which was centred principally upon hysteria, was allied to an explanation of repression and the genesis of the hysterical unconscious.

This explanatory aspect seems to have disappeared completely in 1905. Seduction is omnipresent in the text but its role is strictly circumscribed.

Seduction comes about on the basis of a (subsequent) physiological theory of the general erotogeneity of the body.

It is limited to forms of somatic contact between the adult and the child that have no *communicative* function; it is a matter of simple excitations of the erotogenic zones, without any contribution of fantasy on the part of the adult. At several points Freud even seems to want to insist on the mechanical aspect of exciting actions, leaving out altogether the relational aspect:

> The anatomical situation of this region, the secretions in which it is bathed, the washing and rubbing to which it is subjected in the course of a child's toilet, as well as accidental stimulation (such as the movement of intestinal worms in the case of girls), make it inevitable that the pleasurable feeling which this part of the body is capable of producing should be noticed by children even during earliest infancy, and should give rise to a need for its repetition (p. 188).

Permit me to put a *personal development* into play here, since I have myself proposed what I call 'the general theory of seduction'. For me, there is no question of denying the notion of a general excitability (*Reizbarkeit*) in every living being, especially at the level of the cutaneous envelope, and in particular with respect to the body's places of entry and exit. How can we deny in the child that which exists for every organism, even a monocellular ball of protoplasm? But the assimilation of this general *Reizbarkeit* to a *Verführbarkeit* (seducibility) risks being misleading, insofar as it implies the prior presence of sexuality within the organism. Yet we know that precisely in the child, the little human being, the hormonal conditions of sexuality that we find at the pubertal period are practically absent.

In our view, the properly sexual character of the 'sexual life of the child' remains impossible to define on a purely physiological basis. It is inseparable from the appearance of the sexual fantasy, which is itself correlative to the intervention of the other (the sexual adult).

C) *Another line* concerning seduction is no less strange or interesting: *that regarding the object.*

The Three Essays *and the Theory of Seduction*

We know how much the notion of the object and of object relations has become predominant within a certain approach to psychoanalysis. Here, in the *Three Essays*, we are so to speak at the starting point of this evolution, and matters are not always clarified. It is doubtless evident from the first that the object in question is that of the *sexual drive* and the sexual drive alone. This problem is never confused with that of the perceptual object in general, as conceived by either Piaget or even Winnicott.

However, the *total object / partial object question* remains open and not clear-cut. In the first of the *Three Essays*, 'object' is used to refer to a total person, and Freud works extensively under the heading of 'aberrations in respect of the object', particularly homosexual object choice. As regards this first appearance of the choice of object as person, Freud expresses reservations very early on about the notion of an intrinsic link between the drive and the sex of the object: the following note, which admittedly dates from 1915, is characteristic of this conception:

> [P]sychoanalysis considers that a choice of an object independently of its sex – freedom to range equally over male and female objects – as it is found in childhood, in primitive states of society, is the original basis from which, as a result of the restriction in one direction or another, both the normal and the inverted types develop (pp. 146–7).

This veritable indifference inherent in the drive with regard to the sex of the total object warrants emphasis. It is, to be sure, related to the notion of bisexuality; but the question goes further and rejoins the question of the truly essential separation that Freud seeks to maintain between 'drive' and 'object'.

But let us first of all go back to the *simpler question* of whether by sexual object Freud understands the *total object* (a person) or *a partial object* (a part of the body). We notice that the perspective will change completely between the First Essay (total object) and the Third. In the latter the object will suddenly become the part object of the component drive: for the nursling infant this is, quintessentially, the breast.

In fact one would have great difficulty synthesising the two points of view – total/partial. This is because Freud *centres hardly any of the theory of the infantile drive on the relation to the object*. One could even say that he initially considers the *object as inessential* to the search for excitation and pleasure connected to the erotogenic zones. Genital synthesis, the connection with procreation – these are essentially pubertal developments. Freud sketches a mysterious, almost mystical conception of the sexual drive in itself; auto-erotism is an almost original state, one that is without external object and in which another part of the body can be taken as a partner in a sort of mirror relation.

The most surprising passage is found in the first Essay, at the end of the chapter on the "Deviations in respect of the sexual object":

> The most general conclusion that follows from all these discussions seems, however, to be this. Under a great number of conditions and in surprisingly numerous individuals, the nature and importance of the sexual object recedes into the background. What is essential and constant in the sexual drive is something else (p. 149).

This passage is completed by a no less surprising note, dating from 1910 but in the same vein, where Freud opposes the ancients' high estimation for the drive itself to our overly exclusive preoccupation with the object:

> The most striking distinction between the erotic life of antiquity and our own no doubt lies in the fact that the ancients laid the stress upon the drive itself, whereas we emphasize its object. The ancients glo-

> rified the drive and were prepared on its account to honour even an inferior object; while we despise the drive activity in itself, and find excuses for it only in the merits of the object (p. 149 n. 1).

It is not at all easy to imagine what Freud means by "the drive itself" or even "what is essential and constant in the sexual drive". A drive whose sole aim is pleasure and which is auto-erotic, that is to say, with no object beyond the subject's own body. (Unfortunately, the question of fantasy and the 'internal' fantasmatic object are not invoked at all, even in the reversal that leads from sucking at the breast to thumb sucking).

To maximise the surprise it is important to put this drive/object opposition into contact with the passage that follows. It concerns the effects of seduction on the drive itself:

> Moreover, the effects of seduction do not help to reveal the early history of the sexual drive; they rather confuse our view of it by presenting children prematurely with a sexual object for which the infantile sexual drive at first shows no need (p. 191).

The main point here is the remarkable comment, epistemological in nature, that *seduction confuses our view* (*verwirrt unsere Einsicht*) and prevents us from understanding what the drive really is, and that it does so by erroneously introducing the object into a process where it has no role to play.

What better way of experiencing how Freud is at once close to – yet far from – the *solution as we conceive it*. We too think that it is by seduction that the other intervenes in infantile sexuality, but far from this observation putting Freud on the path towards the genesis of sexuality, the precocious object introduced by seduction becomes a sort of inopportune artefact. If one considers that the drive is already to be regarded as a deviant instinct, seduction would introduce a still more serious epistemological deviation.

D) But all of this will undergo a further alteration that is not easily compatible with the above. It has to do with the Third Essay, "The Transformations of Puberty", in which Freud picks up afresh the question of the object.

To be sure, Freud begins in a way that is consistent with the earlier ideas – with their paradoxical character:

> The sexual drive has hitherto [i.e. before puberty] been predominantly auto-erotic; it now finds a sexual object. Its activity has been hitherto derived from a number of separate drives and erotogenic zones, which, independently of one another, have pursued a certain sort of pleasure as their sole sexual aim (p. 207).

But some pages further on there appears the chapter on "*die Objektfindung*" ("The Finding of an Object") which *inverts the entire perspective*. I am referring to the first paragraph of this chapter, which concludes with the famous formula "*die Objektfindung ist eigentlich eine Wiederfindung*" ("The finding of an object is in fact a refinding of it" (p. 222)).

Within a few lines, and in apparent contradiction with the passages from the Second Essay, Freud maintains:

1) that the sexual drive in general has a first object, beyond the subject's own body: the mother's breast;
2) that auto-erotism is not an original state that the influence of seduction would "confuse", but a secondary state that appears with the loss of the breast: "As a rule the sexual instinct then becomes auto-erotic" (p. 222).

The Three Essays *and the Theory of Seduction*

The chapter that follows again resumes, over two long pages, the theme of seduction – seduction by the nurse, by those dispensing care, and of course by the mother above all. Freud gives the greatest credit to this seduction, attributing to it the awakening and the strength of the sexual drive in the future adult:

> A mother would probably be horrified if she were made aware that all her marks of affection were rousing her child's drive and preparing for its later intensity (p. 223).

Let us emphasise several points in the light of this.

One the one hand, this seduction appears here as a regular, even universal, phenomenon, since it depends not only on the direct excitation of the genital zones, which is "unavoidable in nursery care", but also on the simple relation of affection:

> [T]he sexual drive is not aroused only by direct excitation of the genital zone. What we call affection will unfailingly show its effects one day on the genital zones as well (p. 223).[6]

On the other hand, this infantile seduction has a double effect: it "prepar[es] for [the] later intensity" of the sexual drive, but it is also at the origin of numerous relations of sexual love with the diverse 'people who look after the child', in particular the mother. It is difficult to reconcile this passage with the aforementioned claim that the sexual life of the individual knows no object before puberty.

---

6 One cannot fail to see here the prefiguration of an idea that we have developed at length in the article "Sexuality and Attachment in Metapsychology" (this volume): the relation of attachment (and the messages which relate to it) constitutes 'the carrier wave' which the sexual unconscious on the part of the adult comes to 'compromise'. Freudian "affection" is the earliest name for the contemporary term 'attachment'.

Moreover, Freud maintains that the 'finding of an object', which is the main theme of this chapter, merely succeeds an original 'finding' of the maternal breast. The object is thus 'introduced', let us say, with breastfeeding. But at no point does Freud allow himself to *wonder whether it is not a matter of a first seduction.*

First of all, he considers the *'Saugen'* (sucking, suckling) as an *activity* purely on the child's part; it is only much later, with the *Leonardo* paper and with the interrogation of the passivity inherent in the vulture fantasy, that he will wonder whether this *Saugen* does not in reality correspond to a *Saügen* (giving suck), thereby introducing the question of activity on the part of the mother.

Moreover, Freud remains resistant to the idea that the woman's *breast* is *a major erotogenic zone*. Introducing this idea would bring into play the entire relation of seduction within what is commonly called 'the experience of satisfaction'.

On our view, the maternal unconscious is in play in the act of the *Saügen*. Taking a step further we can ask what *passes*, with the introduction of the breast, as a partially unconscious message from the mother to the child. Yet it is essential to recognise that this first page on the 'finding of the object' remains silent with respect to seduction by breastfeeding, even though seduction in general is very much present throughout the Second and Third Essays.

Conclusion

In our first part we showed that the notion of generalised sexuality and that of an infantile polymorphous perversity that remains present, in purely latent and unconscious manner, in the adult, could answer one of the major objections that Freud poses in 'falsifying' the theory of seduction. Every adult, especially in the presence of the small child, sees this 'perverse' sexuality (in the most general sense of the term) awaken within him – which cannot but be channelled into the earliest messages sent to the child from the adult.

In our second part, we continued to hold to the first version of 1905. The Second and Third Essays are virtually invaded with the notion of seduction. While the drive is described as being, in its essence, indifferent to the question of the object until puberty, the object will be *introduced*, and in a way that is (according to Freud) illegitimate, by the almost inevitable seductions coming from the adult that introduce a disturbance, at once real and epistemological, into a clear vision of the drive. But although here he rightly recognises – and as if in spite of himself – the intersubjective role of seduction, Freud doesn't seize the opportunity to use this idea to analyse the first introduction of an object, the *breast*, as the very prototype of a seduction by the maternal other. On his account, the active protagonist in this experience is the nursling and not the mother.

Finally, although he *generalises the facts of seduction* to normal childhood, and thus emphasises their immense importance, Freud does not arrive at *a metapsychological theory* that would assign seduction a foundational role in the theory of normal repression, the genesis of the unconscious and the eruption of the sexual drive.

Many elements are still missing: the idea of an early communication between the adult and the child; the idea that the messages of the adult other are in a position of asymmetry with regard to those of the child, the adult messages being infiltrated by the infantile sexual unconscious of the transmitter. Also missing is any attempt to describe the child's treatment of these enigmatic messages deriving from the adult (translation – repression).

However general might be the presence of the facts of seduction within the *Three Essays* of 1905, we note that the occasion is not used to develop a general *theory* of normal seduction that would be situated as an extension of the restricted, psychopathological *theory*, outlined in the years 1895–1897.

15

FREUD AND PHILOSOPHY[1]

The general nature of this question risks simply leading us back to aporias, namely:
Which Freud exactly?
And *what* philosophy?

Which Freud? We shall, of course, refrain from putting Freud 'on the couch', as they say… But there does perhaps exist an intermediate level, which I shall further try to define as that of the *exigency*. An uncontrollable exigency that makes up the originality of an otherwise unpredictable intellectual trajectory. This Freud of the *exigency* is not purely subjective. It is found – and can be demonstrated – in the written work and its equilibrium.

What Freud *says* and what he *does* vis-à-vis philosophy can only leave us perplexed.

Here, Paul-Laurent Assoun's little work *Freud, la philosophie et les philosophes*[2] provides the necessary reference points. In it, we find the double-handed language and the double attitude which Freud displays in relation to philosophy – what Assoun calls Freud's 'double

---

[1] Introductory remarks to a discussion organised by the "France Culture" radio station, February 25, 2006, at the Bibliothèque nationale de France.
[2] (Paris: Presses Universitaires de France, 1976).

speech'. Out of a dozen examples, two quotations will suffice: "I most secretly nourish the hope of arriving, via these same paths, at my initial goal of philosophy";[3] but many years later (in 1925): "I have carefully avoided any contact with philosophy proper. This avoidance has been greatly facilitated by constitutional incapacity".[4]

All of this, at least as far as explicit statements are concerned, forms part of an intellectual autobiography that Freud elaborated and modified ceaselessly. But what does he say from a more thoroughly argued point of view? *The standpoint on philosophy* is clearly set out in the chapter on "The Question of a *Weltanschauung*" in the *New Introductory Lectures* (1933). Here the uniform and universal point of view characteristic of all world systems is rejected, and both its internal connection to narcissism and the aim of comforting those who live by those systems are explicitly brought forward as decisive arguments. But the principal critique is in fact reserved for the *religious* view of the world; the philosophical view remains relatively inoffensive, of interest only to a restricted elite, and therefore having little influence on the course of the world.

While claiming repeatedly that he is "not properly competent to judge [the different systems]",[5] Freud does not refrain from offering opinions on Marxism and its active branch, Bolshevism. But – and this is no less interesting for us – he also breaks a few spears against the intellectual "nihilism" of those he calls "anarchists", those who claim that "we find only what we need and see only what we want to see": "the relativity theory of modern physics seems to have gone to their head" (ibid., pp. 175–6). Without taking Freud as an authority here, let us simply note that he already arraigns, after his own fashion, what is nowadays called 'postmodernism'. This is a postmodernism

---
3 *The Complete Letters of Sigmund Freud to Wilhelm Fliess: 1887–1904*, trans. Jeffrey M. Masson (Cambridge Mass. and London: Harvard University Press, 1985), letter dated 1 January 1896.
4 *An Autobiographical Study* (1925d), SE 20, p. 59.
5 "Lecture 35: The Question of a *Weltanschauung*", *New Introductory Lectures on Psychoanalysis* (1933a), SE 22, p. 175.

that continues to thrive, maintaining that 'anything goes', and which, in order to attack psychoanalysis from the rear, does not fail to assert that if all hermeneutic keys are valid then psychoanalysis now has no privilege above any other 'narrative schema', that it is only one narrative among others.

To return to 'world views', let us clearly observe that Freud will not reject them all but will subscribe explicitly to what he calls the "scientific *Weltanshauung*", to which he allies psychoanalysis. *It too* is characterised by its uniform ambition, but – and this is an essential difference – this aim is not only conceived as a programme whose accomplishment is to be found displaced unceasingly towards the future. Without wishing to develop the characteristics of science here, let us note its absolutist aspects, which Freud in no way rejects: "truth cannot be tolerant … it admits of no compromises or limitations"; it "proced[es] with rejections and dismissals" (ibid., p. 160). This last view would return us directly to *Popper's* notion of falsification; a Popper whose epistemology – beyond his uninformed critique of what he claimed to be psychoanalysis but which actually boiled down to a somewhat simplistic Adlerism – shows many points of contact with Freud's.

Freud compares this vision of science, with which he fully concurs, to that of philosophy, which, he says, is "not opposed to science". Philosophy "works in part by the same methods" (ibid.), but it goes wrong in seeking, by means of positive *assertions*, to fill the gaps in the unity at which it aims, whereas for science such a unity always remains a regulative and programmatic principle.

We would not wish to leave Freud's reflection at this point, pointing at the absolutist and systematic character of philosophical world systems: for *on the one hand, on the side of philosophy*, the uniform, totalising aim represents just one aspect of things, best illustrated by Hegelianism, which Freud detests so much as to fail to recognise its dialectical moving force. It will suffice to mention Kierkegaard, without listing the great number of modern philosophers for whom the 'Weltanschauung' or 'world vision' is the least of their concerns.

But *on the other hand, on the side of Freud himself,* another term will be advanced and will be ceaselessly repeated by him: namely *'speculation'*, to which he willingly admits dedicating himself, even if he does so without abandoning 'patient observation'. I shall simply mention some of the great texts that contain a speculative dimension – *Totem and Taboo, Civilisation and its Discontents* and many others – in order to pause for a few moments over the text that is paradigmatic among them: *Beyond the Pleasure Principle*, where speculation is defined as "an attempt to follow out an idea consistently, out of curiosity to see where it will lead".[6] Here one could see precisely Popper's procedure of *conjecture*, where the imagination can be given free reign, to be followed by *refutation or falsification* of the conjecture based on one or another of its results. But this speculation – which in the case of *Beyond the Pleasure Principle* is metacosmological – does not for the most part lead to refutations or solidly grounded findings. It will lead, a few years later, to a formulation that sounds like an absolute, beyond all proof: "To begin with it was only tentatively that I put forward the views that I have developed here, but in the course of time they have gained such a hold upon me that I can no longer think in any other way".[7]

Exigency. This is the term I now propose to describe what pushes Freud in a single direction, which is constantly at work in him throughout all his 'goings-astray'. In the case of *Beyond the Pleasure Principle* it is the exigency of the 'death drive' – a notion that will, to be sure, undergo further elaboration. But primarily it is the exigency of the *unconscious*, encountered in the practice of analysis.

To speak of the Freudian discovery is not to speak of analysis as merely the updating of a procedure to access in a new way phe-

---

6 *Beyond the Pleasure Principle* (1920g), SE 18, p. 25.
7 *Civilisation and its Discontents* (1930a), SE 21, p. 119.

nomena that are already recognised but just poorly understood – in a word, a psychology supplied with revitalised instruments. Psychoanalysis is the simultaneous inauguration of a new *procedure* and a new *domain of being*.

Psychoanalysis, Freud will say – and I am barely glossing his words – is a specific procedure that allows access to hitherto unknown entities, unconscious entities. It is thus comprised at once of a new method and a new object. At the same time, the exigency of which I speak is not an exigency belonging to the researcher: it is the *very pressure exerted by his object*.

Such is the meaning of the *realism* of the unconscious – as opposed to all hermeneutic conceptions – which the following very particular characteristics denote:

alien-ness [*étrangèreté*],[8] as also designated by the well-known formula 'internal foreign body' [*corps étranger interne*];

atemporality, and, more exactly, the exclusion of temporalisation;

the absence of coordination;

the absence of negation;

also, of course, the *sexual character* of the unconscious, to be understood here in the sense of polymorphous infantile sexuality.

In *support of his theory of the unconscious* Freud is sometimes led to refer to philosophers, in a genealogy that is not entirely free of confusions. The reference to Kant is rudimentary at best. The reference to Schopenhauer reintroduces the idea of a primal unconscious, an 'unconscious will', as the bedrock of our conscious life. We cannot deny that Freud himself states on several occasions that 'everything which is conscious has first been unconscious' and that 'the primary precedes the secondary'. These are all propositions that it is important we oppose.

---

8 [*Editor*: Laplanche's term is literally 'stranger-ness', which we have translated in hyphenated form as 'alien-ness' to enable the reader to hear the noun in Laplanche's neologism and to preserve the sense of the irreducibility of the *other* as alien.]

I am well aware that by issuing such reservations I am pleading on behalf of one Freud against another: the Freud of the experience and the exigency of alterity, against the Freud of a Ptolemaic, ipsocentrist re-centring that re-emerges ceaselessly and boils down to a formula of the following kind: in the depths and at the origin of man, flush out the instinctual id: "Nothing has entered into you from without; it is only a part of yourself which you do not recognise".[9] Such would be the formula I reject.

Two further remarks to finish up:

1) It is not for nothing that the exigency of the *death drive* should impose itself towards the end of the Freudian oeuvre. I recall Freud's own statement: "I can no longer think in any other way". However, this exigency is not a pure lived experience, a subjective constraint. It is a constraint that is at once legible in the very structure of the Freudian oeuvre and in its evolution. Since *Life and Death in Psychoanalysis*, I have tried to pose the question, "Why the death drive?"[10] Now, the explanation can be found in the drift taken by Freud's work during the years around 1915, a drift that tends to make one forget the uncontrollable, irreconcilable aspect of the sexual drive, which Freud names "*Lucifer Amor*" in the letters to Fliess.[11] It is a drift that, among other things, is consolidated by the place accorded to a sexuality unified under the aegis of 'the Eros of the divine Plato' – a term very difficult to reconcile with the 'polymorphous sexuality' situated at the origin of our being and of our symptoms. As such, the death drive may be deciphered as a reaffirmation of the heterogeneity of the sexual within us, the infantile sexuality that is unbound and in need of binding.

2) Nor is it without significance that the discovery of the unconscious, in the earliest years, should be accompanied by a clini-

---

9 Cf. "A Difficulty in the Path of Psychoanalysis" (1917a), *SE* 17, p. 142.
10 *Life and Death in Psychoanalysis*, trans. Jeffrey Mehlman (Baltimore: Johns Hopkins UP, 1977), pp. 103–124.
11 *The Complete Letters of Sigmund Freud to Wilhelm Fliess: 1887–1904*, letter dated 10 July, 1900.

cal and theoretical attempt to detect the source of that alterity in the enigmatic message of the adult other, a message infiltrated by the sexual unconscious *of the adult*. I am referring here to the *theory of seduction*, which is inseparable from the exigency of the unconscious as *other* within us. Heir to the sexual asymmetry of the adult-*infans* relation – an asymmetry that is characteristic of what may be referred to as the 'fundamental anthropological situation' – the unconscious forever reminds us that we do not gravitate around ourselves nor even around an instinct-based id that is genetic in nature.

From the beginning we gravitate around the enigmatic other, the sexual adult other of our childhood, that other who is, moreover, enigmatic to himself.

For this reason, psychoanalysis – which is itself but a tiny part of our forever unfinished knowledge of the cosmos – is a body of knowledge which we might describe as 'wounded', opened up from the first by the enigma of the experience of the unconscious.

This in no way implies that psychoanalysis has to renounce the rationalist option. A *wounded rationalism*: this would be one of the possible formulas for referring to Freud's philosophy, in the knowledge that that very wound is a stimulating element.

16

IN DEBATE WITH FREUD[1]

The Freud that concerns me is neither the name, which is sported like a 'badge' by the divergent psychoanalytic movements, nor, conversely, the individual, for whose biographies I have very little appetite, especially those that claim to be psychoanalytic. It is above all what he himself wanted to be: the Freud of the written and published oeuvre. This does not mean that I want to transform this oeuvre into a sacred text.

It is an oeuvre of debates, of second thoughts, of certainties but also of doubts. A text written in German, which we (as an entire team: André Bourguignon Pierre Cotet, Janine Altounian, François Robert) gave ourselves the task of publishing in French in an *Œuvres complètes* as faithful as possible to the original. The fidelity of the translator: this means resisting unceasingly and to the greatest extent possible the adage according to which 'every translator is a traitor' and 'every translation an interpretation'. On the basis of principles such as these, it becomes too easy to give up truly translating. I propose in contrast a form of translation that far from imposing an interpretation, remains open to the most various, even the most offensive interpretations on the part of the reader. 'Doing justice' to a great text, means not mask-

---

[1] First published in the weekly *Le Point*, April 20, 2006, no. 1753.

ing but restoring its contradictions, its weaknesses, its moments of hesitation and imprecision, and even its incoherences.

Freud the thinker is the man of a *discovery*, and I shall insist on this aspect first of all. Here we have a researcher between thirty and forty years old, highly cultured and endowed with solid scientific experience, moved by an unshakeable positivist rationalism and an equally unshakeable ambition – he sometimes sees himself in the role of a 'conquistador', a Christopher Columbus of psychopathology – who decides to put into practice the method of investigation developed by his elder colleague Joseph Breuer. As a method it consists in inducing the patient to speak 'freely', by agreeing to reveal his most incongruous thoughts.

But at this point the application of a simple 'method' will change everything: it ceases to be a matter of ameliorating the existing psychopathology with the aid of a new instrument. The method known as 'free associations' suddenly opens onto a *new object*: that which Freud names the Unconscious. Not that this *terra incognita* can ever be charted, as was the America of the conquerors; but it does allow itself to be inferred, supposed and reconstructed on the basis of its effects: dreams, daydreams, parapraxes, slips, jokes… In order to refer to it, Freud employs strange terms that bear witness to its otherness: the unconscious acts within us as an 'internal foreign body' (one imagines a kind of implant, deposited by a neurosurgeon). The unconscious manifests itself in the neurotic as a 'reminiscence', that is to say as a memory that would remain forever cut off from its sources. Freud is also certain that the unconscious is bound to our earliest childhood, and that it is indissociable from 'infantile sexuality'. A sexuality whose trail he picks up in each case he analyzes, a sexuality so different from our adult sexuality (which nowadays one speaks of as being liberated) that one would even hesitate to employ the same term to refer to it. This polymorphous, anarchic, infantile 'sexual', which seeks excitation more than satisfaction, is destined for (more or less total) repression within each of us.

One finds in Freud's texts the most varied genres and styles, from the most elegant and almost novelistic, through to the weightiness of the 'academic' thinker trained in the discipline of the Germanic Universities. Beyond this diversity, however, I want to stress that, from the years 1880–1890, it is as though he is haunted by an *exigency* that is drawing him on. And this is imposed upon him not by his own thought, but by his very object, just as it imposes itself on any psychoanalyst who constrains himself to use the Freudian method.

I have sometimes employed the image of a mountaineer seeking to conquer a Himalayan summit that is almost inaccessible and lost among the clouds. Seeking the 'right track' is everything, but it is also inevitable that our man might take a wrong path leading to a 'sheer drop'. Should we turn back and retrace our steps? Or should we get out the climbing pegs?

Speaking personally, it is these decisive junctions, these points of 'going astray' in the Freudian oeuvre which fascinate me, and I have set myself the task of opening up a discussion of just what is at play in such moments: what then becomes of the *exigency* which magnetizes the entire movement of this strange body of thought? For me it is a matter of putting Freud back to work, of making his work 'work' (of making it creak perhaps) by working with it.

I shall cite only one example, that of a decisive moment: with the publication of his first analytic cases (the *Studies on Hysteria*), Freud simultaneously constructs an exceptionally audacious theory aimed at nothing less than explaining the origin of the unconscious in 'the hysteric', by means of the details and the metamorphoses of the complex interpersonal relationship between the infant and the adult who first opens it up to life, its first 'other', so to speak. Then abruptly, on September 21, 1897, posing objections drawn from clinical work, from theory and also from simple common sense (but what 'common sense' applies to psychoanalysis?), he renounces this theory known as the 'theory of seduction'. In a rather sheep-like fashion, most historians see in this a favourable announcement: of the future birth of the theory of 'fantasy' and the 'Oedipus complex'. But the negative aspect of this *volte-face* goes unremarked: an *hereditary* theory of the prehistoric or 'phylogenetic' origins of the human psyche regains the entire terrain. This is a path leading to impasses that will recur throughout the length of Freud's oeuvre. It asserts the acquisition and genetic inscription of lived scenes from prehistory that will be transmitted through the unconscious of every human being. This would be the case for the famous 'murder of the father', even though there is no evidence that it could be memorized and *acquired* during the prehistory of mankind.

It is therefore worthwhile thoroughly to re-examine the difficulties of the 'theory of seduction' and to see whether more recent advances with respect to preverbal communication between the very young child and the adult would allow us to enlarge the bases of this supposedly obsolete theory.

Many are the points in Freud's oeuvre that call for re-examination and for a new 'work'. I shall cite only that much debated idea of the 'death drive'.

Is this oeuvre worth the effort? Well, isn't it a proof of its vitality that it is able to give rise to such debates? Freud's oeuvre is, for me at least, the site of an *unfaithful fidelity*: fidelity of translation first of all, which alone permits the infidelity of discussion, for one can only discuss an author if one's understanding is based very closely on what he actually says. But fidelity also to the *exigency* of the object that our practice as psychoanalysts reveals: this object which keeps knocking at the door, this intruder, this other within us which we still refer to using the same word as Freud: 'the Unconscious'.

17

PSYCHOANALYSIS AND PSYCHOTHERAPY[1]

Since this question has been so muddled by considerations that are important but, in spite of everything, mainly extrinsic (that of the analytic 'setting' in particular), I shall try to be brief and clear.

1. I shall distinguish the psychoanalytic *act* – what the psychoanalyst does *as a psychoanalyst* – and the current *practice* of psychoanalysts – what they do in the treatment and, more generally, in the relationship with any patient.

2. The psychoanalytic act can be conveniently divided into *situation* and *method*, both of which are essential.

The *situation* is one of radical asymmetry. This has lent itself to all sorts of misunderstandings, including what Ferenczi formulated as 'professional hypocrisy'. We know that nowadays this asymmetry has been swept aside by the idea that the position of the analyst has no privilege, any more than does the position of the observer in physics. This is the famous 'transference-countertransference' refrain that is never missing from conference papers.

However, the inspired invention of the analytic situation cannot be properly understood unless it is coupled with a conception

---

[1] First published in *Le Carnet psy*, 108, May 2006. Response to an investigation coordinated by Daniel Widlöcher.

of the 'fundamental anthropological situation' (adult-*infans*) as originary asymmetry, another name for which is 'seduction'.

It is only in relation to infantile asymmetry that the 'unbearable' analytic asymmetry can be explained and justified. 'Neutrality' is not primarily a refusal to give the other help, counsel, knowledge, etc. It is sustained only by what we must call the internal 'refusal'[2] of the analyst: an understanding perhaps of his own unconscious mechanisms, a respect for unconscious alterity and also a sense of his limits, which implies a rejection of any aim to master, to fashion the other, of any *poïesis*.

The transference, if we wish to retain its analytic specificity, can only be conceived within the framework of this situation that basically puts the subject back as close as possible to the enigmas that were offered to him in his childhood. In addition to the enigmas of the internal other (the unconscious), it is the 'treatment' of the enigmas of the external other (adults, parents) that is, in the most favourable cases, put to work again.

3. The *method*, as its name indicates, is *analytic*. It aims to bring into the open elements that are hidden – unconscious or bordering the unconscious – or defensive, in the utterances, the acts and the transference of the analysand. As such, the psychoanalytic method has a destructuring aim. It seeks hidden elements where they are least expected. It undermines the coherent unities upon which an entire life might have been organized (ideologies, visions of oneself and others, narrative schemas, personal romances, etc.), in order to identify their separated components.

The method of psychoanalysis is based upon *free association*

---

2 [*Editor*: '*Refusement*' – this is a neologism invented by Laplanche to translate Freud's *Versagung*, which Strachey translates as 'frustration' in the *Standard Edition*. Where 'frustration' refers to the lack of an external object of satisfaction, '*refusement*' refers to a subject who refuses a desired object or mode of satisfaction, often to himself. Here Laplanche applies the term to the analyst, whose refusal to advise or control the analysand or to know in advance the significance of his symptoms and behaviour is sustained by a similar refusal with regard to his own internal other.]

(which we might more accurately call the 'associative-dissociative' method), upon the analyst's *interpretations* – by which I refer to the means of underlining, of 'pointing out' the presence of an unusual element, close to the unconscious (as in Freud's "Constructions in Analysis")[3] – and on the reconstructions of a defence process. The psychoanalytic act is thus due to the joint action of the analysand and the analyst, united in the method.

4. *Strictly speaking*, neither any psychotherapy nor any psychoanalysis has ever cured anyone; the latter a *fortiori*, even if it has the appearance of a well-dug excavation site. But let us not forget that this field of excavation is unceasingly reorganized and reconstituted by the patient. *The only psychotherapist is our 'patient' and more generally any human being* who constitutes himself from his first days as *subject of a story*, by temporalising himself, by memorizing, by 'writing' or rewriting his history in a more or less coherent way. The 'subject', then, of an interior narration, which may be single stemmed or may branch out. (This explains why the only true 'report' of a case is that of the patient himself).

5. Freud said nothing other than this (which one hardly hears these days), when he stated that the 'synthesis' (which he was reproached for not concerning himself with) – today one would name it 'reconstruction', 'structuring', 'subjectivation', etc. – was not his province, and that, as in chemistry, the disjoined elements always had a tendency to reassemble themselves again spontaneously. The remark always remains pertinent, not as a formula for indifference or for the refusal of help, but as a test of the essential delimitation between psychoanalysis and psychotherapy.

6. How to apply this criterion to the thousand contemporary forms of practice, whether or not they are related to psychoanalysis?

Within the psychoanalysis of neuroses such as we always practise it today, psychotherapy and psychoanalysis are continuously coexistent.

---

3 (1937d), *SE* 23, pp. 257–69.

A small portion of the time and effort of the patient and the analyst is aimed at 'analyzing'. I include in this act the 'treatment' of defences, intimately bound to the unconscious fantasies. Most of the time of a psychoanalysis is devoted to giving form and narrative to what the analysis has discovered – is devoted, therefore, to 'psychotherapy'.

A process of putting-into-narrative in which the analyst is not uninvolved, if necessary proposing forms of binding, narrative and partial schemas – 'Oedipal', 'castratory' or otherwise – but always with caution. We need, however, to emphasise that, for Freud, the 'becoming conscious' of an unconscious element was sufficient in itself to open the way to a new synthesis. We have, I think, retreated from this 'physicalist' view, thanks to such concepts as narrativity, personal history, even subjectivation, which give a much richer content to the Freudian notion of 'working through' as being precisely the 'psychotherapeutic' moment of the treatment.

7. Let us summarize:

All psychoanalysis is devoted primarily to psychotherapy: to the self-narration of the subject, with the more or less active assistance of the analyst.

But the psychoanalytic *act* – sometimes quite rare – is something else. A work of unbinding, it tries to make new materials surface for a profoundly renewed narration; and of course, we shall not be surprised that the psychoanalyst is also cautious and sparing: for isn't his work of unbinding allied with that of the sexual death drive?

8. *Psychotherapies* are multiple. The fact that they might or might not be practised by analysts, or even without any explicit reference to psychoanalysis, has little to do with their nature.

a) There are the psychoanalyses that risk slipping towards psychotherapy pure and simple.

The self-structuring or self-narration persist, but they work on second-hand material, 'recycling' it. The result is not negligible, but the unconscious foundations are seldom exposed. To put it in terms of 'translation', one translates starting from an existing translation, with little reference to the original text.

b) A good number of the psychotherapies carried out by analysts fall into this category, because they are not equipped from the outset with the methodological means that enable the sounding-out of the unconscious.

c) I think that the majority of so-called non-analytic psychotherapies fall into the same category. Listening to someone with attention and a 'containing' attitude often allows them important progress in their self-narration. According to the statistics, the results are comparable to those of 'analytic' psychotherapies (carried out by analysts), and it would be necessary to verify this without prejudice. Let us note carefully that the 'evaluations' in question do not take into account the psychoanalyses carried out according to the 'analytic' method.

d) I leave aside, of course, those (psycho?)therapies aimed at rectifying a neurotic behaviour by means of a veritable dressage or training (Cognitive Behavioural Therapy).

e) The psychotherapy of the psychoses and *serious* 'borderline' cases, as they're known, poses an entirely different precondition: the very problem of indication. Is it right to help 'unbind' what is already inadequately bound? Here the perspective changes radically: the psychotherapist is apparently invited to take part 'creatively' in construction, by bringing to bear his schemas, even his own materials. His 'involvement' is maximum, to the point that one may wonder whether the reported cases are not unique specimens to which the therapist has devoted the major part of his time and attention. The *multiplicity* of approaches and theorizations in the published cases shows that most of the time it is the idiosyncrasy of the therapist-analyst that is to the fore – his unconscious underpinnings, his values, his very existence. There are as many therapists of psychoses as there are individuals, and the theories carry no real weight since they can do little but dress up a practice that is above all individual.

I shall add a dampener here: no one is totally insane; a neurotic, repressed part always exists (cf. Freud: "The Splitting of the

Ego"). To this extent the cautious analysis of this neurotic part can have a beneficial follow-on effect for the whole of the person, including the psychotic part.[4]

Conclusion

I have sought above all to show that psychoanalysis and psychotherapy are not separate fields but that in any psychoanalysis there is inevitably something of analysis and something of psychotherapy.

"I dressed him; God healed him".[5] I transpose this into:

"I debrided his wounds; he healed them in his own way."

---

4 See the diagram in "Three Meanings of the Term 'Unconscious' in the Framework of the General Theory of Seduction", in this volume.
5 [*Trans*: A saying attributed to the sixteenth-century French surgeon Ambroise Paré apropos of his own successful means of dressing patients' wounds].

18

INCEST AND INFANTILE SEXUALITY[1]

Introduction: It is for me a great honour to be invited to give this *Festvortrag* in Vienna for Freud's 150th anniversary, and also an occasion of great emotion.[2]

Freud, our master in all things!

I have just written a little article called "In Debate with Freud".[3] I shall define my approach with two formulas:

I am interested above all in what Freud openly formulated: with the written work, which I, together with the entire team of the French *Œuvres complètes*, seek to translate as rigorously as possible.

My attitude is that of a 'faithful infidelity'. A fidelity with respect to reading and translation, restoring to Freud what he meant – including his contradictions and his turning points; an infidelity with respect to the interpretation of Freud's 'goings astray', in order to try to find what I call 'New Foundations for Psychoanalysis'.

Freud remained dominated by the exigency of his discovery:

---

1 Delivered at the formal meeting of the two Vienna Psychoanalytic Societies on May 6, 2006, for Freud's 150th anniversary.
2 I should like to thank the organizers of this celebration, the Wiener Psychoanalytische Vereinigung and the Wiener Arbeitskreis für Psychoanalyse, and in particular Mrs. Daphne Stock who so attentively assisted me during the preparation for this event.
3 Essay 16 in this volume.

'the unconscious'; let us follow him in this exigency!

Incest and infantile sexuality: it is perilous to try to link up two notions – two psychoanalytic observations, each as well-established as the other – which, apparently at least, do not intersect.

Infantile sexuality, even if it is often neglected or pushed into the background and by analysts themselves, remains for us a fundamental acquisition that no one dare challenge; and yet, from the simple chronological point of view, it is very far removed from the classical problem of incest. It is a given, and a theorization, which relates primarily to the very first months and years of life. In particular, it emerges before any designation of the kinship categories that remain essential if one is to speak of incest: father, mother, sister, uncle, etc. In terms of its sources at least, infantile sexuality is considered to be pregenital and related to the most diverse erotogenic zones. In the first edition of the *Three Essays*, it corresponds to the period of auto-erotism, theorized by Freud on the basis of observations by the paediatrician Lindner, according to the following schema: the earliest relations with the adult, the model for which remains the act of sucking at the mother's breast, are as it were turned back by the child upon itself, for example in the form of thumb-sucking. This is what I have previously referred to as 'auto-time', a veritable crucible where infantile sexuality is generated, as well as a schema that is valid for far more than the 'oral drive' alone.

Conversely, *incest* (at the initiative of the child), and the taboo from which it is indissociable, is located by Freud in later years – say, towards the ages of 2 or 3 – and is in fact regarded as contemporary with the Oedipus complex. Like the Oedipus, it presupposes the lexicon, the nomenclature of the 'object-persons' within the field of kinship relations. Like the Oedipus, even if it occurs in the infantile period the contents of the incest fantasy show that it is located in the world of adults, the very theatre where the drama of Oedipus the King is played out: for marrying the mother is a much more meaningful act by which to define incest than having intimate relations with her in childhood. Moreover, as many ethnological examples show, the act of marrying a woman does not necessarily involve any reference to sexuality.

From a juridical point of view, France lacks a penalty for and even a definition of incest. The only coherent definition is that given by the *Robert* dictionary: "Sexual relationships between a man and a woman who are related or linked to a degree which prohibits marriage".[4] We can see that it refers incest explicitly to *matrimonial* considerations. We may also note that the prohibition relates only to adult persons, and these days, in Western civilisation, is without conceivable penal sanction.

The dialogue with anthropology still remains indispensable, and for Freud above all.

Freud's central theory regarding incest remains anthropological, located in prehistory, and of course centred on adult sexuality. I shall rapidly recapitulate what is called the 'founding myth' of *Totem and Taboo*, although it bears a stronger relation to parricide than to incest.[5] In a nutshell, an all-powerful 'father of the horde' – who has rights over the life and death of all, and sexual rights over all the women – is one day assassinated by an alliance of the sons, who – so as not to fall back into the same lawless world – subsequently issue the prohibition against the murder of the father, and against sexual relationships with mothers and sisters. Freud once referred to this construction as our "scientific myth",[6] an oxymoron by which he only redoubles the difficulty, offering us the choice between a 'hard', 'scientific' version, and a 'soft', 'mythological', version of this outline of origins. But I think it necessary to recall that right up until the end

---

4 *Le Nouveau Petit Robert de la langue française* (Paris: Le Robert, 2010), p. 1299; our translation.
5 Freud's best synthesis on the question of incest is found in *Moses and Monotheism* (1939a), SE 23, pp. 81–83.
6 Sigmund Freud, *Group Psychology and the Analysis of the Ego* (1921c), SE 18, p. 135.

(until *Moses*) Freud will stick constantly with the 'hard', factual, historical version, and with the notion of the phylogenetic transmission of this original situation. He is thus faced with difficulties – which he doesn't duck – concerning the affirmation of phylogenesis, something he never gave up. The references to phylogenesis in his work are multiple and almost continuous, from the letter of 21 September 1897, where he announces the powerful resurgence of the 'hereditary factor', until *Moses*, where he accepts without any difficulty the notion that the scene of the father's murder could be reproduced thousands of times, finally to be inscribed in the memory of the species.

One of the interesting texts on this trajectory is "Overview of the Transference Neuroses" (1915),[7] a manuscript originally addressed to Ferenczi, in which the factual and theoretical question is tackled at its root: for example, given that they had no descendents, how could brothers castrated by the father transmit the imagined scenarios? I simply quote the last sentence of "Overview": "In sum, we are not at the end, but rather at the beginning, of an understanding of this phylogenetic factor" (ibid., p. 20).

If problems connected with phylogenesis create difficulties for psychoanalysis in relation to history and prehistory, psychoanalysis is nevertheless, and of necessity, engaged in a dialogue with anthropology. However, even if *Totem and Taboo* is a text that demands to be debated on an equal footing with other great anthropological texts, the discussion will come to an abrupt end for lack of true common ground.

The incest prohibition as far as the anthropologists are concerned is a law imposed on one or more kinship groups; it bears principally upon exchange, exogamy and their social outcome: procreation. It is focused on sisters (or 'classificatory' sisters), who cannot marry within the group. In contradistinction, *the psychoanalytic incest prohibition* remains narrowly coextensive with the Oedipal triangle, the

---

[7] In Sigmund Freud, *A Phylogenetic Fantasy: Overview of the Transference Neuroses*, trans. Axel Hoffer and Peter T Hoffer, ed. Ilse Grubrich-Simitis (Cambridge, Mass & London: Harvard, 1987).

references to more removed kinship, such as sisters, being treated as extensions (displacements) of the basic Oedipus. The major form of incest is always considered to be mother-son incest. But on both sides, among the majority of anthropologist-ethnologists and analysts, various points are widely underestimated: father-daughter incest, homosexual incest, and above all the multiplicity within any given society of sexual prohibitions and restrictions of all types, which are quite different from incest – even if the latter does remain a major element within a potentially abundant lexicon.

But in order to see the whole picture, let us return to incest and its prohibition as they are understood, as an unwritten Vulgate, within the analytic community:

— the 'scientific myth' of *Totem and Taboo* is maintained, but the stress is laid on the *myth* aspect rather than on the reference to *science* (prehistory);

— phylogenesis is hardly ever invoked, but still less is it discussed or refuted, it is maintained, on hold, as a kind of relic, a Freudian caprice, a taboo piece of the theory;

— it is affirmed, with hardly any proof, that the incest taboo ensures the maintenance of the difference between the sexes and the difference between the generations, although one might rather say that it depends on them;

— for certain analysts, incest and its taboo would be a 'primal fantasy', an object of what is known as primal repression. With such terms as 'primal' the reference to the dark night of origins is incontrovertible, as it is in all mythic narratives.

Let us return again to the status of the *Totem and Taboo* myth. First and foremost, it is tightly intricated with the Oedipus complex, and it is asserted that each is inscribed within phylogenesis. In this sense, the myth would be central to the constitution of the Unconscious, as its kernel. There thus exists a double option with regard to myth in general: either it is universal by right, 'primal' (and it would be absolutely necessary to give some idea of its prehistoric genesis, which, according to

Freud, is bound to the first real act: "In the beginning was the deed");[8] or – and this is my position – it is a structure that varies greatly according to the multiple contingencies of kinship relations, and provides, as Levi-Strauss puts it so well, a solution that enables the "[relief] of intellectual uneasiness and even existential anxiety".[9]

The fact that a 'structure' (be it the Oedipus, incest or castration) has a widespread incidence, does not necessarily imply that, from the metapsychological point of view, it is buried in the unconscious. It belongs to the domain of the preconscious in its task of helping to put into narrative the – conscious-preconscious, unconscious – history of the subject, and therefore of the analysand.

I see that, so far, I have only sidestepped my main theme of how to bring together and articulate the incest prohibition with what is called the polymorphous sexuality of the child. To say that these are connected is to say that they are able to coexist. However, this is hardly possible if one wishes to locate the problem of incest at the age where it could be conceptualised by the child in a given society – that is to say, at the age when the child has at his disposal the corresponding categories of Father, Mother, Sister, Brother, Aunt, etc.

In fact, the aporia remains absolute for as long as we cling to the perspective of only one of the protagonists. If by 'ego' we refer, as do the anthropologists, to the character from whose point of view one places oneself in order to contemplate the entire process, there is no doubt that in the classical psychoanalytic conception this ego is the child, as much within the oedipal triangle as within the incest/taboo configuration of incest.

But this problem already becomes more acute with Melanie

---

8 [*Editor:* A quotation from Goethe's *Faust* (Part 1, scene 3) that concludes Freud's *Totem and Taboo* (1912-13), *SE* 13, p.161].

9 Claude Lévi-Strauss, *The Jealous Potter*, trans. Bénédicte Chorier (Chicago and London: Chicago UP, 1988), p. 171. For further developments, see Jean Laplanche, "La psychanalyse, mythes et théorie", in *Entre séduction et inspiration: l'homme* (Paris: Presses Universitaires de France, 1999).

Klein: we see the drives and even the Oedipus targeting the parents, slip to the earliest age (the paranoid phase) in the child's fantasies.

With Lacan, we witness a complete reversal of the situation. At first the child is the object of the desire of the mother, and does not manifest any inclination to behave as an 'ego' in the above sense. Hence the famous Lacanian schema of the 'preoedipal triangle': mother–child–phallus. For Lacan, incest is explicitly conceived as being perpetrated by the mother. We know that from this point of view it would be the father who brings forth the 'cut' (between mother and child), the incest prohibition and the Law. It would take too long to carry out a close criticism of this position. Let us simply say that it provides, in new terms, another formulation of what Margaret Mahler referred to as the symbiotic phase. However, all conceptions of primitive symbiosis or absolute primary narcissism are contradicted by the many modern observations of a precocious and reciprocal communication, on the model of what is today called attachment, between the adult dispenser of care (*die Pflegeperson*) and the *infans* (literally, without language).

My own position is very different from Lacan's. I do not insist on the centrality of the desire of the mother, which would encompass everything from the beginning and to which the paternal 'metaphor' or function would put an end. However prevalent may be the classic familial positions of father, mother and child, it seems necessary to distance oneself from them in order to bring to the fore what I call the 'fundamental anthropological situation'. Following Ferenczi's thoroughly innovative suggestions concerning what occurs 'between the child and the adult', I think that vis-à-vis the first years of life and the sexuality connected to them, the central point to consider is not, fundamentally, the relation between the child and the two parents (insofar as they are related by blood) but the fact that those who raise the child are *adults* ("the person in charge of [the child] … as a rule, [the] mother" ["die Pflegeperson … in der Regel doch die Mutter"],

Freud says in the *Three Essays*),[10] which means that the *kinship* relation is not determinant in the first situation in which the *infans* finds itself. What matters above all is the absolute difference of age and development, together with its corollary: a fledgling child who has no *innate* sexual drives (there is no proof of their existence) and an adult who is inhabited not just by his adult, genital sexuality but also by infantile sexuality derived from his own childhood.

In *On Dreams*, Freud writes: "almost every civilized man retains the infantile forms of sexual life in some respect or other. We can thus understand how it is that repressed infantile sexual wishes provide the most frequent and strongest motive-forces for the constructions of dreams".[11] Besides the dream, however, the major situation capable of reactivating (*regen*) the adult's dormant infantile sexuality is actually that of caring for a child: in this situation, reciprocity and asymmetry coexist. The reciprocity pertains to the adult/*infans* exchanges on the level of self-preservation or attachment. The asymmetry derives from the fact that only the adult harbours within him a repressed infantile sexual unconscious, and that this unconscious will try to infiltrate the self-preservative communication, to the point of rendering it almost unintelligible. Such are what I call the 'enigmatic messages' addressed to the child.

But we must not overlook the following point: no individual is in possession of the means of translating all adult messages imbued with sexuality, and therefore of partially repressing them. In some cases, infantile sexuality is both translated and repressed. In others, it remains in the form of untranslated traces, ready to be acted out in perversions.

Let us leave these theoretical considerations in order to note what we see around us: the multiplication of sexual abuses committed against children by adults. I shall not here enter into historical

---

10 *Three Essays on the Theory of Sexuality* (1905d), SE 7, p. 223..
11 *On Dreams* (1901a), SE 5, p. 682.

considerations as to whether these abuses are now more numerous than was formerly the case, or just more extensively disclosed in media reports and legal charges.

What is, in any case, striking is the effacement of incest as such compared to sexual crime committed by adults. In France, by the way, incest is not in itself a crime (a father and an adult daughter are perfectly able to cohabit) but merely one aggravating factor, tucked away within offences that may be committed upon a minor 'by a person in authority'. A single example, among the horrible headlines with which the press assails us: "Four year old child raped at home". Whether the abuse is committed by the father or a more distant relative or a neighbour makes no difference to the horror of the crime.

On the other hand, without having to enter here into the detail of the acts committed – from molestation through to sodomy and fellatio, up to torture and murder – it is hard to resist the psychoanalytic notion of a perverse acting out of fantasies that have their origin in the infantile sexuality of the adult. I shall add only one point: I once wondered whether the phrase 'sexual crime' mightn't be glossed by the term 'crime *qua* sexual', by which I mean that from rape through to the most diverse crimes – crimes of passion, gratuitous crimes, gangster-related or terrorist crime – the infantile sexual root in the adult author of the crime could be justifiably evoked and explored by the psychoanalyst.

To stick within the frame of our society as it is evolving, one thus sees that the incest prohibition is being diluted in the underlying evolution of the family: widespread divorce, recomposed families, multiple adoptions, homosexual unions with or without children who are adopted or conceived by biomedical artifice. On the horizon not of science fiction but of the evolution of genetics, we are forced to await the appearance of parthenogenesis or human cloning. The analyst must be wary about approving or condemning all such prospects, if he is willing to imagine that, one day perhaps, an individual will come for a consultation who has no *biological* father or mother, but who would have been cared for in his earliest days by benevolent adults.

Perhaps, then, we will see the term incest fade little by little and become indefinable – but this would not prevent sexual crime from thriving.

In order to draw towards a conclusion, I initiate here two reflections on major themes: an anthropological theme and a clinico-theoretical theme.

The anthropological theme is entitled 'drive renunciation' (*Triebverzicht*). It again takes support from Freud, in a line of texts that form a guiding thread throughout his entire oeuvre.

The kick-off, it seems to me, occurs with a small text from Draft N. I reproduce it here for an immediate gloss:

> May 31, 1897: 'Holiness' is something based on the fact that human beings, for the benefit of the larger community, have sacrificed a portion of their sexual liberty and their liberty to indulge in perversions. The horror of incest (something impious) is based on the fact that as a result of community of sexual life (even in childhood) the members of a family hold together permanently and become incapable of contact with strangers. Thus incest is antisocial – civilization consists in this progressive renunciation. Contrariwise the 'superman'.[12]

I shall underline only those words which anticipate the developments to come: "*sacrificing*" a portion of sexual liberty; "*sexual liberty and the liberty to indulge in perversions*"; "the sexual community: *even in childhood*"; "*renunciation*".

In this passage, drive renunciation is already set forth as being

---

12 "Draft N" (1950 [31st May, 1897]), *SE* 1, p. 257.

necessary for cultural progress. The interpretation of the incest taboo seems to head in the direction of Lévi-Strauss's theory: it would be a correlate of the accession to the larger community.[13]

The theme of drive renunciation will be found in almost the same terms as Draft N[14] in the 1908 text, "'Civilized' Sexual Morality and Modern Nervous Illness".[15] A text that sounds nowadays like a warning cry, or even a cry of contained despair, in the face of so-called 'Victorian' morals. But here the renunciation, far from being limited to 'perverse' sexuality, includes the entirety of sexual relationships, except for those that aim at procreation within marriage. Yet, in spite of this manifest denunciation, Freud takes great care not to dictate precepts, not to recommend 'sexual freedom', and still less to abandon the idea of a *necessary* 'drive renunciation' (*Triebverzicht*).

This need for drive renunciation will henceforth run throughout the oeuvre. By way of example, let us cite "The Acquisition and Control of Fire",[16] where the cultural hero (Prometheus), far from being a rebel mounting an attack on behalf of 'sexual freedom', is the one who imposes renunciation on his subjects. And of course there's *Civilization and Its Discontents*, whose meanderings I shall refrain from following, and finally the *Moses*. What emerges from all the Freudian texts, from first to last, is that some aspect of irreconcilability (*Unverträglichkeit*) exists between sexuality and a human development towards the civilized state. It remains necessary to grasp the irreconcilable elements 'on both sides'.

---

13 In the *Three Essays* we find a passage that prefigures Lévi-Strauss's theses on this point very exactly: "Respect for [the incest] barrier is essentially a cultural demand made by society. Society must defend itself against the danger that the interests which it needs for the establishment of higher social units may be swallowed up by the family; and for this reason, in the case of every individual, but in particular of adolescent boys, it seeks by all possible means to loosen their connection to the family – a connection which, in their childhood, is the only important one", op.cit., p. 225.
14 Did Freud keep a copy of this part of the correspondence with Fliess?
15 (1908d), *SE* 9, pp. 177–204.
16 (1932a), *SE* 22, pp. 183–93.

On the side of the sexual, Freud is relatively clear: what is by nature irreconcilable is the polymorphously perverse infantile sexual drive. But with what is this drive irreconcilable? Here we encounter two answers – the one external, the other internal – both of which can be preserved.

On the one hand, it is *irreconcilable with culture*, with society in general. A formula that has the disadvantage of granting 'society' a kind of force in itself, an energy, and also an intention: that of reproducing itself.

On the other hand, it is *irreconcilable … with itself*. The infantile sexual drive, with its *unbinding*, anarchic function, with its pursuit of excitation rather than satisfaction, is, so to speak, self-destructive. Following the rules of the primary process alone, it cannot in itself, after depletion, tend towards anything other than a 'zero level', and even to the psychical and possibly physical annihilation of the individual. Here, you may recognize our interpretation of the 'death drive' as the 'sexual death drive'.

But, conversely, 'renunciation' does not mean annihilation. For pregenital sexuality the paths are open to repression (which is always partial) and translation, to narrativisation and being put to use – which amounts to nothing less than sublimation, if we are willing to withdraw the 'sublime' aspect and to see in sublimation the movement of symbolization-translation that is available to most human beings. The primary objective of the sublimations is, quite simply, genital sexuality, insofar as it appears able to integrate the perverse infantile components.

I cannot finish this anthropological section without evoking the person of Maurice Godelier, a major French ethnologist-anthropologist. The virtue of his principal work, *Les métamorphoses de le parenté*,[17] consists in the fact that for the first time – or one of the rare times – we have an anthropologist who doesn't neglect sexuality in the Freudian sense – sexuality as the search for pleasure – to the exclusive benefit of desexualized concepts such as reproduction, marriage and exchange.

---

17 Maurice Godelier, , *Les métamorphoses de le parenté* (Paris: Fayard, 2004).

Maurice Godelier has the merit of recognising from the very start that the 'misuses of sex' are much more numerous than simply incest.[18]

One could perhaps summarize his position as follows: incest (together with its taboo) is a 'central'[19] concept among the most diverse peoples, quite definable (because of the positivity of kinship relations) and likely to encompass or to serve as a 'screen' (*Deck*), in the Freudian sense of the term, for stigmatizing a much broader range of practices. Godelier thinks that the existence of such prohibitions is essential to a regulated use of reproductive sexuality within society. But, informed by a kind of reverence for 'society' and its 'power' (which he conceives of as veritable entelechies), he fails to see that in the individual psyche these prohibitions work above all against the anarchic functioning of the sexual death drive.

My final development, which is clinical and metapsychological, has more importance for us as psychoanalysts.

It is essential that we hold firm on several points:

1) *"The neuroses are – so to say - the negative of perversions"*[20] – a Freudian formula which is obviously directed at infantile sexuality, and which implies a radical difference of status between the sexual contents in the normal-neurotic and those in the perverse psychopath.

2) *The fundamental anthropological situation* is the human given *par excellence*, beyond even the Oedipus complex.

3) The adult/*infans* and, subsequently, adult/child relation, are at once the *birthplace of polymorphous drive sexuality*, the very site where sexual crimes can occur, and perhaps even (if our generalisation is accepted) the site of crimes in general.

---

18 Godelier can certainly be reproached for having appropriated a little too hastily the Freudian concept of polymorphously perverse sexuality and, in a general way, for neglecting the Freudian contribution, apart from the myth of the primal father.
19 "Incest occupies a central place among the multiple uses of the sex which each society rejects as being wicked" (Godelier, *Les metamorphoses*, ibid., p. 419).
20 "The Sexual Aberrations", *Three Essays on the Theory of Sexuality*, op.cit., p.165.

From saying this to saying, as the title of a recent book suggests, "All Paedophiles?",[21] there is of course a step that I absolutely refuse to take. A confusion which would quickly lead to this eminently practical, even ethical question: is it necessary to hunt down and to condemn any intrusion of adult sexuality into the 'innocent' being of the child, even to dedicate oneself to denying infantile sexuality and the Freudian discovery? We know the absurdities, the paralogisms and the witch hunts of all kinds which have their origin in the confusion of an already difficult question: the delimitation between messages that, through symptoms, slips or parapraxes, are infiltrated (and inescapably so) by the unconscious infantile sexuality of the adult, and sexual acts to which the child is forced to submit, in which the message part is increasingly thin, and unbound violence is increased – the sign of psychopathic perversion and ultimately the pressure of the death drive.

Here, given the wanderings and digressions of the courts, of public opinion and of experts of all kinds, it appears imperative, above all for the psychoanalyst, who deliberately situates himself apart from the domain of action (and apart from prescriptive speech of whatever kind), to find some theoretical reference points to frame his clinical views and even his therapeutic interventions.

The model suggested is thus deliberately theoretical, at once dynamic and topographic. It is that of the 'third topography' initially outlined by Freud in his article on "The Splitting of the Ego in the Process of Defence",[22] subsequently refined by Christophe Dejours[23] and completed or modified by myself in "Three Meanings of the Term 'Unconscious' in the Framework of the General Theory of Seduction".[24] I present the diagrams from that text here, but can only comment on them briefly.

---

21 Elsa Guiol, *Tous pédophiles?* (Paris: Editions de la Martiniere, 2005).
22 *SE* 23, pp. 271–278.
23 Christophe Dejours, *Le corps d'abord* (Paris: Payot, 2001 [1986]).
24 Present volume, essay 10.

Incest and Infantile Sexuality

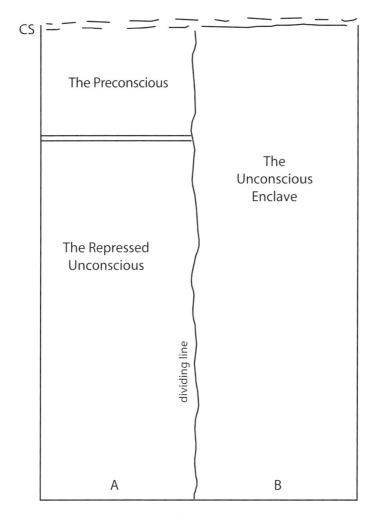

Figure 1

Incest and Infantile Sexuality

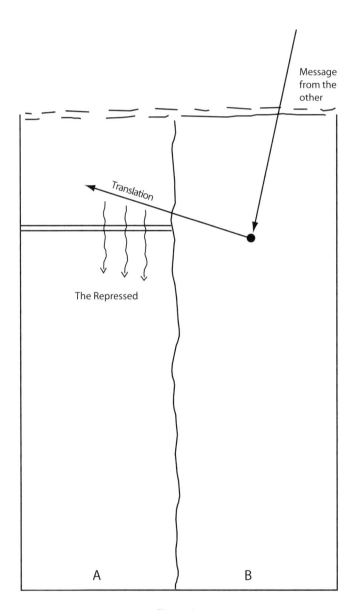

Figure 2

Incest and Infantile Sexuality

The compromised and sexualized message coming from the adult other knows two fates once it reaches the child. Either it remains 'enclaved' [*enclavé*] - 'inserted / enclosed',[25] in the 'amential' state, which is to say untreated, unsymbolized, untranslated by the small child [see side B, figures 1 and 2]; or it is translated (a process which takes place after a waiting period), included in the history of the subject. In the latter case, there remains a repressed unconscious residue. What remains *permanently* in the unconscious enclave is obviously not the same type of communication as what can be translated. With the former we have something violent and unassimilable (barely a message at all), and with the latter a type of the return of the repressed.

When the subject becomes adult, he reiterates this alternative with respect to his own *'infans'*. In the one situation, there is a conscious-preconscious message addressed to the child and compromised by a return of the sexual *repressed* (the *repressed unconscious*), but without being completely untranslatable: this is what I call the 'enigmatic message'. In the other situation, we have the perverse, psychopathic even psychotic acting out, itself derived from an old 'enclaved' (*enclavé*) acting out from which all psychic elaboration has been excluded: this is what we nowadays see appearing in the media and in the courts.

This topography is obviously only schematic and, fortunately for the possibilities of psychotherapy, the two processes can be entangled with or contaminated by each other: in my view, there is no perverse acting out in which we cannot grasp some small scrap or fragment of message. On the other hand, the fresh 'treatment' of the repressed unconscious (in particular by the analysis) can give rise to a forceful movement in the unconscious enclave.[26]

---

25 [*Editor:* Lacking verbal forms in English for the English noun 'enclave' (the French has *enclaver, enclavé*), we have specified the double and linked meanings of 'insertion / enclosure.' See note 6, essay 10]}.

26 [*Editor*: Clearly Laplanche intends a verbal parallel both in the text and in the diagrams in order to point to the conceptual contrast between *'l'inconscient refoulé'* (the repressed unconscious) and *'l'inconscient enclavé'* which we have translated as 'the unconscious enclave'].

Finally, insertion-enclosure [*enclavement*] and the resultant exclusion of any psychic elaboration can be transmitted from 'generation' to 'generation'.[27] Indeed, even if we observe forms of transmission of the perverse suffering-acting out that involve reiteration without elaboration, such a 'transgenerational' process, as it is sometimes called, never occurs in a mechanical and linear way. The vicissitudes always remain individual and particular, even though they are marked with a common seal, and each reorientation in the lineage would only be possible by the intervention of real, fortuitous circumstances. A new translation of the unconscious enclave always remains conceivable.

Having put all of this forward for further reflection, I should not wish to finish without insisting on the central, Freudian point: drive renunciation (*Triebverzicht*) far from being a dictat of the superego is the cultural destiny of every human being, translating and putting into narrative form for himself the messages of the other, including their most enigmatic sexual aspects.

---

[27] Here, I am not simply speaking about genetic parent-child 'generations' but of transmission-reiteration, whatever the kinship ties may be.

19

CASTRATION AND OEDIPUS AS CODES AND NARRATIVE SCHEMAS[1]

Castration and Oedipus, which Freud refers to as 'complexes', are organized sets of representations of fantasies, affects and drive impulses. Freud also employs the terms 'configuration', 'situation', etc.

These situations would be real situations, really lived by the child in relation to his human surroundings.

But it should be noted at the outset that for Freud these situations, right down to certain details, are determined, prefigured, by phylogenetic inheritance. Thus the fantasy of castration is classified among the 'primal fantasies' inscribed through phylogenesis. As to the Oedipus complex, which can be regarded as the much broader situation encompassing the primal fantasies, its phylogenetic origin is explicitly affirmed in "The Dissolution of the Oedipus Complex": "Although the majority of human beings go through the Oedipus complex as an individual experience, it is nevertheless a phenomenon that is determined and laid down by heredity and is bound to pass away according to programme when the next pre-ordained phase of development sets in".[2] There is no use in blinding ourselves to those

---

1 Paris, July 2006.
2 (1924d), *SE* 19, p. 174.

aspects of the classical Freud that are in line with a certain developmental psychology.

As regards *phylogenesis* and the mode of acquisition of the complexes in question, it should be stressed that Freud never denied that his ideas were in conflict with the reigning theories of acquisition. According to Freud, such acquisition is accomplished neither in the Darwinian nor in the Lamarkian mode. These two modes are supposed to bring to the species (in different ways) a survival advantage: mutations and the selection of the strongest, according to Darwin; adaptation to the environment according to Lamarck. For Freud it is something else entirely: a kind of inscription in the memory of the species, conceived of as a little like the memory of the individual. A lived experience that exerts a very strong impression on the collective mind, or is repeated thousands of times (or even both), is inscribed in the collective memory as a lived sequence of events that will subsequently impregnate individual memories and come back to life in the existences of individuals. So it is, for example, for the famous 'Murder of the father', one of the pillars of the Oedipus, which is not absent as a desire in any of the 'children of men'.

It is remarkable that this theory of a collective memory[3] founded on the force and the repetition of the original impression, continues to live on in the arsenal of presuppositions kept by many psychoanalysts, without ever being called into question itself.

It is remarkable too that Freud allowed his admiration for Darwin to coexist with a theory of engrammation – of mental inscription –which is so foreign to that of natural selection.

Let us first consider separately the concepts of castration and the Oedipus complex. Such a separation is conceptually possible;

---

3 "In my opinion there is an almost complete conformity in this respect between the individual and the group: in the group too an impression of the past is retained in unconscious memory traces", Sigmund Freud, *Moses and Monotheism* (1939a), *SE* 23, p. 94.

indeed 'castration' itself comprises two distinct aspects: on the one hand, the perception of – and reaction to – the anatomical difference of the sexes; on the other hand, the attribution of this difference to a cutting-off, itself the correlative of a conflict.

I have for a long time placed emphasis on this 'anatomical difference of the sexes', so as to distinguish its characteristics clearly.[4] First of all, it is an anatomical difference, and not physiological or biological. (As such, the notion of, for example, the 'biological' foundation of the 'refusal of femininity' disappears). It relates to the morphology of the organs and not to their functioning. Moreover, this difference is not a scientific, but a purely popular and essentially visual difference. I have stressed the idea that with the transition to the upright posture in humanoids, only the male external organs remained perceptible. But this anthropological consideration, with its evolutionist overtones, is not the essential thing. What counts, what is striking about the *representations* of man and woman, is the presence or absence of visible genitals. Greek statuary is only the most developed example here.

Freud returned on several occasions to the child's perception of difference. He often introduced nuances with regard to the more or less universal consequences attributed by the child to this 'perception'. And yet what is perception of a 'lack'? One would here run up against the aporias developed by Bergson apropos of the idea of nothingness. It can be seen that Freud had trouble separating the idea of the difference of the sexes from that of a cutting-off of one of the genital organs.

It fell, however, to two authors,[5] who for a long time carried out analytical observations on young children, to supply new observations that better enable the establishment of this distinction between 'castration' as difference and castration as the consequence

---

4 Cf. "Gender, Sex and the *Sexual*" in this volume.
5 Herman Roiphe and Eleanor Galenson *The Infantile Origins of Sexual Identity* (New York: International Universities Press, 1981).

of a removal of one of the two genital organs. To be sure, their ideas are not always conceptually precise, in spite of the meticulousness of their observations. In any case, the conclusion is obvious: it would be advisable to envisage, prior to the oedipal period at which a close connection comes into play between the Oedipus and castration, an 'early genital' phase, unconnected to the person of the parents, where "sexual difference and the new genital sensations" (ibid., p. 285.) come into play in their own right. To this phase belongs by rights, with variations according to both sexes, the awareness or the taking into account of boy/girl difference, such as Freud himself defines it: presence or absence of the phallus. This phase would be connected to an 'early castration reaction', but where castration is perceived as a danger without being ascribed to a castrating (oedipal) figure. It is certainly on this point regarding the 'early castration reaction' that the authors are least explicit, but their observations leave no doubt about the threat that is frequently connected to the perception of difference. Undoubtedly this threat is explained by the authors in relation to their fidelity to the Mahlerean theses concerning the process of 'separation-individuation' and its dangers. Thus "the emergence of the genital phase, including the pre-oedipal castration reaction, reactivates and becomes fused with the earlier fears of both object and anal loss"(ibid.).

Also extremely interesting is the divergent description of the way in which the boy and the girl treat castration: denial, or symbolization.

It remains the case that if one takes into account the way in which the authors describe the experience of the difference, two different paths appear, just as in Freud himself: either the absence is immediately attributed to a possible cutting-off, to a 'castration' (which means, from a logical point of view, that something is separated from a larger totality: the penis from the body); or presence and absence coexist like two opposed terms (1 and 0), as Freud will set forth in an extraordinarily abrupt formula for the little girl: "She has seen it and knows that she is without it and wants to have it".[6]

This opposition of the 0 and the 1 is what will guide part of our subsequent considerations. First of all, though, I cannot move on without a more thorough discussion of the Oedipus complex and the position that is given to it in psychoanalysis as well as in myth.

I shall start from a banal consideration: the one to whom action is attributed in the Oedipus ('ego' in the anthropological sense) is Oedipus himself: in the mythical version, King Oedipus; in the psychoanalytic version, the child vis-à-vis the parental couple. Oedipus is the *initiator* of the murder and of the incest. From the sexual point of view in particular this supposes in the child an innate incestuous sexual desire, which moreover accords with the phylogenetic hypothesis.

I have on several occasions developed the idea of a fundamental anthropological situation (FAS), a situation in which an *infans* [literally, without language], who is not supplied with sexual drives, is *from the beginnings* of life confronted with an *adult* who harbours within himself not only mature sexual experience, but also the more or less well integrated remainders (repressed – sublimated) of his infantile sexuality. It should be added, moreover, that this situation is from the outset one of *communication*, adult and child communicating on the level of care and attachment, while on the side of the adult, and of the adult alone, sexual signals are able to come to light sporadically.

If, to simplify things, it is admitted that the adult in question is generally the father or the mother, one sees that there is, so to speak, a misattribution with respect to the initiation of the complex. The initiator of messages bearing sexuality is unquestionably the parent (or the adult). The incestuous one, potentially, is the adult. I am obviously not speaking here about *actual acts of sexual abuse*, which do raise some complex metapsychological problems, but about the normal adult or banal neurotic.

---

6 "Some Psychical Consequences of the Anatomical Distinction Between the Sexes" (1925j), *SE* 19, p. 252.

How could the initiation of the Oedipus – and of incest – be thus turned around so as to be transferred from the adult to the child? Obviously by the identification of the child with the aggressor: the victim of the incest makes himself its subject.

Greek mythology gives us at least two occurrences of this inversion: the Oedipus myth itself includes as a prelude a paedophilic episode committed by the father of Oedipus, but on another child. The second episode, the 'classical' Oedipus, consequently seems like the manifest reversal of the first episode, of passivity into activity.

Consider too the myth of Phaedra. The Queen has the intention to commit incest with her (step)son. Then seeing that she is about to be found out, she accuses Hippolytus of having courted her. The murder of Hippolytus by his own jealous father completes the total inversion of the situation.

It is thus easy to decipher the reversal, which makes of the paedophilia a desire for incest, for which the child is responsible.

It is necessary within this framework to point out again the double position of the castration complex: its independent position, on the one hand, where it acts as a code based on presence/absence; and on the other hand, its position of intrication with the Oedipus complex, where it enters into the *story* as principal punishment for the crime. This double position, as independent code and as fragment of a 'narrative schema', will be deployed when it comes to the treatment of the fundamental anthropological situation.

The FAS is characterised by enigmatic messages sent by the adult, and which the child (after a period of latency) will have to 'treat', to 'translate'.

Up to now we have identified at least two types of message: those bound to sexual excitation within the framework of the care given to the child; others bound to the assignment of a gender to the child, where we have located 'identification by the social network'.

These two types of message are treated by the child with the assistance offered by the (essentially human) environment. As such, we attribute the greatest importance to the perception of the *difference* between the sexes for translating and elaborating the *diversity* of the genders, which is itself offered from the very outset by the immediate social environment. Translated into the presence or absence of the penis, the difference between the genders will assert itself right up to the 'Oedipus complex'.

We are, however, far from affirming with Freud that the Oedipus complex is a 'situation'; and still less a situation that is initiated by the child. The Oedipus complex was and remains a myth, from its Sophoclean version to its Freudian and post-Freudian versions.

It helps the child to put into narrative – at the price of his own culpability – the often much more raw sexual messages that are conveyed to him by the parent, the adult. Sexually speaking, it proposes a much watered down version of these messages, even if it is not without a certain stimulating value in itself.

Vanquishing the father, marrying the mother – here are aims that, beyond any sexuality, have an obvious affirmative value: which is the reason Marie Delcourt once subtitled a book on Oedipus "the legend of the conqueror".[7]

These romances, these scenarios that vary according to the individual, would thus be of the order of culturally transmitted narrative schemas and not, as classical theory would have it, of phylogenetic, supposedly 'primal' fantasies.

To conclude, one may wonder about the validity of the code/narrative-schema dualism. Clearly the first term refers to a restricted number of elements (2 in castration!) suitable for transcribing a given message. This is, of course, at the expense of the richness and the fidelity of the translation. 'Narrative schema' refers to a theory of nar-

---

7 Marie Delcourt, *Oedipe ou la légende du conquérant* (Paris: Les Belles Lettres, 1981 [orig. 1944]).

rativity in which the restricted code is submitted to scenarios that are more or less rich, popular and flexible. It is perfectly possible, however, to speak about a history 'translated into Oedipus', because its elements are relatively fixed, their relations sufficiently predictable, so that the passage from one 'romance' to another is possible. The 'remakes'[8] of a film are sometimes superior to and richer than the original version, sometimes inferior. There is nothing to prohibit each human from trying. Translation? 'New version'. For us the 'translational' hypothesis remains for now the most reliable, and is not without linguistic foundation (Jakobson).

The idea of an 'aid to translation', and of its sociocultural origin, coming to the service of a 'drive to translate', is further corroborated by the psychoanalytic study of *fairytales*. Their narrative schemas are relatively fixed and limited in number, their oedipal and castration themes, just like those related to infantile sexuality, are easily recognizable. The child's need always to hear again and in the same terms the same tales, supports the need to reaffirm the accuracy of the translation.

---

8 [*Trans*. In English in the original].

BIBLIOGRAPHY

Abbreviations
SE *The Standard Edition of the Complete Psychological Works of Sigmund Freud*, ed. and trans. James Strachey et al, vols. 1-24, London: The Hogarth Press, 1953-74. The references to Freud's works carry a lower case letter after each date, which follows the listing of the works for each year of publication in the *Standard Edition*.

GW *Gesammelte Werke*, eds. Anna Freud with Marie Bonaparte et al, vols. 1-17, London: Imago Publishing Co., 1940-52; vol. 18 Frankfurt am Maine: Fischer Verlag, 1968.

When more than one date appears in a given entry, the date immediately after the author's name is the date of first publication, followed by the date of composition in square brackets where this is significantly different. Except for the Freud references, the date of the first English translation is given at the end of the reference.

André, Jacques (1995), *Aux origines féminines de la sexualité* (Paris: Presses Universitaires de France).

Assoun, Paul-Laurent (1976), *Freud, la philosophie et les philosophes* (Paris: Presses Universitaires de France).

Balint, Michael (1935), "Critical Notes on the Theory of the Pregenital Organisations of the Libido", in *Primary Love and Psychoanalytic Technique* (London: The Hogarth Press, 1952).
———(1951), "On Love and Hate", in *Primary Love and Psychoanalytic Technique* (London: The Hogarth Press, 1952).
———(1952), "Early Developmental States of the Ego. Primary Object Love", in *Primary Love and Psychoanalytic Technique* (London: The Hogarth Press, 1952).

de Beauvoir, Simone (1949), *The Second Sex*, trans. H.M. Parshley (London: Picador, 1988).

Bourguignon, André (1968), "Neurophysiologie du rêve et théorie psychanalytique", *La Psychiatrie de l'enfant*, vol. 11, no. 1.

Butler, Judith (1990), *Gender Trouble: Feminism and the Subversion of Identity* (London and New York: Routledge).
———(1993), *Bodies that Matter: On the Discursive Limits of Sex*, (London and New York: Routledge).

Hua, Cai (2001), *A Society without Fathers or Husbands: The Na of China*, trans. Asti Hustvedt (New York: Zone Books).

Carroy, H. (1903–1909), *Dictionnaire biographique international des écrivains*, vols. 1-4 (Paris: G. Olms, 1987).

Corbett, Greville (1991), *Gender* (Cambridge: Cambridge University Press).

Costes, Alain (2003), *Lacan: Le fourvoiement linguistique* (Paris: Presses Universitaires de France).

Dejours, Christophe (1986), *Le corps d'abord* (Paris: Payot, 2001).

Delcourt, Marie (1944), *Oedipe ou la légende du conquérant* (Paris: Les Belles Lettres, 1981).

Dornes, Martin (1996), "La théorie de Margaret Mahler reconsidérée", in *Psyche*, vol. 50, no. 11. Reprinted in Martin Dornes, *Psychanalyse et psychologie du première âge* (Paris: Presses Universitaires de France, 2002).

Fenichel, Otto (1946), *The Psychoanalytic Theory of Neurosis* (London: Routledge, 1946).

Ferenczi, Sàndor (1933), "Confusion of Tongues between Adult and the Child: The Language of Tenderness and of Passion", in *Sandor Ferenczi: Selected Writings*, ed. Julia Borossa (Harmondsworth: Penguin Books, 1999).
———(1969), "Attention During the Narration of Dreams", *Further Contributions to the Theory and Technique of Psychoanalysis*, trans. Jane Isabel Suttie et al. (London: The Hogarth Press).
———(1969),"To Whom does one Relate one's Dream?", *Further Contributions to the Theory and Technique of Psychoanalysis*, trans. Jane Isabel Suttie et al. (London: The Hogarth Press).

Feyerabend, Paul (1975), *Against Method* (London: Verso, 2010).

Florence, Jean (1978), *L'identification dans la théorie freudienne* (Universités Saint-Louis: Brussels).

Fox, Robin (1967), *Kinship and Marriage: An Anthropological Perspective* (Harmondsworth: Penguin Books).

Freud, Sigmund (1896c), "The Aetiology of Hysteria", *SE* 3.
———(1898a), "Sexuality in the Aetiology of the Neuroses", *SE* 3.
———(1900a), *The Interpretation of Dreams*, *SE* 4 and 5.
———(1901a), *On Dreams*, *SE* 5.

———(1905d), *Three Essays on the Theory of Sexuality, SE* 7.
———(1908c), "On the Sexual Theories of Children", *SE* 9.
———(1908d), "'Civilised' Sexual Morality and Modern Nervous Illness", *SE* 9
———(1909d), "Notes Upon a Case of Obsessional Neurosis", *SE* 10.
———(1911c), "Psycho-Analytic Notes on an Autobiographical Account of a Case of Paranoia (Dementia Paranoides)", *SE* 12.
———(1912d), "On the Universal Tendency to Debasement in the Sphere of Love" *SE* 11.
———(1912–13), *Totem and Taboo, SE* 13.
———(1914c), "On Narcissism: An Introduction", *SE* 14.
———(1914g), "Remembering, Repeating and Working Through", *SE* 12.
———(1915c), "Instincts and their Vicissitudes", *SE* 14.
———(1915e), "The Unconscious", *SE*. 14.
———(1915f)"A Case of Paranoia Running Counter to the Psychoanalytic Theory of the Disease", *SE* 14.
———(1916-17), "Lecture 15: Uncertainties and Criticisms", *Introductory Lectures on Psychoanalysis, SE* 16.
———(1916-17), "Lecture 25: Anxiety", *Introductory Lectures on Psychoanalysis, SE* 16.
———(1916-17), "Lecture 26: The Libido Theory and Narcissism", *Introductory Lectures on Psychoanalysis, SE* 16.
———(1917a), "A Difficulty in the Path of Analysis", *SE* 17.
———(1917d), "A Metapsychological Supplement to the Theory of Dreams", *SE* 14.
———(1917e), "Mourning and Melancholia", *SE* 14.
———(1919a), "Lines of Advance in Psycho-Analytic Therapy", *SE* 17.
———(1919e), "A Child is Being Beaten", *SE* 17.
———(1920a), "The Psychogenesis of a Case of Homosexuality in a Woman", *SE* 18.
———(1920g), *Beyond the Pleasure Principle, SE* 18.
———(1921c), *Group Psychology and the Analysis of the Ego, SE* 18.
———(1922a), "Dreams and Telepathy", *SE* 18.
———(1923a), "Two Encyclopedia Articles", *SE* 18.
———(1923b), *The Ego and the Id, SE* 19.
———(1923c), "Remarks on the Theory and Practice of Dream-Interpretation", *SE* 19.
———(1924d), "The Dissolution of the Oedipus Complex"
———(1925d), *An Autobiographical Study, SE* 20.
———(1925h), "Negation", *SE* 19
———(1925i), "Some Additional Notes on Dream-Interpretation as a Whole", *SE* 19.
———(1925j), "Some Psychical Consequences of the Anatomical Distinction Between the Sexes", *SE* 19.
———(1930a), *Civilisation and its Discontents, SE* 21.
———(1932a), "The Acquisition and Control of Fire", *SE* 22.

———(1933a), "Lecture 33: Femininity", *New Introductory Lectures on Psycho-Analysis*, SE 22.

———(1933a), "Lecture 35: The Question of a *Weltanschauung*", *New Introductory Lectures on Psychoanalysis*, SE 22.

———(1937c), "Analysis Terminable and Interminable", *SE* 23.

———(1937d), "Constructions in Analysis", *SE* 23.

———(1939a), *Moses and Monotheism*, SE 23.

———(1940a), *An Outline of Psychoanalysis*, SE 23.

———(1950 [31st May, 1897]), "Draft N", *Fliess Papers*, SE 1.

———(1950a [1895]), *Project for a Scientific Psychology*, SE 1.

———(1985 [1915]), *A Phylogenetic Fantasy: Overview of the Transference Neuroses*, trans. Axel Hoffer and Peter T Hoffer, ed. Ilse Grubrich-Simitis (Cambridge, Mass. & London: Harvard).

———(1985), *The Complete Letters of Sigmund Freud to Wilhelm Fliess*: 1887–1904, ed. and trans. J. M. Masson (Cambridge, Mass. & London: Harvard UP).

Godelier, Maurice (2004), *Les métamorphoses de le parenté* (Paris: Fayard).

Golse, Bernard (2004), review of *L'avenir de la psychanalyse*, in *Le Carnet psy* no 94, November.

Gortais, Jean "Le concept de symbiose en psychanalyse", in *Psychanalyse à l'Université*, vol. 12, no. 46.

Granger, Bernard (2004), *L'avenir de la psychanalyse: débat entre Daniel Widlöcher and Jacques-Alain Miller* (Paris: Le Cavalier Bleu).

de la Grasserie, Raoul (1898), "La catégorie psychologique de la classification, révélée par le langage", *Revue philosophique*, vol. 45.

Green, André (1979), "L'enfant modèle", in *Nouvelle revue de psychanalyse*, vol. 19.

Guiol, Elsa (2005), *Tous pédophiles?* (Paris: Editions de la Martiniere).

Gutton, Philippe (2003), *Le pubertaire* (Paris: Presses Universitaires de France).

Heimann, Paula (1950), "On Counter-Transference", *International Journal of Psycho-Analysis*, vol. 31.

Hirata, Helena, Laborie, Françoise, Ledoaré Hélène, Senotier, Danièle (2000), *Dictionnaire critique du féminisme*, (Paris: Presses Universitaires de France).

Holmes, Jeremy (1996), *Attachment, Intimacy, Autonomy: Using Attachment Theory in Adult Psychotherapy* (New York: Jason Aronson).

Jakobson, Roman (1959), "On the Linguistic Aspects of Translation", in *The Translation Studies Reader*, ed. Lawrence Venuti (New York & London: Routledge, 2000).

Kernberg, Otto (1995), *Love Relations* (New Haven and London: Yale University Press).

Klein, Melanie (1952), "On Observing the Behaviour of Young Infants", in *Envy and Gratitude and Other Works 1946–1963* (London: Hogarth, 1975).

Lab, Pierre (1969), "La conflit intra-psychique", in *La théorie psychanalytique*, ed. Sacha Nacht (Paris: Presses Universitaires de France).

Lacan, Jacques (1959), "On a Question Prior to any Possible Treatment of Psychosis", in *Écrits*, trans. Bruce Fink (New York: WW Norton).
———(1966), *Écrits* (Paris: Editions du Seuil).
———(1979), "Le Séminaire, Livre XXIV: L'insu que sait de l'une bévue s'aile à mourre, 1976–1977", in *Ornicar?* Vol. 17.
———(2005), *Écrits* trans. Bruce Fink (New York: WW Norton).

Lagache, Daniel (1949), *L'unité de la psychologie: Psychologie expérimentale et psychologie clinique* (Paris: Presses Universitaires de France, 2004).
———(1961), "La psychanalyse et la structure de la personnalité", in *Œuvres IV* (Paris: Presses Universitaires de France 1986).

Laplanche, Jean (1970), *Life and Death in Psychoanalysis*, trans. Jeffrey Mehlman (Baltimore: Johns Hopkins UP, 1977).
———(1980), *Problématiques I: L'Angoisse* (Paris: Presses Universitaires de France).
———(1980), *Problématiques II: Castrations-Symbolisations*, (Paris: Presses Universitaires de France).
———(1980), *Problématiques III: La Sublimation* (Paris: Presses Universitaires de France).
———(1987), *Problématiques IV: Le baquet: Transcendance du transfert* (Paris: Presses Universitaires de France.
———(1988), "The Wall and the Arcade" in *Jean Laplanche: Seduction, Translation, Drives*, ed. John Fletcher and Martin Stanton (London: Institute of Contemporary Arts, London, 1992).
———(1989), *New Foundations for Psychoanalysis*, trans. David Macey (Oxford: Blackwell).
———(1989), "Terminologie raisonnée", in *Traduire Freud*, eds. André Bourguignon, Pierre Cotet, Jean Laplanche and François Robert (Paris: Universitaires de France).
———(1990), "Implantation, Intromission", in *Essays on Otherness*, ed. John Fletcher (London: Routledge, 1999).

———(1992), *La révolution copernicienne inachevée: travaux 1967-92* (Paris: Aubier).
———(1992), "The Freud Museum Seminar", in *Jean Laplanche: Seduction, Translation, Drives*, ed. John Fletcher and Martin Stanton (London: Institute of Contemporary Arts).
———(1993), *Le fourvoiement biologisant de la sexualité chez Freud* (Paris: Synthélabo).
———(1993), "Exigency and Going Astray", trans. Vincent Ladmiral and Nicholas Ray, *Psychoanalysis, Culture and Society*, vol. 11, 2006.
———(1993), "Short Treatise on the Unconscious", in *Essays on Otherness*, ed. John Fletcher (London: Routledge, 1999).
———(1994), "La psychanalyse dans la communauté scientifique", in *Entre séduction et inspiration: l'homme* (Paris: Quadridge/Presses Universitaires de France, 1999).
———(1996), "La psychanalyse, mythes et théorie", in *Entre séduction et inspiration: l'homme* (Paris: Presses Universitaires de France, 1999).
———(1999), "Sublimation and/or Inspiration", trans. John Fletcher and Luke Thurston, in *New Formations*, no. 48, Winter 2002–3).
———(1999), "La parabole Chouraqui" in *Le Primat de l'autre* (Paris: Flammarion).
———(1999), "Notes on Afterwardsness" in *Essays on Otherness*, ed. John Fletcher (London & New York: Routledge).
———(2006), *Problématiques VI: l'après-coup* (Paris: Presses Universitaires de France, 2006.
———(2006), *Problématiques VII: Le fourvoiement biologisant de la sexualité chez Freud* (Paris: Presses Universitaires de France).
———(2006), "The So-Called Death Drive: A Sexual Drive", in *The British Journal of Psychotherapy*, vol. 20, no. 4, 2006.

Laplanche, Jean and Pontalis, Jean-Bertrand (1973), *The Language of Psychoanalysis*, trans. Donald Nicholson-Smith (London: The Hogarth Press).

Lavie, Jean-Claude (1972),"Parler à l'analyste", *La Nouvelle Revue de Psychanalyse*, vol. 5.

Legendre, Pierre (2000), *Le crime du Caporal Lortie* (Paris: Flammarion).

Lévi-Strauss, Claude (1949), *The Elementary Structures of Kinship*, trans. J.H. Bell, J.R. von Sturmer and Rodney Needham (Great Britain: Eyre and Spottiswoode, 1969).
———(1962), *The Savage Mind*, trans. John and Doreen Weightman (Chicago and London: Chicago UP, 1968).
———(1962), *Totemism*, trans. Rodney Needham (Boston: Beacon Press, 1963).
———(1985), *The Jealous Potter*, trans. Bénédicte Chorier (Chicago and London: Chicago University Press, 1988).

Lévy-Friesacher, Christine (19830, *Meynert-Freud, 'l'amentia'* (Paris: Presses

Universitaires de France).

Lichtenstein, Henry (1961), "Identity and Sexuality", *Journal of the American Psychoanalytic Association*, vol. 9.

Lorenz, Konrad (1970-1), *Studies in Animal and Human Behaviour*, 2 vols. (Cambridge Mass.: Harvard University Press, 1970 and 1971).

Lyotard, Jean-François (1971), *Discours, Figure* (Paris: Klincksieck).

Margueritat, Danielle (1998), "L'analyste et le rêveur", in *Le Fait de l'analyse*, no. 4.

Matthieu, Nicole-Claude (1991), "Trois modes de conceptualisation du rapport entre sexe et genre", in *L'anatomie politique*, (Paris: Côté femmes).

de Melo Carvalho, Maria Teresa (1996), *Paul Federn, une autre voie pour la théorie du moi* (Paris: Presses Universitaires de France).

Mendel, Gérard (1988), *La psychanalyse revisitée* (Paris: Le Découverte).

Miller, Jacques-Alain and Daniel Widlöcher (2004) *L'avenir de la psychanalyse: débat entre Daniel Widlöcher and Jacques-Alain Miller* (Paris: Cavalier Bleu, 2004).

Montagner, Hubert (2000), "L'attachement", in *Le Carnet psy,* October, no. 48.

Nunberg, Herman and Federn, Ernst (1962–1975), *Minutes of the Vienna Psychoanalytic Society*, eds. Herman Nunberg and Ernst Federn, trans. Margaret Nunberg with the assistance of H. Collins (New York: International Universities Press, 1962–1975), vols. 1-4.

Oppenheimer, Agnès, "Le meilleur des mondes possible. À propos du projet de R. Schafer", in *Psychanalyse à l'Université, vol. 9*, no. 35.

Osborne, Peter (1996) ed., *A Critical Sense*, ed. Peter (London and New York: Routledge).

Person, Ethel Spector (1999), *The Sexual Century*, (New Haven and London: Yale University Press).

Person, Ethel and Ovesey, Lionel (1983), "Psychoanalytic Theories of Gender Identity", in *The Journal of the American Academy of Psychoanalysis*, vol. 11.

Popper, Karl (1935), *The Logic of Scientific Discovery* (London: Routledge, 2002).
———(1963), *Conjectures and Refutations: The Growth of Scientific Knowledge* (London: Routledge).

Reiche, Reimut (1997), "Gender ohne Sex", *Psyche*, 9/10.

Renard, Michel (1969), "La narcissisme", in *La théorie psychanalytique*, ed. Sacha Nacht (Paris: Presses Universitaires de France).

Robert, Paul (2010), *Le Nouveau Petit Robert de la langue française* (Paris: Le Robert).

Roiphe, Herman and Galenson, Eleanor (1981), *Infantile Origins of Sexual Identity* (Connecticut: International Universities Press).

Simon, Bennet (1992), "Incest: see under Oedipus complex: The History of an Error in Psychoanalysis", in *The Journal of the American Psychoanalytic Association*, vol. 40.

Spinoza, Benedict de (1677), *Ethics, Demonstrated in Geometrical Order* in *The Essential Spinoza: Ethics and Related Writings*, trans. Samuel Shirley, ed. Michael L. Morgan (Indianapolis: Hackett Publishing Company, 2006).

Stoller, Robert (1968), *Sex and Gender* (London: The Hogarth Press).
———(1975), *Perversion: the Erotic form of Hatred* (London: Karnac 1986);
———(1985), *Presentations of Gender* (New Haven and London: Yale University Press).

Tarelho, Luiz Carlos (1999), *Paranoïa et la théorie de la séduction généralisée* (Paris: Presses Universitaires de France).

Tinbergen, Nikolaas (1951), *The Study of Instinct* (Oxford: Clarendon).

Viderman, Serge (1970), *La construction de l'espace analytique* (Paris: Denoël).

Widlöcher, Daniel (2001), *Sexualité infantile et attachement* ed. Daniel Widlöcher (Paris: Presses Universitaires de France).
———(2001), "Primary Love and Infantile Sexuality: An Eternal Debate", trans. Susan Fairfield, in *Infantile Sexuality and Attachment* (London: Karnac, 2002).

Wittgenstein, Ludwig (1921), *Tractatus Logico-Philosophicus*, trans. Brian McGuiness and David Pears (New York & London: Routledge, 2001).